THE COMIC BOOK HISTORY OF THE COCKTAIL

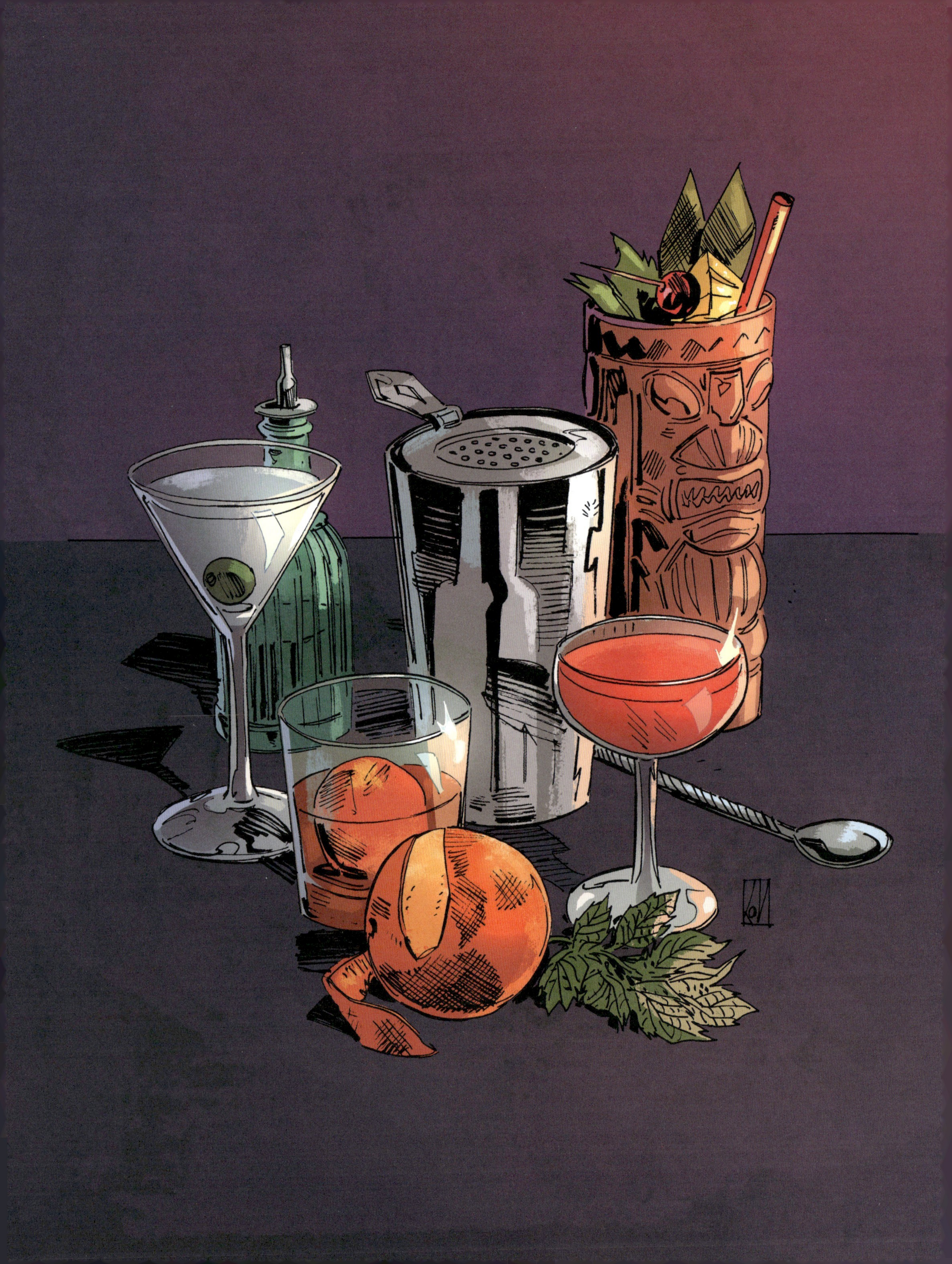

THE
COMIC BOOK
HISTORY
OF THE
COCKTAIL

FIVE CENTURIES OF MIXING DRINKS AND CARRYING ON

DAVID WONDRICH

ILLUSTRATED BY DEAN KOTZ

TEN SPEED GRAPHIC
An imprint of TEN SPEED PRESS
California | New York

CONTENTS

INTRODUCTION	**THE WORLD COCKTAILS MADE**	1
	CHASER: HOW TO DISTILL SPIRITS	
CHAPTER I	**TO THE BOTTOM OF THE (PUNCH) BOWL**	8
	MIXOLOGY: A BOWL OF PUNCH	
	CHASER: RUM AND ARRACK	
CHAPTER II	**AMERICA'S FIRST: THE MIGHTY JULEP**	19
	MIXOLOGY: THE BRANDY JULEP	
	CHASER: BRANDY	
	MIXOLOGY: THE SIDECAR	
CHAPTER III	**COCKING THE TAIL**	27
	MIXOLOGY: THE IMPROVED HOLLAND GIN COCKTAIL AND THE PINK GIN	
	CHASER: GIN	
CHAPTER IV	**AMERICAN DRINKS IN ENDLESS PROFUSION**	37
	MIXOLOGY: THE SHERRY COBBLER AND THE NEW YORK SOUR	
CHAPTER V	**THE PROFESSOR: JEREMIAH P. THOMAS**	46
	MIXOLOGY: THE BLUE BLAZER	
	CHASER: RYE AND BOURBON	
CHAPTER VI	**THE AMERICAN BAR VENTURES FORTH**	56
	MIXOLOGY: THE SHORT DRINK, AKA PRINCE OF WALES	

| CHAPTER VII | **THE NEW TESTAMENT, OR THE COCKTAIL 2.0** | 66 |

MIXOLOGY: THE DRY MARTINI
CHASER: VERMOUTH

| CHAPTER VIII | **THE BLAST AND THE SPARK** | 79 |

MIXOLOGY: THE HANKY PANKY
CHASER: COCKTAIL BOOKS

| CHAPTER IX | **PROHIBITION AND REPEAL** | 86 |

MIXOLOGY: THE FRENCH 75
CHASER: HOLLYWOOD DISCOVERS THE COCKTAIL
MIXOLOGY: THE MOSCOW MULE

| CHAPTER X | **CUBA AND THE TROPICAL COCKTAIL** | 99 |

MIXOLOGY: THE BENJAMIN MENÉNDEZ SPECIAL
AND MR. CHING'S ZOMBIE
CHASER: THE COCKTAIL AND THE TWO WORLD WARS,
1914–1918 AND 1939–1945

| CHAPTER XI | **DOPOGUERRA** | 113 |

MIXOLOGY: THE SATURN
CHASERS: CAMPARI AND VODKA

| CHAPTER XII | **THE SO-CALLED DARK AGES** | 125 |

MIXOLOGY: THE AMARETTO SOUR (NO. 2)

| CHAPTER XIII | **A BOOZY RENAISSANCE** | 135 |

A PARTING GLASS 148

MIXOLOGY: EL PANETÙN AND THE TRUSTY NAIL
RECIPES: SOME DRINKS I HAVE ENJOYED (AND HOW TO MIX THEM)
DATES, NOTES, AND FURTHER READING

ACKNOWLEDGMENTS 166

ABOUT THE CONTRIBUTORS 166

INDEX 167

INTRODUCTION

THE WORLD COCKTAILS MADE

It's time.

That time when, all around the globe, people gather to toast the day that is done; to welcome the night as it fills in the empty spaces and wipes away the should-have-dones and might-have-beens; to recharge and refresh and take solace in human companionship and let a little, icy pool of diluted ethanol flavored with various herbs, spices, and fruits help massage them into a state of relaxation.

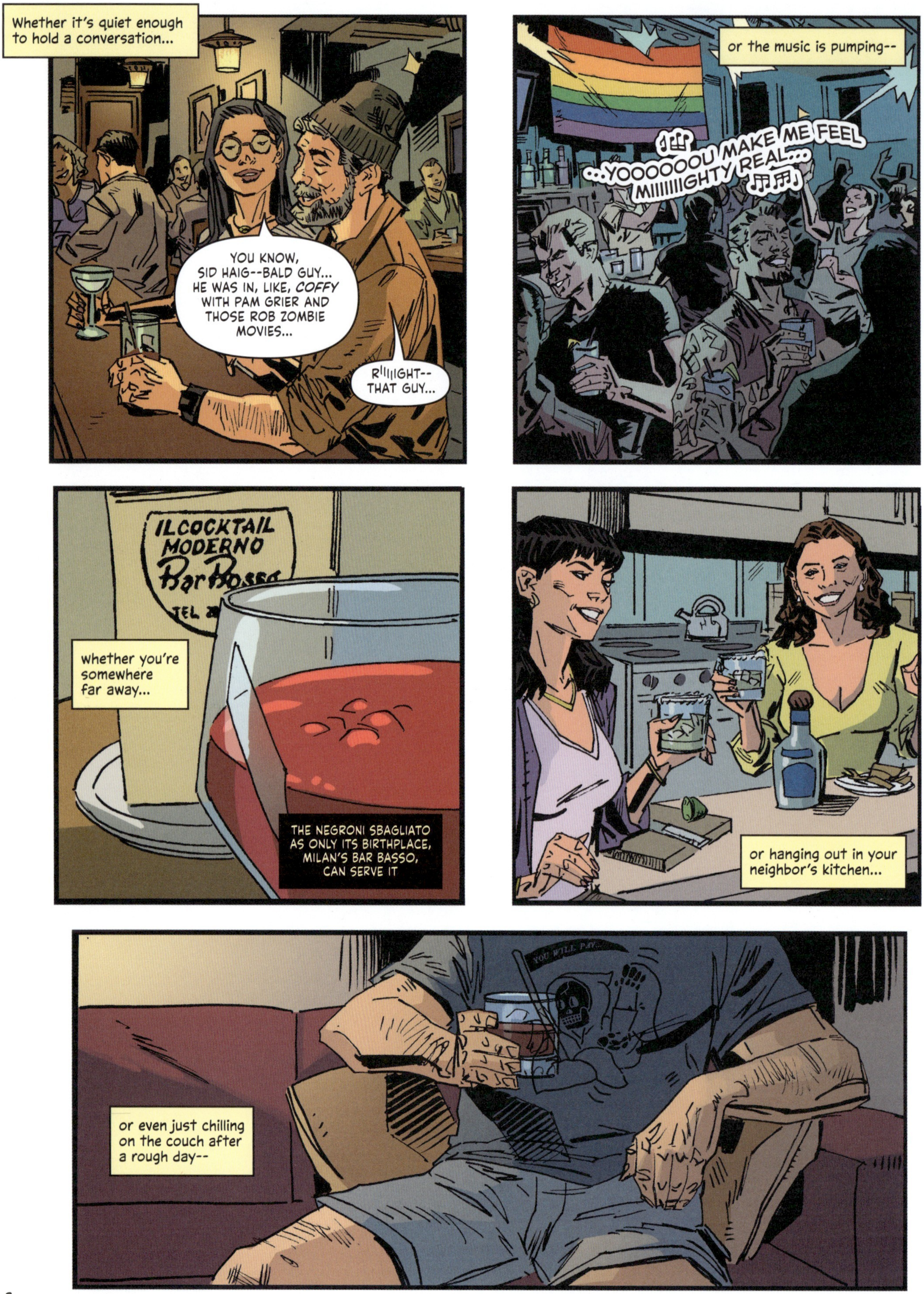

Whether it's quiet enough to hold a conversation...
YOU KNOW, SID HAIG--BALD GUY... HE WAS IN, LIKE, *COFFY* WITH PAM GRIER AND THOSE ROB ZOMBIE MOVIES...
R'''IGHT-- THAT GUY...
or the music is pumping--
...YOOOOOOU MAKE ME FEEL MIIIIIIGHTY REAL...
ILCOCKTAIL MODERNO
whether you're somewhere far away...
THE NEGRONI SBAGLIATO AS ONLY ITS BIRTHPLACE, MILAN'S BAR BASSO, CAN SERVE IT
or hanging out in your neighbor's kitchen...
or even just chilling on the couch after a rough day--

whether you're sipping something simple...

TI' PUNCH, A SPECIALTY OF THE FRENCH CARIBBEAN

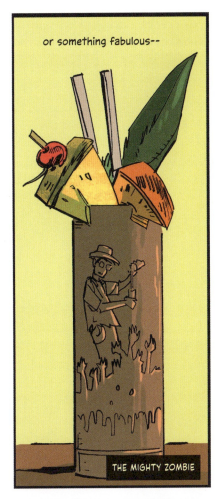

or something fabulous--

THE MIGHTY ZOMBIE

something bedrock classic...

NEW ORLEANS'S BELOVED SAZERAC COCKTAIL

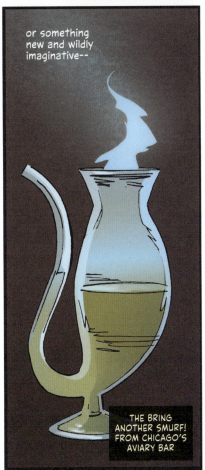

or something new and wildly imaginative--

THE BRING ANOTHER SMURF! FROM CHICAGO'S AVIARY BAR

something sweet and sexy, like a well-made Cosmopolitan...

or, what the hell, a trusty old G&T--

With every sip you take, you add yourself as a new link in a long chain of cocktail drinkers. A chain that stretches back to...

the 1920s and Prohibition?

A GIN BUCK*

the Gilded Age of the 1890s?

"THE ONLY WILLIAM" STIRS UP A WHISPERS OF THE FOREST.

the 1850s?

JERRY THOMAS THROWS HIS FAMOUS BLUE BLAZER.

the 1770s?

VIRGINIA'S ORIGINAL MINT JULEP

the 1690s?

CANARY WINE AND STOUGHTON'S BITTERS

the 1620s?

A BOWL OF RACK PUNCH IN INDIA

This book is the story of that chain.

*SQUEEZE HALF A LIME INTO AN ICE-FILLED HIGHBALL GLASS. ADD TWO OUNCES LONDON DRY GIN, TOP OFF WITH GINGER ALE, AND STIR.

First, a little prehistory...

KING MIDAS'S TOMB

Like its subject, the history of the cocktail is a mixture--stirred together from hefty slugs of the stories of mixed drinks and of bars and bartenders, spiked with some good, stiff dashes of the history of distilled spirits.

Each of those parts is very old. The subjects of King Midas of Phrygia were mixing drinks some twenty-seven hundred years ago.

Seven centuries later, Roman cities were dotted with lively *popinae* (bars) staffed with wisecracking *caupones* (bartenders); in fact, at Pompeii another beautifully preserved bar has just been uncovered.

Some time after that, Han dynasty Chinese revelers were knocking back spirits distilled from grain.

As far as we can tell, though, the Chinese weren't mixing those spirits into an early version of the Manhattan, the Romans stuck to wine, and those Phrygian drinks were mixed from beer, wine, and mead--no spirits and none of that special, bracing kick that we expect from a true cocktail.

A BAR IN POMPEII, FIRST CENTURY CE

A HAN DYNASTY DISTILLERY

The modern art of mixology--the word is an American one from the 1850s, and if it's a bit silly, it's not as silly as "the fine art of mixing drinks," which is the alternative--doesn't really step up until distilled spirits make it into everyday use.

Until people needed a practical and pleasant-drinking way of taming the liquid fire lurking in the bottle. (For a quick look at distillation, see page 7.)

Whenever and wherever distillation was invented (it's an open question), it's safe to say that drinking spirits as a regular activity first caught on in Asia, spreading through India, China, and their neighboring regions around 1000–1200 CE.

Distillation started spreading through Europe in the twelfth century but didn't become truly widespread until the fifteenth century (it would hit the Americas and parts of Africa in the sixteenth century).

In Europe, at least, we know how people drank their spirits thanks to the remarkable report on distillation and its uses written by Michele Savonarola, an Italian physician, in the 1440s.

By then, spirits had gone from a rare and precious medicine taken by rich people in small doses to something, as Savonarola said, even "sold in the piazzas to the poor and wretched."

The most common way of drinking them was straight, in shots, but it was also common to mix one part of this aqua vitae (water of life) to three parts wine, water, or beer--in order of preference.

ITALIAN STILL, CIRCA FIFTEENTH CENTURY

On the other side of the world, as far as we can tell, things were pretty much the same: in the early seventeenth century, the Mughal emperor Jahangir drank six cups a day of mixed wine and palm arrack, the local spirit.

TRADITIONAL INDIAN STILL, CIRCA 200 BCE-PRESENT

Although this mix of wine and booze would in time give us our ports, sherries, Madeiras, and other delicious, fortified wines, as a drink mixed on the spot, it's still a pretty dull way to drink spirits. At the beginning of the seventeenth century, we found something better. Much, much better.

JAHANGIR, 1569-1627

CHASER: HOW TO DISTILL SPIRITS

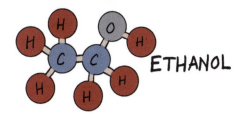
ETHANOL

Spirits begin where beer and wine leave off. In those, once the yeasts have eaten all the sugar in your grape juice or boiled barley water and excreted it as C_2H_5OH (aka ethanol, or alcohol to you and me) and CO_2, you just drink the result.

Ethanol is lighter than water and turns to steam at a lower temperature: 173°F (78°C) as opposed to 212°F (100°C). If you heat wine or beer to a temperature in between, you can turn most of the alcohol into steam while leaving most of the water behind.

Find a way to corral that ethanol-rich steam and prevent it from dispersing in the air...

...and then bring it into contact with enough cool water or air to turn it back into liquid, and you've got something much more potent, transportable, and longer lasting than beer or wine.

Humans are clever and over the centuries have figured out dozens and dozens of different forms of stills to do that--some of them most elaborate, others very simple indeed.

CHAPTER I

TO THE BOTTOM OF THE (PUNCH) BOWL

India, England, and Around the World ~ 1600–1850

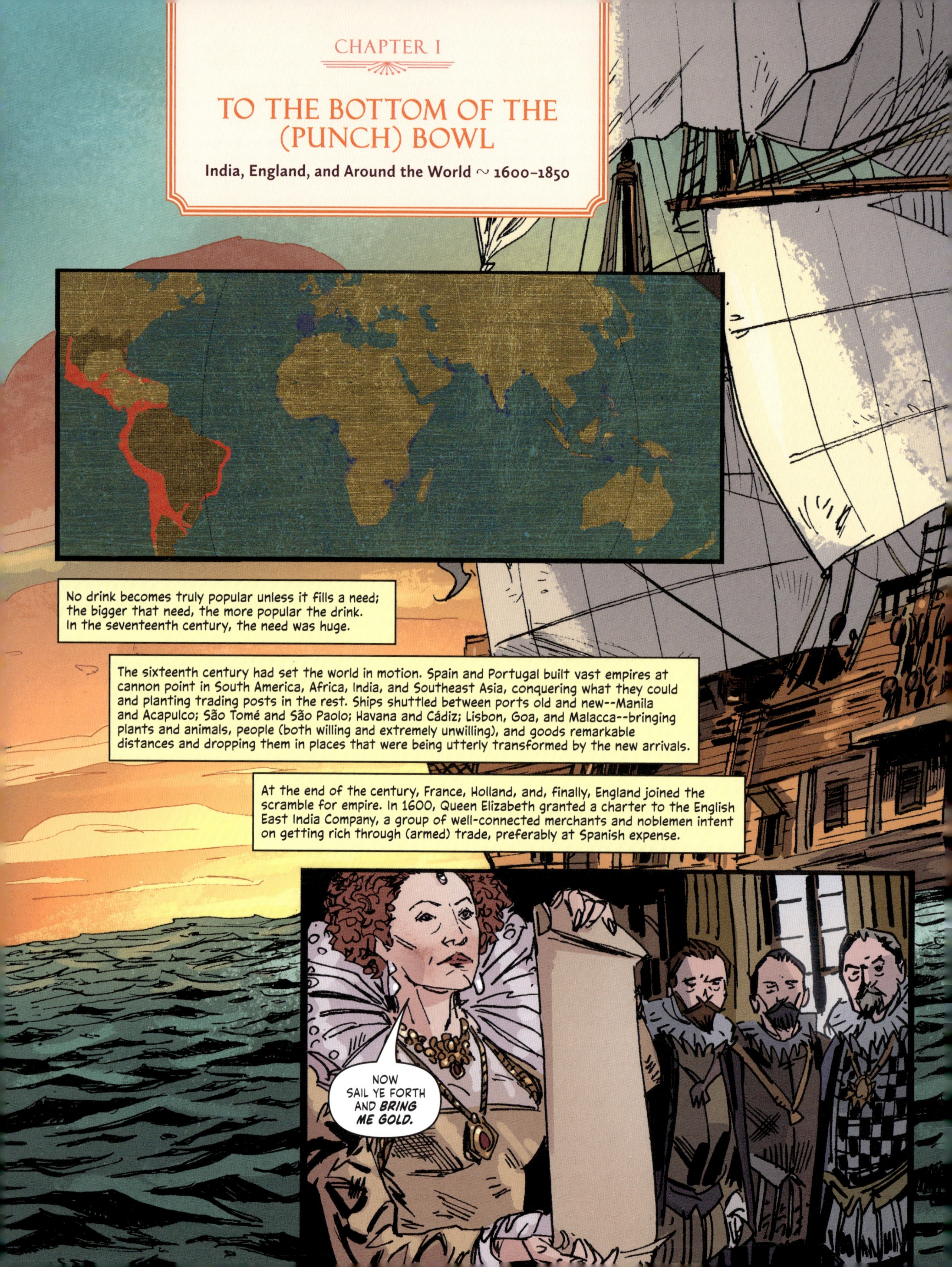

No drink becomes truly popular unless it fills a need; the bigger that need, the more popular the drink. In the seventeenth century, the need was huge.
The sixteenth century had set the world in motion. Spain and Portugal built vast empires at cannon point in South America, Africa, India, and Southeast Asia, conquering what they could and planting trading posts in the rest. Ships shuttled between ports old and new--Manila and Acapulco; São Tomé and São Paolo; Havana and Cádiz; Lisbon, Goa, and Malacca--bringing plants and animals, people (both willing and extremely unwilling), and goods remarkable distances and dropping them in places that were being utterly transformed by the new arrivals.
At the end of the century, France, Holland, and, finally, England joined the scramble for empire. In 1600, Queen Elizabeth granted a charter to the English East India Company, a group of well-connected merchants and noblemen intent on getting rich through (armed) trade, preferably at Spanish expense.
NOW SAIL YE FORTH AND ***BRING ME GOLD.***

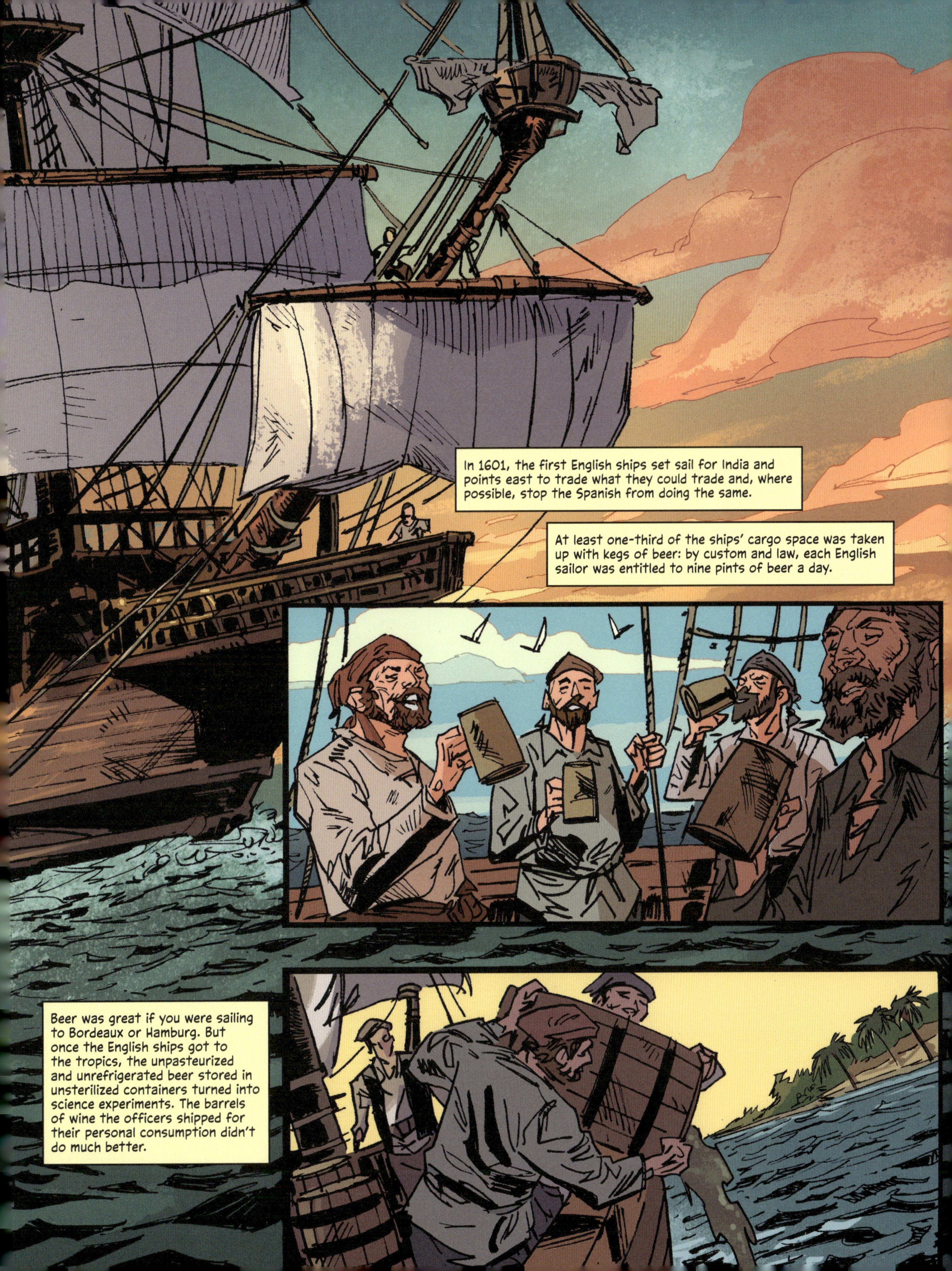
In 1601, the first English ships set sail for India and points east to trade what they could trade and, where possible, stop the Spanish from doing the same.
At least one-third of the ships' cargo space was taken up with kegs of beer: by custom and law, each English sailor was entitled to nine pints of beer a day.
Beer was great if you were sailing to Bordeaux or Hamburg. But once the English ships got to the tropics, the unpasteurized and unrefrigerated beer stored in unsterilized containers turned into science experiments. The barrels of wine the officers shipped for their personal consumption didn't do much better.

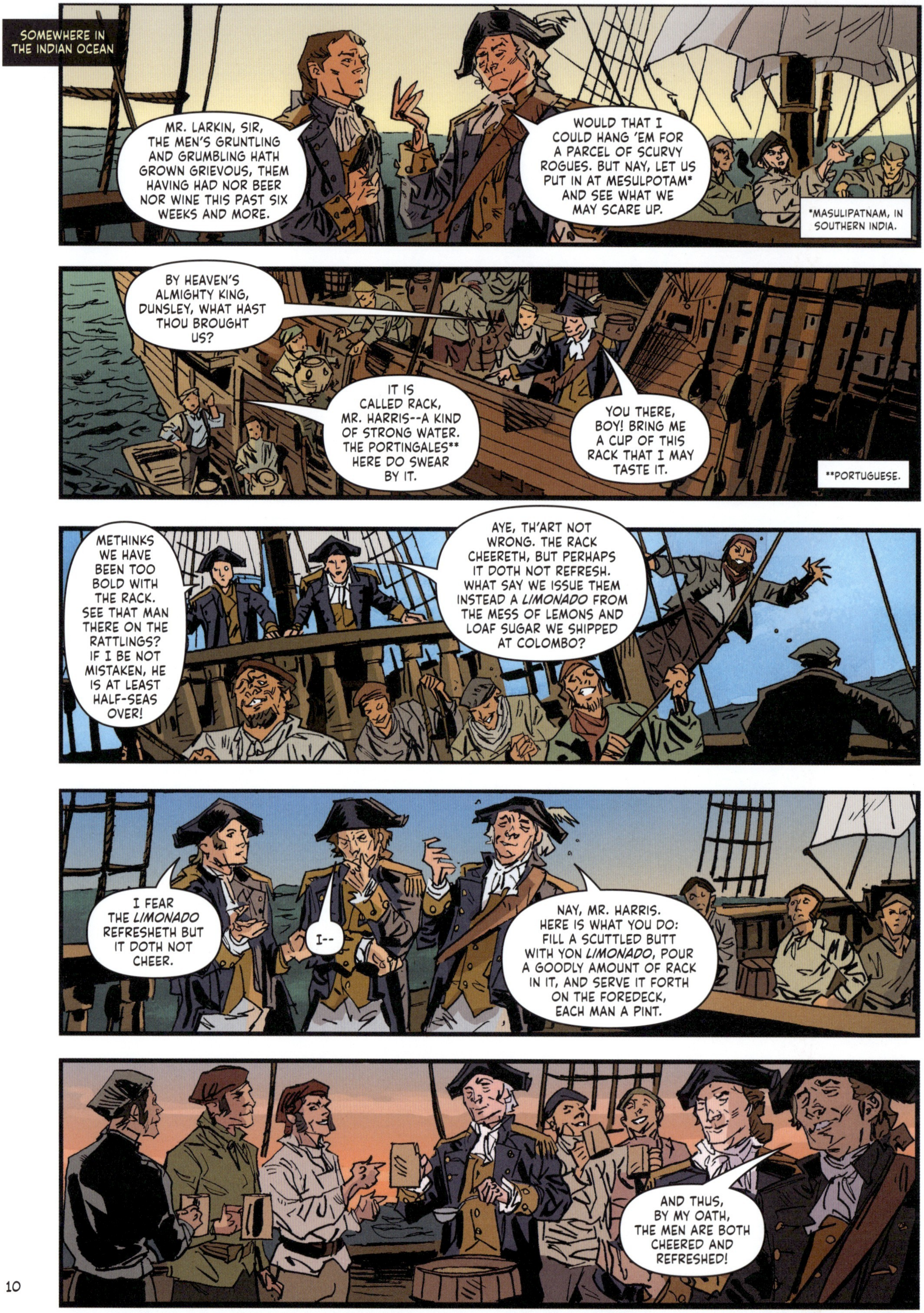
SOMEWHERE IN THE INDIAN OCEAN
MR. LARKIN, SIR, THE MEN'S GRUNTLING AND GRUMBLING HATH GROWN GRIEVOUS, THEM HAVING HAD NOR BEER NOR WINE THIS PAST SIX WEEKS AND MORE.
WOULD THAT I COULD HANG 'EM FOR A PARCEL OF SCURVY ROGUES. BUT NAY, LET US PUT IN AT MESULPOTAM* AND SEE WHAT WE MAY SCARE UP.
*MASULIPATNAM, IN SOUTHERN INDIA.
BY HEAVEN'S ALMIGHTY KING, DUNSLEY, WHAT HAST THOU BROUGHT US?
IT IS CALLED RACK, MR. HARRIS--A KIND OF STRONG WATER. THE PORTINGALES** HERE DO SWEAR BY IT.
YOU THERE, BOY! BRING ME A CUP OF THIS RACK THAT I MAY TASTE IT.
**PORTUGUESE.
METHINKS WE HAVE BEEN TOO BOLD WITH THE RACK. SEE THAT MAN THERE ON THE RATTLINGS? IF I BE NOT MISTAKEN, HE IS AT LEAST HALF-SEAS OVER!
AYE, TH'ART NOT WRONG. THE RACK CHEERETH, BUT PERHAPS IT DOTH NOT REFRESH. WHAT SAY WE ISSUE THEM INSTEAD A *LIMONADO* FROM THE MESS OF LEMONS AND LOAF SUGAR WE SHIPPED AT COLOMBO?
I FEAR THE *LIMONADO* REFRESHETH BUT IT DOTH NOT CHEER.
I--
NAY, MR. HARRIS. HERE IS WHAT YOU DO: FILL A SCUTTLED BUTT WITH YON *LIMONADO*, POUR A GOODLY AMOUNT OF RACK IN IT, AND SERVE IT FORTH ON THE FOREDECK, EACH MAN A PINT.
AND THUS, BY MY OATH, THE MEN ARE BOTH CHEERED AND REFRESHED!

Well, it could have happened like that.

The fact is, all we know is that the East India Company sailed to Asia and started drinking punch there. It doesn't seem to have been an Indian drink, although it might have been. But exactly how it came together? It's not in the existing records.

It may have started with one Captain Larkin, a known arrack-swiller who, by 1622, had a concoction named after him that's almost certainly our drink. As "punch" (recorded in 1632), it quickly traveled around the known world.

We can't say if it was the "factors"--traders--in the East India Company's "factories" in India who taught the sailors to make punch or if the factors were taught to do it by the sailors, but they all sure drank a lot of it.

By the 1660s, the company's India hands who managed to survive their tropical sojourns had brought punch back to London, where it was adopted by the new coffeehouses (they weren't licensed to sell beer or wine, you see, but punch wasn't beer or wine).

Meanwhile, punch drinking had also swept through Britain's colonies in North America and the Caribbean, where wine was an expensive luxury and it was often too hot to make and keep beer.

In America, the fuel for those punch sessions was rum, a spirit that the English had adopted from the Portuguese and Spanish. But while those had left it to the enslaved workers and small farmers who had invented it, the British in Barbados industrialized its production and folded it into their brutal, exploitative, and very, very profitable sugar industry.

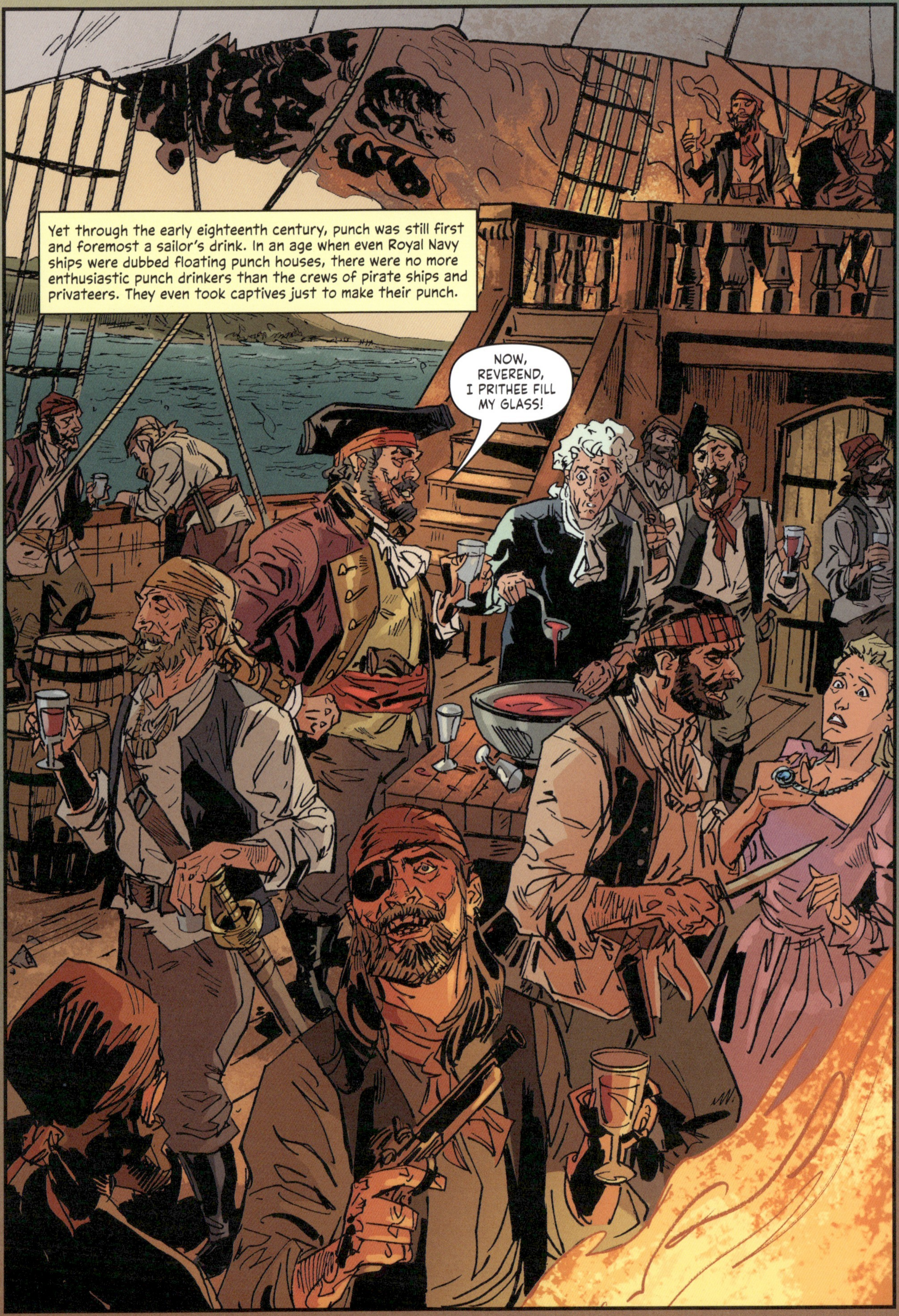
Yet through the early eighteenth century, punch was still first and foremost a sailor's drink. In an age when even Royal Navy ships were dubbed floating punch houses, there were no more enthusiastic punch drinkers than the crews of pirate ships and privateers. They even took captives just to make their punch.
NOW, REVEREND, I PRITHEE FILL MY GLASS!

Elsewhere, things were changing. In 1731, James Ashley, a thirty-three-year-old cheesemonger from the English Midlands, opened the London Punch House near St. Paul's Cathedral and transformed the history of mixology.

By buying his French brandy, Jamaican rum, and Batavia arrack wholesale by the barrel, Ashley was able to charge 25 percent less than the going price for a bowl of punch. Between that and his willingness to sell it in amounts as small as a single glass, his painted boast was unusually close to the truth.

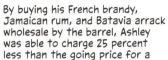

PRO BONO PUBLICO
JAMES ASHLEY IN 1731 FIRST REDUCED THE PRICE OF PUNCH RAISED ITS REPUTATION AND BROUGHT IT INTO UNIVERSAL ESTEEM

"AND, HETTY, MIND HOW YOU DRAW THAT-- STREWTH BUT I DID FIND THE STUFF SLOPPED ABOUT YESTERDAY."

"KITTY, MY DEAR, ANOTHER FLORIN BOWL OF THE BRANDY PUNCH FOR LORD GOSFORD'S TABLE, IF YOU PLEASE."

A punch house like Ashley's, which was widely imitated in all of its aspects, was a center of city life, a place where clubs--most of which were nothing more than loose, informal groups of friends--met regularly to drink and eat and smoke and talk, talk, talk, talk, talk.

Women drank punch, too--just not in the big public rooms where the men did. In the early eighteenth century, London even had a Ladies' Punch Club that met near fashionable St. James. In general, such doings were kept on the q.t.

As the fashionable social drink of its age, punch quickly began to evolve.

It soon became a mark of advanced punch making to extract the sweet, fragrant oil from the peels of the lemons or oranges used to make the drink, whether by infusing them in the booze or by scraping them on the dense loaf sugar used then.

GENTLEMEN, LET OUR DRINK BE AS THE WORLD DESCRIBED BY OVID, WHERE EARTH AND AIR AND WATER AND FIRE WERE ALL JUMBLED UP TOGETHER WITH NO DEITY TO SORT THEM OUT. LET US DRINK OUR WINE IN OUR PUNCH!

Others found better things with which to dilute their punches than plain water: soda water, tea, champagne, or any other wine.

In Paris, where punch making was creeping into the confectioner's art, the chic thing to do was to replace the sugar with various syrups and liqueurs.

Not to be outdone, the Germans and Austrians and such liked to set theirs on fire. They still do.

Those Parisian confectioners (in fact, many of them were Italians) began experimenting with something much less spectacular than fire but ultimately more useful: ice. The punch you would find at a place such as the famous Café Tortoni would resemble an alcoholic sorbet, where rum or brandy was cushioned by fruit syrups, juices, and champagne. Pas mal--not bad.

Every American social club had its own punch recipe. Some clubs, such as Philadelphia's State in Schuylkill Fishing Club, became famous for them.

Unlike at most such clubs, the State in Schuylkill's members and their guests were their own servants and responsible for mixing its famous Fish House Punch, fueled by a potent mix of Jamaican rum, French brandy, and American peach brandy.

In Virginia, home to innumerable clubs of its own, the ingredients tended to be a little more luxurious. When Jasper Crouch, Richmond's top caterer, made punch for the Quoit Club, where prominent citizens met to throw iron rings at posts, eat barbecued pig, and drink, he used Jamaican rum, too, but with only the oldest cognac and rare Madeira wine.

Where the French used a little champagne to smooth out their punches, groups such as Savannah, Georgia's Chatham Artillery (as much a social club as a militia unit) used a lot, to the point that the Savannah city fathers used to spring Chatham Artillery Punch (brandy, rum, bourbon, lemon, and champagne) on prominent out-of-town visitors to see if they could lay them out. They could.

A rather gentler punch was the creation of Stephen Price, a New Yorker who managed London's exclusive Garrick Club and liked to chill his simple gin punch with iced soda water.

His drink spread to Limmer's Hotel, where one John Collin watched over the rowdy--and very exclusive--barroom. As the John Collins, and then the Tom Collins (from the Old Tom gin Collin made it with), Price's drink became a pillar of mixology.

Like every kind of mixology, punch mixing had its own set of tools.

There were bowls, of course--many of them straight from China and part of the same global trade network that created punch in the first place.

Nobody likes lemon seeds floating in their punch glass. Experts passed the juice through elegant silver strainers.

In the eighteenth century, people were of the opinion that you couldn't have a true bowl of punch without a generous scraping of nutmeg. Gentlemen even carried little, cunningly wrought silver nutmeg graters in their pockets, complete with compartments for the nutmeg.

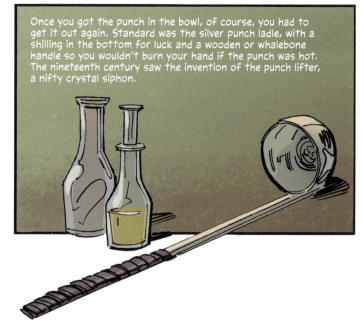

Once you got the punch in the bowl, of course, you had to get it out again. Standard was the silver punch ladle, with a shilling in the bottom for luck and a wooden or whalebone handle so you wouldn't burn your hand if the punch was hot. The nineteenth century saw the invention of the punch lifter, a nifty crystal siphon.

One thing that punch drinkers quickly learned is that punch should be drunk in the small wineglasses of the day (which usually held a mere two ounces) rather than the large beer tankards.

Although weaker than modern cocktails, punch was still plenty strong for a session drink.

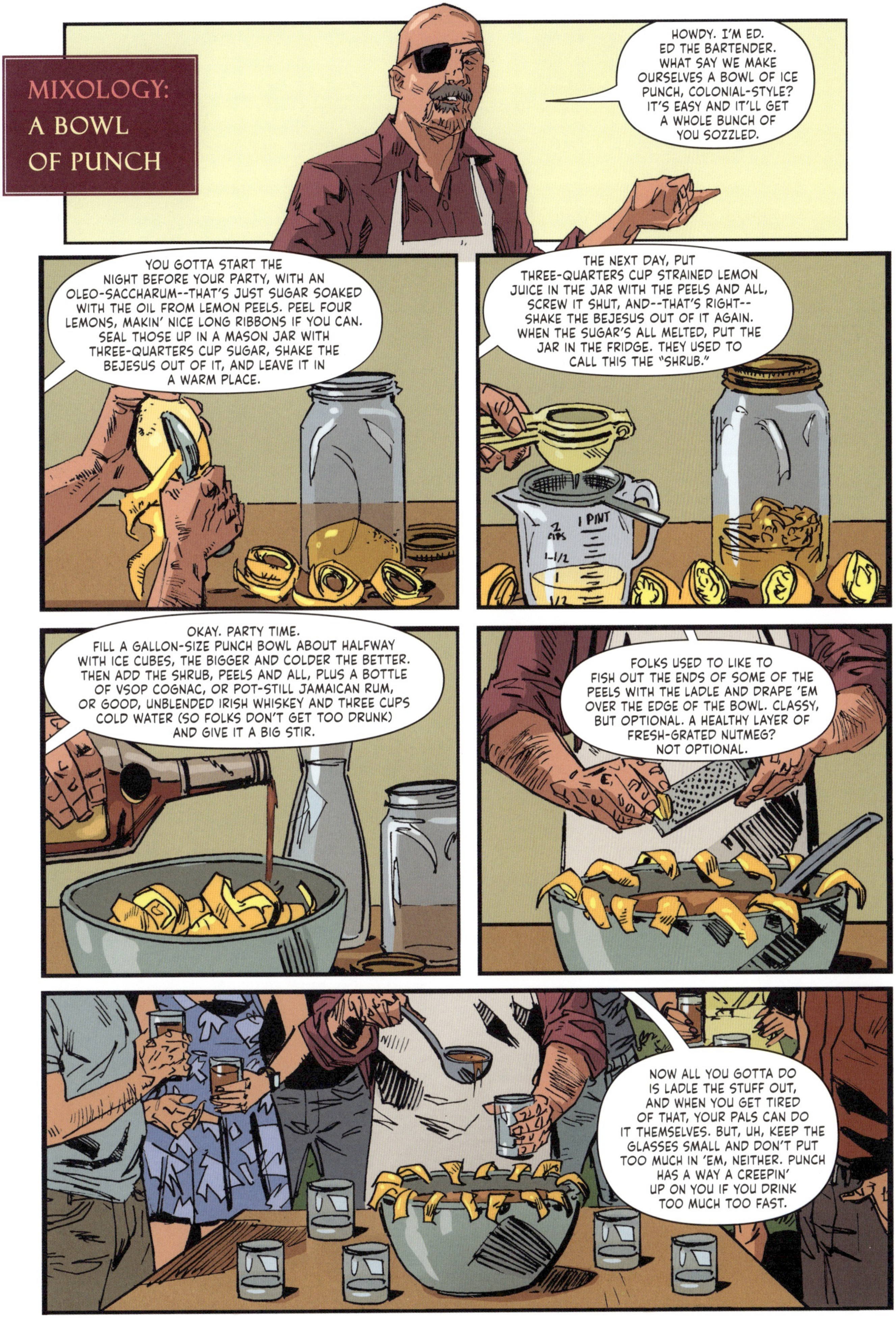
MIXOLOGY: A BOWL OF PUNCH
HOWDY. I'M ED. ED THE BARTENDER. WHAT SAY WE MAKE OURSELVES A BOWL OF ICE PUNCH, COLONIAL-STYLE? IT'S EASY AND IT'LL GET A WHOLE BUNCH OF YOU SOZZLED.
YOU GOTTA START THE NIGHT BEFORE YOUR PARTY, WITH AN OLEO-SACCHARUM--THAT'S JUST SUGAR SOAKED WITH THE OIL FROM LEMON PEELS. PEEL FOUR LEMONS, MAKIN' NICE LONG RIBBONS IF YOU CAN. SEAL THOSE UP IN A MASON JAR WITH THREE-QUARTERS CUP SUGAR, SHAKE THE BEJESUS OUT OF IT, AND LEAVE IT IN A WARM PLACE.
THE NEXT DAY, PUT THREE-QUARTERS CUP STRAINED LEMON JUICE IN THE JAR WITH THE PEELS AND ALL, SCREW IT SHUT, AND--THAT'S RIGHT--SHAKE THE BEJESUS OUT OF IT AGAIN. WHEN THE SUGAR'S ALL MELTED, PUT THE JAR IN THE FRIDGE. THEY USED TO CALL THIS THE "SHRUB."
1 PINT
OKAY. PARTY TIME. FILL A GALLON-SIZE PUNCH BOWL ABOUT HALFWAY WITH ICE CUBES, THE BIGGER AND COLDER THE BETTER. THEN ADD THE SHRUB, PEELS AND ALL, PLUS A BOTTLE OF VSOP COGNAC, OR POT-STILL JAMAICAN RUM, OR GOOD, UNBLENDED IRISH WHISKEY AND THREE CUPS COLD WATER (SO FOLKS DON'T GET TOO DRUNK) AND GIVE IT A BIG STIR.
FOLKS USED TO LIKE TO FISH OUT THE ENDS OF SOME OF THE PEELS WITH THE LADLE AND DRAPE 'EM OVER THE EDGE OF THE BOWL. CLASSY, BUT OPTIONAL. A HEALTHY LAYER OF FRESH-GRATED NUTMEG? NOT OPTIONAL.
NOW ALL YOU GOTTA DO IS LADLE THE STUFF OUT, AND WHEN YOU GET TIRED OF THAT, YOUR PALS CAN DO IT THEMSELVES. BUT, UH, KEEP THE GLASSES SMALL AND DON'T PUT TOO MUCH IN 'EM, NEITHER. PUNCH HAS A WAY A CREEPIN' UP ON YOU IF YOU DRINK TOO MUCH TOO FAST.

CHASER: RUM AND ARRACK

You can turn any spirit into punch, but back when the drink took the world by storm, the spirits that fueled that whirlwind were Caribbean rum and its Dutch-Chinese-Indonesian cousin, Batavia arrack, both based on the leftovers from sugar making.

To make sugar, you had to cut the cane, quickly crush out the juice, and boil it down until it crystallized, skimming off the impurities. This was hot, nasty work. The fields had snakes, the cane mill kept dragging in hands and arms, and the hot syrup stuck like napalm.

In their American colonies, the Spanish and the Portuguese forced enslaved Africans and indigenous people to do it. One of the few "luxuries" that the workers were given was the skimmings from the reducing pans, which their exploiters couldn't sell. The workers learned to ferment it...

...and distill it. The equipment was rudimentary, and the aguardiente, or "burning water," was as funky as it was fiery, but it was better than no booze at all. By the seventeenth century, cane spirit from skimmings, or raw juice, was everywhere in Latin America, and everywhere it was illegal. The colonies were supposed to buy all their spirits from back home, not make their own.

Meanwhile, across the world in the Dutch colony of Batavia (modern Jakarta), people found that if you added molasses--the thick syrup that surrounds the crystallized sugar--to the fermenting palm sap, the local arrack that was distilled from it yielded a stronger spirit, and considerably more of it.

In Barbados, by the 1640s, English sugar planters had begun to hold back the skimmings, boost it with molasses Dutch-style, and distill it. This they could sell to their neighbors and even export to the mainland colonies up north, thus turning industrial waste into pure gold. Kill-devil, they called it.

But it also had a shorter, catchier name: rum.

CHAPTER II

AMERICA'S FIRST: THE MIGHTY JULEP

Virginia and Points North and West ~ 1770–Present

The Cocktail--the reigning king of mixed drinks--is an American creation, but before it assumed the throne, Julep, the son of punch, was the first American-born drink to rule the kingdom.

Dictionaries will tell you that the word "julep" comes from the Persian gulāb, or syrup, and in medieval medicine referred to a thick sugar syrup infused with something medicinal. That could be mint, but it was often something nasty tasting like camphor.

Of course, the immediate origin of the American Mint Julep is a lot less highfalutin.

"WHEN *WILL* WE GET SOME LEMONS?! I GROW WEARY OF THIS INSIPID WASH WATER. LEMON-LESS PUNCH. FAUGH!"

In most of England's North American colonies, citrus fruit had to be imported. When it was gone, you could make your punch without it--that was called Sling--or you could look around for something else to spice up your booze.

We don't know who first put a sprig of mint or two in a glass of Sling (rum, sugar, and water), or even whether they were male or female, white or Black, free or enslaved. It was probably a Virginian, though, and it was before 1770, when the drink turns up in a poem there.

If winters in British America were too cold for lemon trees to grow, they were also cold enough for the ponds and streams to freeze solid. And summers were hot enough to make the effort of cutting and storing that ice worthwhile.

One of the things you could do with that ice was make ice punch, a Philadelphia specialty of the 1780s. While French punch makers like Tortoni used ice-cream-making techniques to freeze liquid punches into big, boozy slushies, in America, where the water was still clean and the winters were cold, American punch makers just put the ice right in the bowl.

Or you could put a chunk or two of ice in a glass of Mint Julep, something that was first recorded at the Wig Wam Gardens in Norfolk, Virginia, in 1807. Good idea--so good that within a decade or so everyone else was doing it, too.

By the 1820s, Yankee ingenuity turned the ice business into a full-fledged industry. From Boston to Savannah, Chicago to New Orleans, cheap ice from New England was there to tame the summer swelter.

FLY-MARKET HOTEL
MURTAGH BYRNE, PROP.

Meanwhile, a new generation of American bartenders took that abundant ice and, starting with the old Mint Julep, built a whole new art of mixing fancy drinks around it. Unfortunately, our group portrait here is mostly imagination; we have pictures of only one or two of them.

THE 1830s "HAIL-STORM" JULEP

1 Othello Pollard (1758?–1838), Boston. **2** Cato Alexander (1780–1858), New York.
3 Orsamus Willard (1792–1876), New York. **4** Jasper Crouch (1800?–1860?), Richmond.
5 Martha King Niblo (1802–1851), New York. **6** Johann George Vennigerholtz (1815–1877), Natchez.
7 William Walker (1790–1853?), Washington, D.C. **8** William Rice (1812–1858?), Philadelphia.
9 Joseph Santini (1817–1874), New Orleans. **10** William Guy (1816–1862), Baltimore.

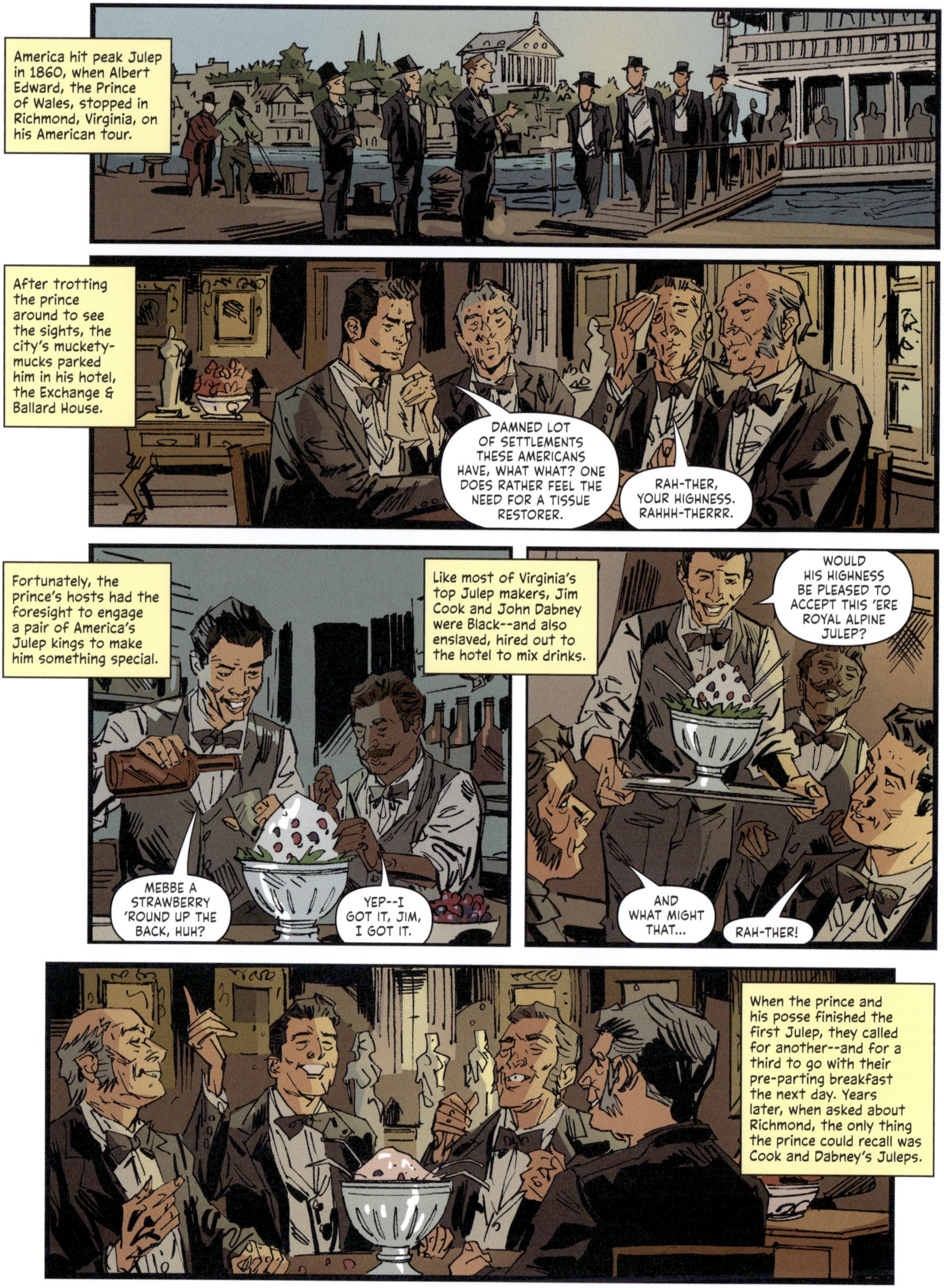
America hit peak Julep in 1860, when Albert Edward, the Prince of Wales, stopped in Richmond, Virginia, on his American tour.
After trotting the prince around to see the sights, the city's muckety-mucks parked him in his hotel, the Exchange & Ballard House.
DAMNED LOT OF SETTLEMENTS THESE AMERICANS HAVE, WHAT WHAT? ONE DOES RATHER FEEL THE NEED FOR A TISSUE RESTORER.
RAH-THER, YOUR HIGHNESS. RAHHH-THERRR.
Fortunately, the prince's hosts had the foresight to engage a pair of America's Julep kings to make him something special.
Like most of Virginia's top Julep makers, Jim Cook and John Dabney were Black--and also enslaved, hired out to the hotel to mix drinks.
MEBBE A STRAWBERRY 'ROUND UP THE BACK, HUH?
YEP--I GOT IT, JIM, I GOT IT.
WOULD HIS HIGHNESS BE PLEASED TO ACCEPT THIS 'ERE ROYAL ALPINE JULEP?
AND WHAT MIGHT THAT...
RAH-THER!
When the prince and his posse finished the first Julep, they called for another--and for a third to go with their pre-parting breakfast the next day. Years later, when asked about Richmond, the only thing the prince could recall was Cook and Dabney's Juleps.

The classic antebellum "Hail-Storm" was a complex drink, made with the most expensive imported and domestic spirits available: cognac, sometimes mixed with Georgia peach brandy (distilled from peaches and barrel aged) or old Monongahela rye, with a float of rich Jamaica rum. Some Juleps incorporated port, sherry, or Madeira as well. Rich folks' drinks.

After the Civil War, in the North, the Julep began a slow fade from everyday bar drink to curiosity. In the South, however, it became a ritual, an item of identity. The Black men who had brought the drink to such epicurean peaks saw their roles reduced from creators to walk-on tray carriers for a much-simplified drink.

With the southern economy in ruins, the new southern Julep was based strictly on local whiskey, partly because American whiskey was way better than it had been in its rough youth, but mostly because it was a hell of a lot cheaper than anything imported.

By the end of the twentieth century, the Julep had become a one-day-a-year drink, slapped together by the thousands on Derby day to be downed by America's would-be debutantes and southern gents.

The twenty-first-century cocktail revolution brought back a lot of old drinks—Punch, the Old-Fashioned—but it hasn't been particularly kind to the Julep, perhaps because it practically takes its own production line. Ironically, you can try the best modern version not in Louisville but in Houston.

ALBA HUERTA AT JULEP, HOUSTON

MIXOLOGY: THE BRANDY JULEP

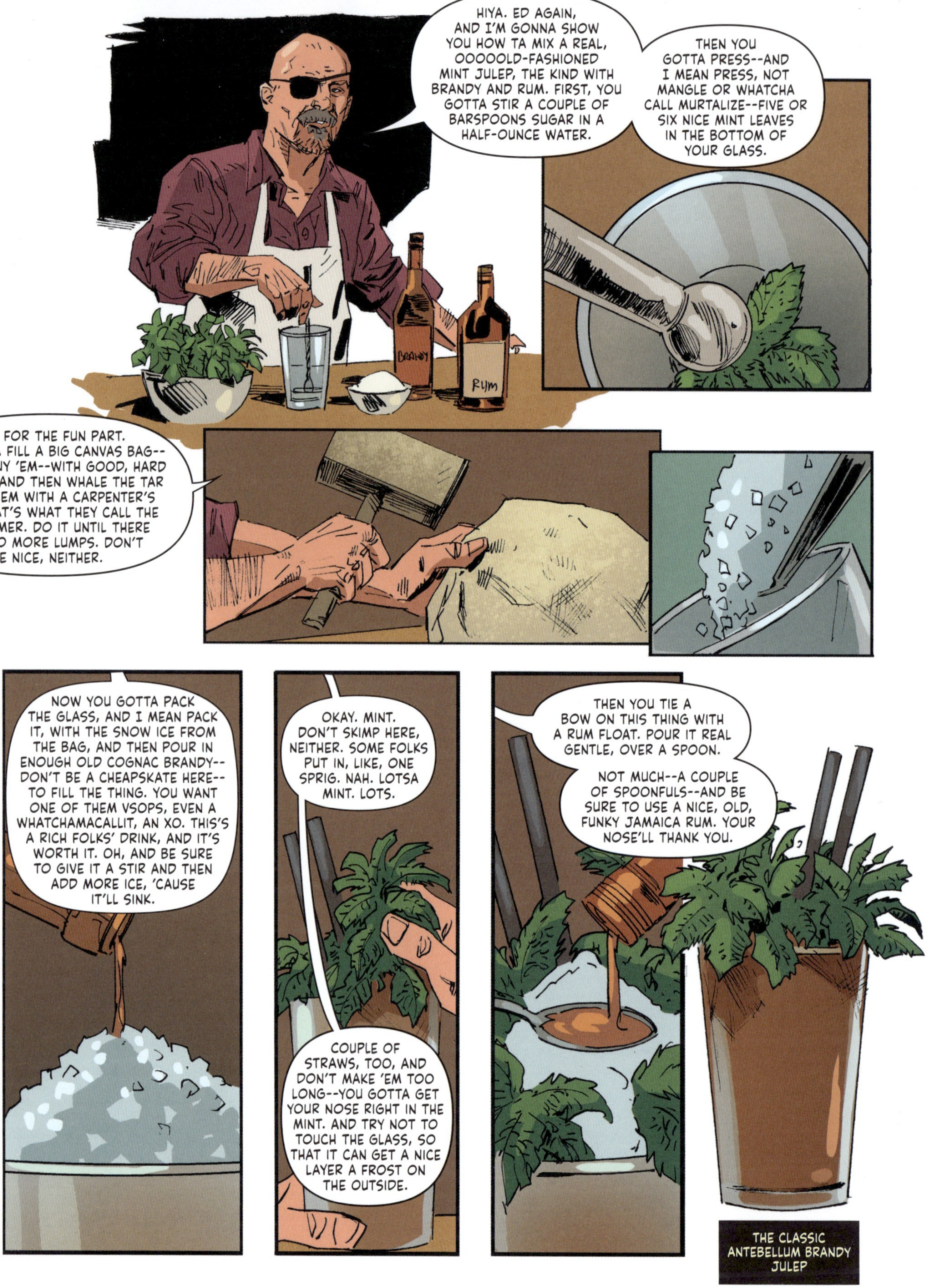
HIYA. ED AGAIN, AND I'M GONNA SHOW YOU HOW TA MIX A REAL, OOOOOLD-FASHIONED MINT JULEP, THE KIND WITH BRANDY AND RUM. FIRST, YOU GOTTA STIR A COUPLE OF BARSPOONS SUGAR IN A HALF-OUNCE WATER.
BRANDY
RUM
THEN YOU GOTTA PRESS--AND I MEAN PRESS, NOT MANGLE OR WHATCHA CALL MURTALIZE--FIVE OR SIX NICE MINT LEAVES IN THE BOTTOM OF YOUR GLASS.
NOW FOR THE FUN PART. YOU GOTTA FILL A BIG CANVAS BAG--YOU CAN BUY 'EM--WITH GOOD, HARD ICE CUBES AND THEN WHALE THE TAR OUTTA THEM WITH A CARPENTER'S MAUL. THAT'S WHAT THEY CALL THE BIG HAMMER. DO IT UNTIL THERE AIN'T NO MORE LUMPS. DON'T BE NICE, NEITHER.
NOW YOU GOTTA PACK THE GLASS, AND I MEAN PACK IT, WITH THE SNOW ICE FROM THE BAG, AND THEN POUR IN ENOUGH OLD COGNAC BRANDY--DON'T BE A CHEAPSKATE HERE--TO FILL THE THING. YOU WANT ONE OF THEM VSOPS, EVEN A WHATCHAMACALLIT, AN XO. THIS'S A RICH FOLKS' DRINK, AND IT'S WORTH IT. OH, AND BE SURE TO GIVE IT A STIR AND THEN ADD MORE ICE, 'CAUSE IT'LL SINK.
OKAY. MINT. DON'T SKIMP HERE, NEITHER. SOME FOLKS PUT IN, LIKE, ONE SPRIG. NAH. LOTSA MINT. LOTS.
COUPLE OF STRAWS, TOO, AND DON'T MAKE 'EM TOO LONG--YOU GOTTA GET YOUR NOSE RIGHT IN THE MINT. AND TRY NOT TO TOUCH THE GLASS, SO THAT IT CAN GET A NICE LAYER A FROST ON THE OUTSIDE.
THEN YOU TIE A BOW ON THIS THING WITH A RUM FLOAT. POUR IT REAL GENTLE, OVER A SPOON.
NOT MUCH--A COUPLE OF SPOONFULS--AND BE SURE TO USE A NICE, OLD, FUNKY JAMAICA RUM. YOUR NOSE'LL THANK YOU.

THE CLASSIC ANTEBELLUM BRANDY JULEP

CHASER: BRANDY

The carefully aged, old, and rich nectar that is a good modern cognac has its roots in the seventeenth century, when some French distillers began deliberately leaving their brandy in oaken barrels for months and even years before shipping them. (Cognac is a type of brandy, just as Pepsi is a type of cola.)

Here's what they learned. If you leave brandy, or any spirit, in a barrel long enough, three things happen. There's EXTRACTION, where the alcohol and water in the booze--both excellent solvents--pull various lignins and tannins and such out of the wood. These things add color, texture, and even a little sweetness. Left too long, though, and the tannins get harsh and bitter.

At the same time, there's OXIDATION, where the air in the barrel breaks down many of the long-chain flavor molecules in the brandy. Some of these followed the alcohol and water through the still; others came from the wood. With pieces of these combining to form new compounds, the brandy stops tasting like grapes and wood and starts tasting like, well, brandy.

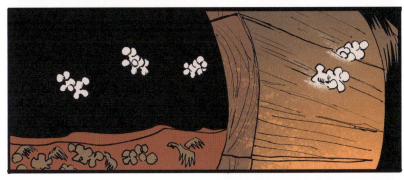

Finally, there's CONCENTRATION. Barrels are porous, and not only does air get in, but also water, alcohol, and other volatile compounds get out.

The heavier compounds that stay behind get more and more concentrated, making the brandy taste thicker and richer.

All of this chemistry means that--as long as it's managed well--you'll end up with brandy that smells like nuts and honey, slides over the tongue like silk, and lingers on the palate like money in the bank. It makes for a fine cocktail, too, if you mix it right.

MIXOLOGY:
THE SIDECAR

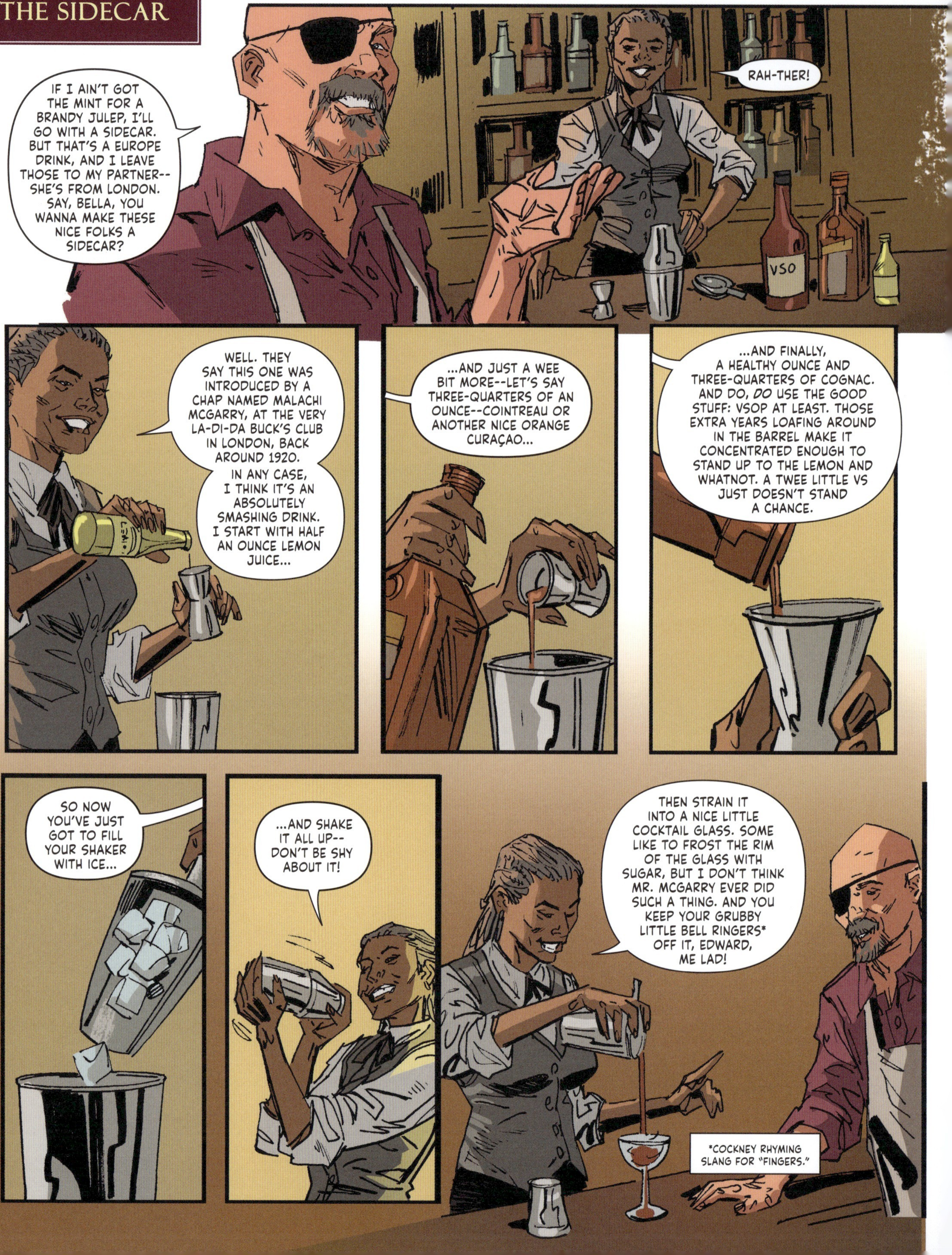
IF I AIN'T GOT THE MINT FOR A BRANDY JULEP, I'LL GO WITH A SIDECAR. BUT THAT'S A EUROPE DRINK, AND I LEAVE THOSE TO MY PARTNER--SHE'S FROM LONDON. SAY, BELLA, YOU WANNA MAKE THESE NICE FOLKS A SIDECAR?
RAH-THER!
VSO
WELL. THEY SAY THIS ONE WAS INTRODUCED BY A CHAP NAMED MALACHI MCGARRY, AT THE VERY LA-DI-DA BUCK'S CLUB IN LONDON, BACK AROUND 1920.
IN ANY CASE, I THINK IT'S AN ABSOLUTELY SMASHING DRINK. I START WITH HALF AN OUNCE LEMON JUICE...
...AND JUST A WEE BIT MORE--LET'S SAY THREE-QUARTERS OF AN OUNCE--COINTREAU OR ANOTHER NICE ORANGE CURAÇAO...
...AND FINALLY, A HEALTHY OUNCE AND THREE-QUARTERS OF COGNAC. AND DO, *DO* USE THE GOOD STUFF: VSOP AT LEAST. THOSE EXTRA YEARS LOAFING AROUND IN THE BARREL MAKE IT CONCENTRATED ENOUGH TO STAND UP TO THE LEMON AND WHATNOT. A TWEE LITTLE VS JUST DOESN'T STAND A CHANCE.
SO NOW YOU'VE JUST GOT TO FILL YOUR SHAKER WITH ICE...
...AND SHAKE IT ALL UP--DON'T BE SHY ABOUT IT!
THEN STRAIN IT INTO A NICE LITTLE COCKTAIL GLASS. SOME LIKE TO FROST THE RIM OF THE GLASS WITH SUGAR, BUT I DON'T THINK MR. MCGARRY EVER DID SUCH A THING. AND YOU KEEP YOUR GRUBBY LITTLE BELL RINGERS* OFF IT, EDWARD, ME LAD!
*COCKNEY RHYMING SLANG FOR "FINGERS."

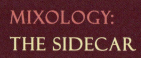

CHAPTER III

COCKING THE TAIL

London, the Hudson Valley, and, Well, Everywhere ~ 1690–1860

In its campaign to establish a new, all-American school of drinking, the Julep had a close partner, one that was also a mix of booze, sugar, water, and a little something extra to make it interesting. Where the Julep's something extra was mint, the Cock-Tail (as the name was originally written) used bitters. Every modern cocktail stands on that simple four-part foundation.

The cocktail's ancestry begins with Purl, an English stomach settler and hangover cure made by steeping wormwood and other bitter herbs in beer or (for Purl Royal) wine. This tasted bitter and brackish and took a couple of weeks to prepare.

In 1690 or 1691, Richard Stoughton, a young London apothecary, came up with a better way to make Purl: an alcoholic extract of herbs with a "pleasant (though bitterish) taste," as his ads claimed. All you had to do was put a couple of spoonfuls into your wine or beer and bam! Purl.

Stoughton was a good businessman and a constant advertiser, and in 1712 he was able to get a royal patent for his Elixir Magnum Stomachicum—or bitters, as everybody took to calling it. But the patent didn't help; the stuff was widely counterfeited: in England, America, Holland—everywhere.

"Wine and Bitters"—Stoughton's bitters plus one of the sweet, fortified wines dominant at the time—was a popular tissue restorer after a night of guzzling Punch. The combination was not that far off from a modern Old-Fashioned.

By the 1760s, those who couldn't afford wine, or whose hangovers laughed at it, took to drinking Gin and Bitters, made with the sweetened, malty gin of the day. The only thing separating this from the American Gin Cocktail of a hundred years later was the ice and the swatch of lemon peel—and, of course, the name.

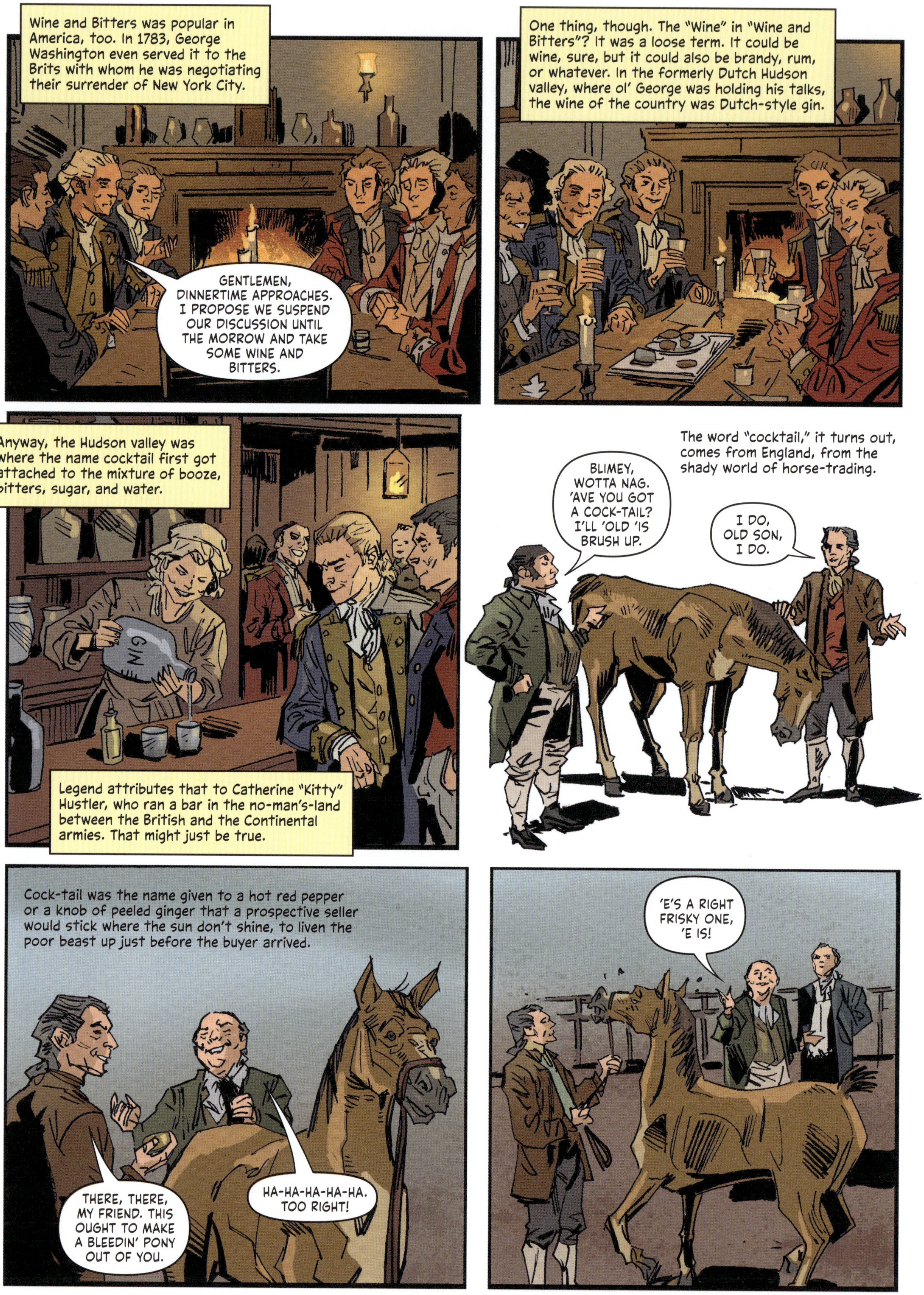
Wine and Bitters was popular in America, too. In 1783, George Washington even served it to the Brits with whom he was negotiating their surrender of New York City.
GENTLEMEN, DINNERTIME APPROACHES. I PROPOSE WE SUSPEND OUR DISCUSSION UNTIL THE MORROW AND TAKE SOME WINE AND BITTERS.
One thing, though. The "Wine" in "Wine and Bitters"? It was a loose term. It could be wine, sure, but it could also be brandy, rum, or whatever. In the formerly Dutch Hudson valley, where ol' George was holding his talks, the wine of the country was Dutch-style gin.
Anyway, the Hudson valley was where the name cocktail first got attached to the mixture of booze, bitters, sugar, and water.
GIN
Legend attributes that to Catherine "Kitty" Hustler, who ran a bar in the no-man's-land between the British and the Continental armies. That might just be true.
The word "cocktail," it turns out, comes from England, from the shady world of horse-trading.
BLIMEY, WOTTA NAG. 'AVE YOU GOT A COCK-TAIL? I'LL 'OLD 'IS BRUSH UP.
I DO, OLD SON, I DO.
Cock-tail was the name given to a hot red pepper or a knob of peeled ginger that a prospective seller would stick where the sun don't shine, to liven the poor beast up just before the buyer arrived.
THERE, THERE, MY FRIEND. THIS OUGHT TO MAKE A BLEEDIN' PONY OUT OF YOU.
HA-HA-HA-HA-HA. TOO RIGHT!
'E'S A RIGHT FRISKY ONE, 'E IS!

At some point in the late eighteenth century, members of the sporting set took to using this cock-tail, in the form of ginger essence or powdered cayenne, to spice up their morning drams.

"I'LL TAKE MY COCK-TAIL BY MOUTH, THANKEE."

Over in America, however, that "cock-tail" came to mean the mixture, not just the thing it was spiced with, and cayenne and ginger yielded to Stoughton's bitters as the preferred spice.

The drink was eventually defined in print in 1806 when Harry Croswell, a newspaper editor in Hudson, New York (some 120 miles north of New York City), answered a reader's query about the strange drink he had mentioned the week before.

One thing remained constant: the drink was still an antifogmatic, which is to say, an eye-opener, a corpse reviver, a phlegm cutter, a pick-me-up--a morning-after drink.

THE PIONEERING CELEBRITY BARTENDER ORSAMUS WILLARD COCKING TAILS AT NEW YORK'S CITY HOTEL, 1817

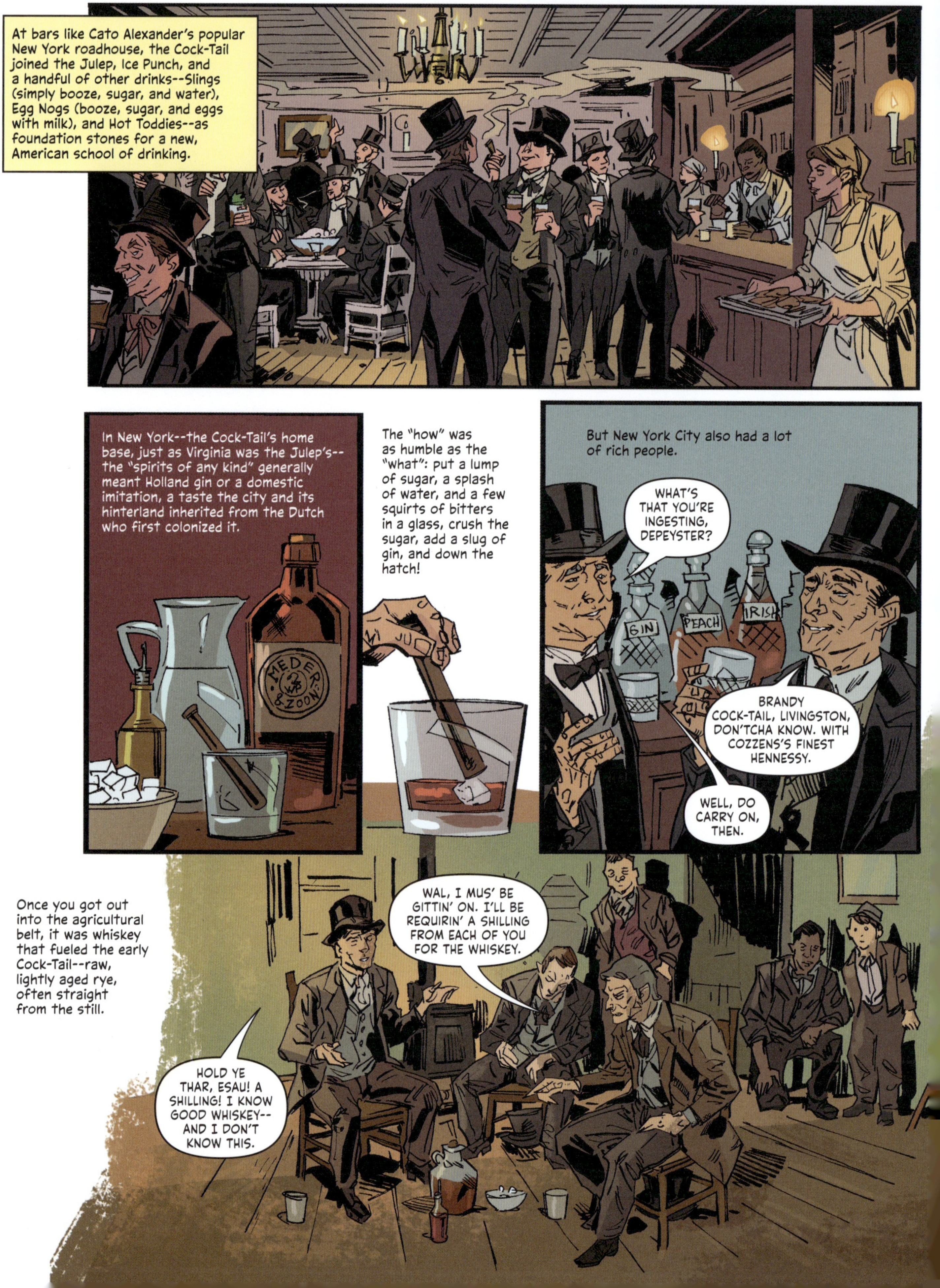
At bars like Cato Alexander's popular New York roadhouse, the Cock-Tail joined the Julep, Ice Punch, and a handful of other drinks--Slings (simply booze, sugar, and water), Egg Nogs (booze, sugar, and eggs with milk), and Hot Toddies--as foundation stones for a new, American school of drinking.
In New York--the Cock-Tail's home base, just as Virginia was the Julep's--the "spirits of any kind" generally meant Holland gin or a domestic imitation, a taste the city and its hinterland inherited from the Dutch who first colonized it.
MEDER &ZOON
The "how" was as humble as the "what": put a lump of sugar, a splash of water, and a few squirts of bitters in a glass, crush the sugar, add a slug of gin, and down the hatch!
But New York City also had a lot of rich people.
WHAT'S THAT YOU'RE INGESTING, DEPEYSTER?
GIN
PEACH
IRISH
BRANDY COCK-TAIL, LIVINGSTON, DON'TCHA KNOW. WITH COZZENS'S FINEST HENNESSY.
WELL, DO CARRY ON, THEN.
Once you got out into the agricultural belt, it was whiskey that fueled the early Cock-Tail--raw, lightly aged rye, often straight from the still.
WAL, I MUS' BE GITTIN' ON. I'LL BE REQUIRIN' A SHILLING FROM EACH OF YOU FOR THE WHISKEY.
HOLD YE THAR, ESAU! A SHILLING! I KNOW GOOD WHISKEY--AND I DON'T KNOW THIS.

During the 1820s, the Cocktail (as it was now being written) spread to every part of the new country, from Balize, Louisiana, where the Mississippi met the Gulf of Mexico...

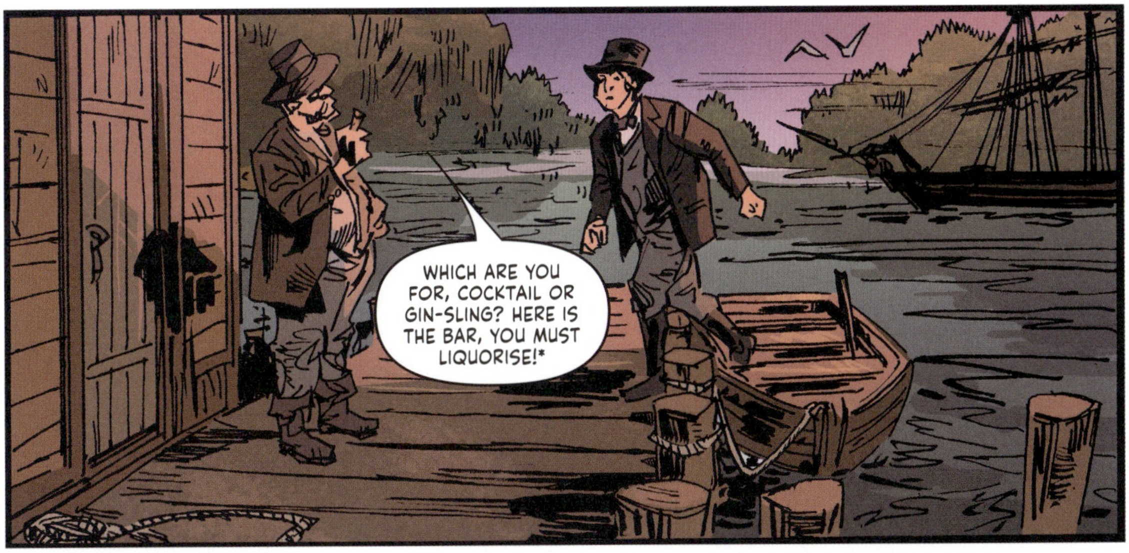
WHICH ARE YOU FOR, COCKTAIL OR GIN-SLING? HERE IS THE BAR, YOU MUST LIQUORISE!*

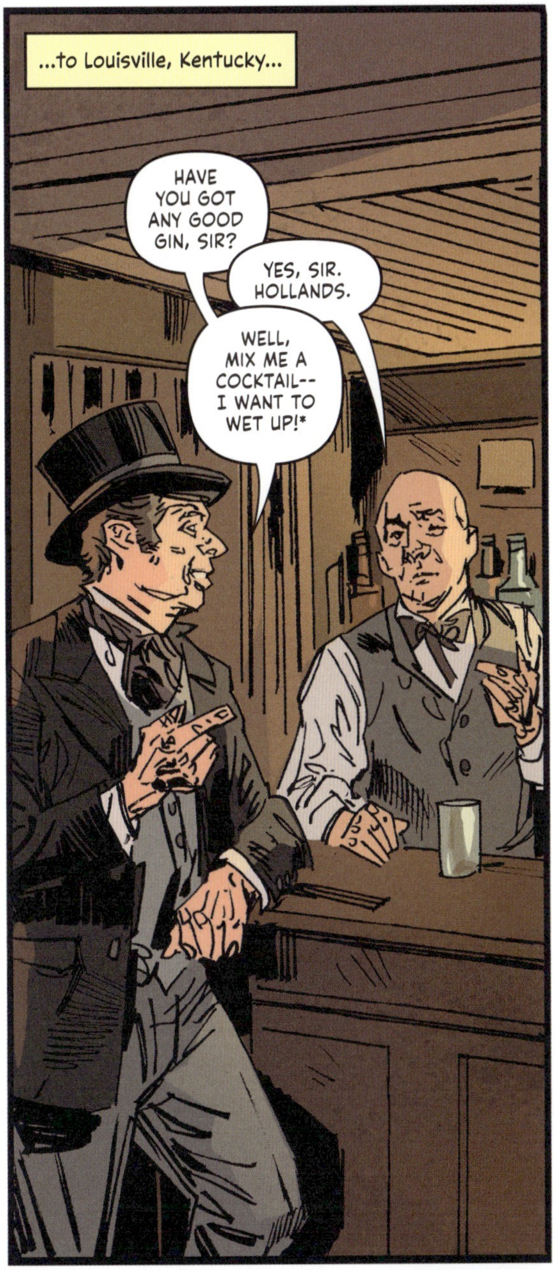
...to Louisville, Kentucky...
HAVE YOU GOT ANY GOOD GIN, SIR?
YES, SIR. HOLLANDS.
WELL, MIX ME A COCKTAIL-- I WANT TO WET UP!*

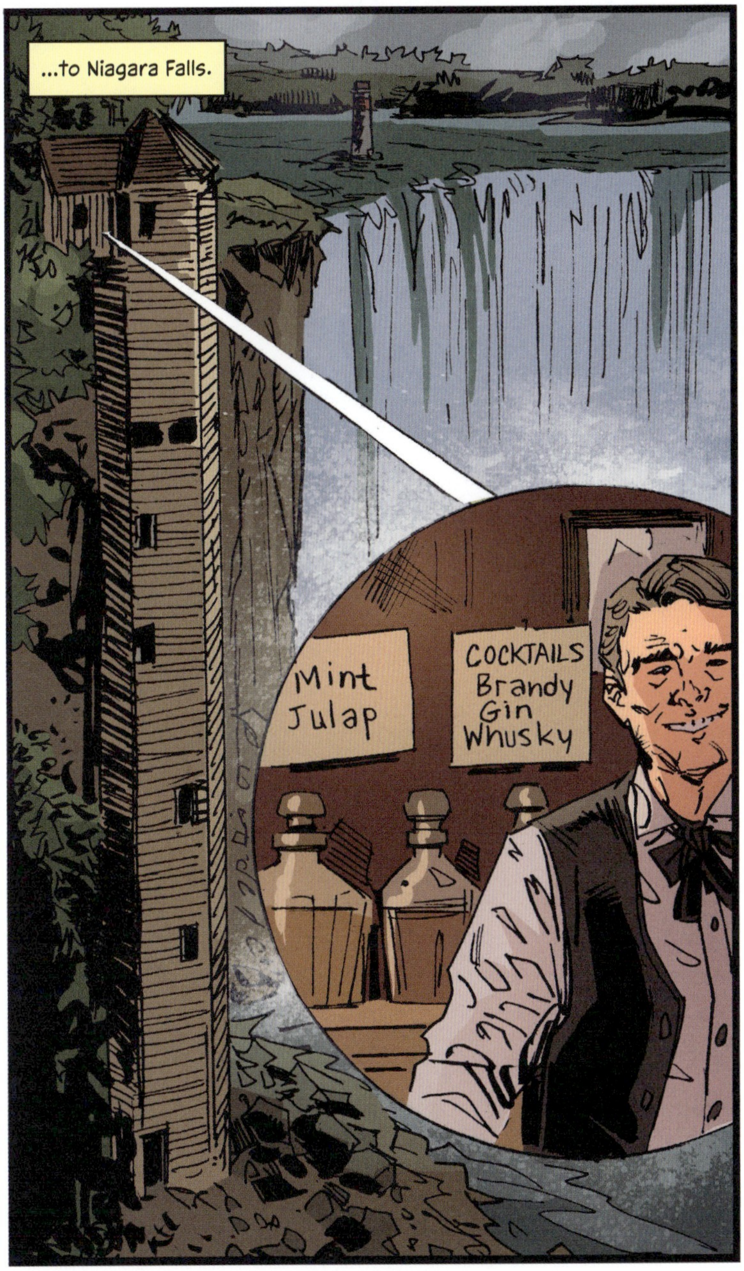
...to Niagara Falls.
Mint Julap
COCKTAILS
Brandy
Gin
Whusky

*DIALOGUE VERBATIM FROM CONTEMPORARY SOURCES.

By the 1830s, American bartending had been focusing on the practice of mixing single-serving iced drinks to order for well over a generation. It had also become a lot more male, with the saucy London-type barmaid yielding to the cocky young man, who made a big show out of mixing drinks.

One of the bartender's flashiest new tricks was to pour the drink from glass to glass in a rapid series of arcs, which got longer and longer as the century went on.

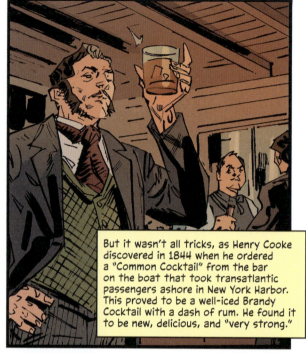

But it wasn't all tricks, as Henry Cooke discovered in 1844 when he ordered a "Common Cocktail" from the bar on the boat that took transatlantic passengers ashore in New York Harbor. This proved to be a well-iced Brandy Cocktail with a dash of rum. He found it to be new, delicious, and "very strong."

Once ice finally made it into the Cocktail, so did other, more exotic things. In 1843, the New York *Sunday Mercury* mentioned a Cocktail "compounded of brandy, sugar, absynthe [sic], bitters and ice," as if the absinthe were an everyday addition.

In New Orleans, the fancy went deep. By the 1850s, at Joseph Santini's famous Jewel of the South, you could get your Cocktail with a splash of maraschino liqueur and a dash of lemon juice, served in a fancy glass lined with lemon peel and rolled in sugar.

By 1860, as America was about to topple into the Civil War, the Cocktail had evolved from a simple Yankee eye-opener, made to be tossed down the gullet by the bleary-eyed, to an exquisitely flavored, iced dewdrop, savored by the discriminating when work was done for the day.

Now you had options. You could have it in the traditional glass or strained into something rather fancier.

You could stick with lump sugar to sweeten your drink or use sugar syrup--or raspberry syrup or even orgeat, made from almonds. Or you could use an alcoholic cordial: maraschino, distilled in Croatia from cherries, and curaçao, flavored with orange peel, were the first to gain popularity.

Epicurean Cocktail drinkers liked theirs fancy, with syrup *and* curaçao, plus a squeeze of lemon oil to give the drink nose appeal.

If you wanted something more refreshing than gin, you could have a Jersey Cocktail, with chilled hard cider instead of the booze, or a Champagne Cocktail, an 1850s creation that is still favored by sporty drinkers.

THE CHAMPAGNE COCKTAIL

Really epicurean Cocktail drinkers took themselves to New Orleans and had one of Santini's Crustas, as he called them.

And if you wanted something more refreshing still, there was the Soda Cocktail, a mix of soda water, sugar, bitters, and ice that was long and refreshing and essentially nonalcoholic (only the bitters had alcohol, and the drink took just a couple of dashes of them).

MIXOLOGY: THE IMPROVED HOLLAND GIN COCKTAIL

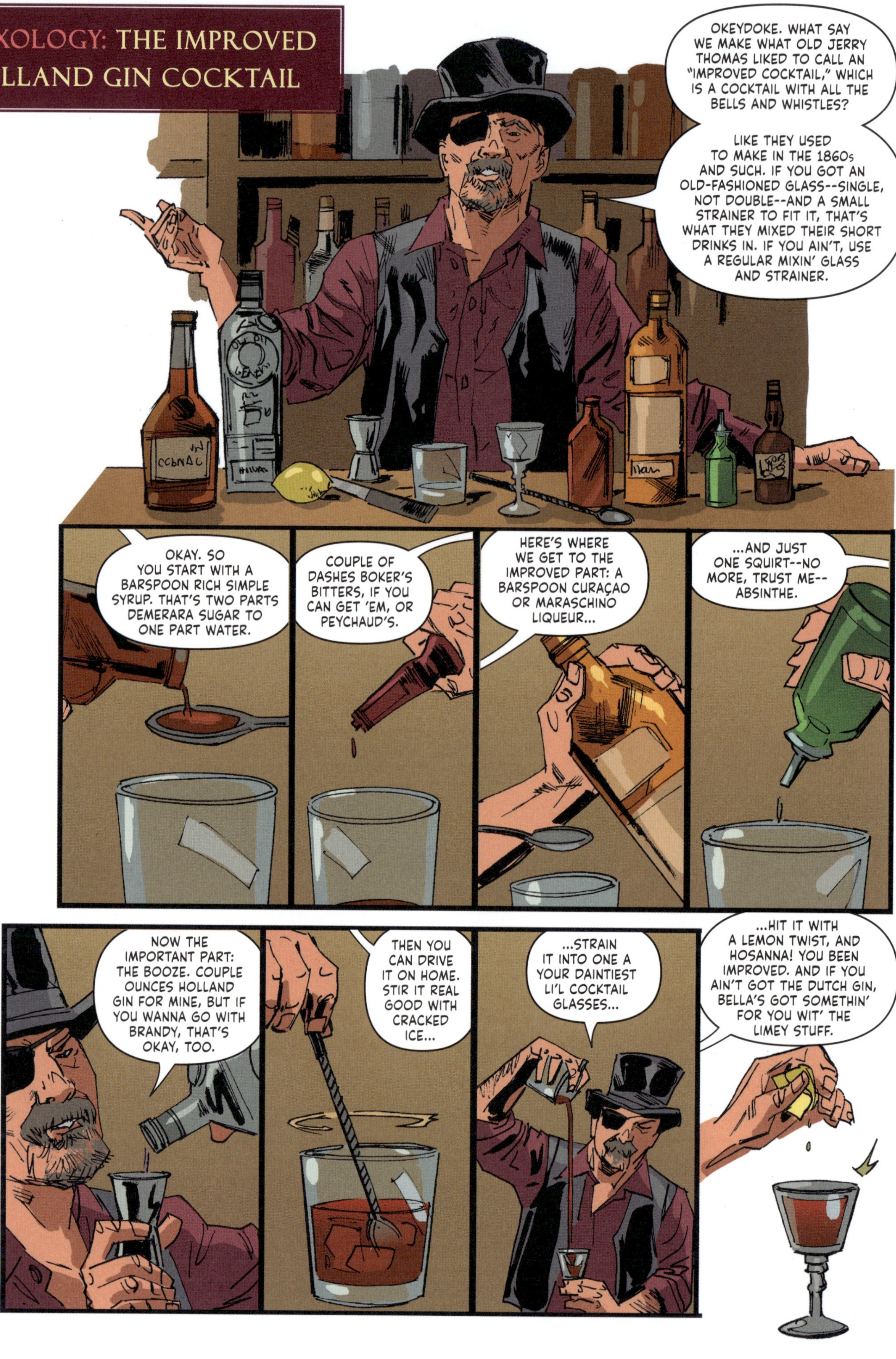

OKEYDOKE. WHAT SAY WE MAKE WHAT OLD JERRY THOMAS LIKED TO CALL AN "IMPROVED COCKTAIL," WHICH IS A COCKTAIL WITH ALL THE BELLS AND WHISTLES?
LIKE THEY USED TO MAKE IN THE 1860s AND SUCH. IF YOU GOT AN OLD-FASHIONED GLASS--SINGLE, NOT DOUBLE--AND A SMALL STRAINER TO FIT IT, THAT'S WHAT THEY MIXED THEIR SHORT DRINKS IN. IF YOU AIN'T, USE A REGULAR MIXIN' GLASS AND STRAINER.
COGNAC
OKAY. SO YOU START WITH A BARSPOON RICH SIMPLE SYRUP. THAT'S TWO PARTS DEMERARA SUGAR TO ONE PART WATER.
COUPLE OF DASHES BOKER'S BITTERS, IF YOU CAN GET 'EM, OR PEYCHAUD'S.
HERE'S WHERE WE GET TO THE IMPROVED PART: A BARSPOON CURAÇAO OR MARASCHINO LIQUEUR...
...AND JUST ONE SQUIRT--NO MORE, TRUST ME--ABSINTHE.
NOW THE IMPORTANT PART: THE BOOZE. COUPLE OUNCES HOLLAND GIN FOR MINE, BUT IF YOU WANNA GO WITH BRANDY, THAT'S OKAY, TOO.
THEN YOU CAN DRIVE IT ON HOME. STIR IT REAL GOOD WITH CRACKED ICE...
...STRAIN IT INTO ONE A YOUR DAINTIEST LI'L COCKTAIL GLASSES...
...HIT IT WITH A LEMON TWIST, AND HOSANNA! YOU BEEN IMPROVED. AND IF YOU AIN'T GOT THE DUTCH GIN, BELLA'S GOT SOMETHIN' FOR YOU WIT' THE LIMEY STUFF.

MIXOLOGY: THE PINK GIN

CHASER: GIN

We owe modern gin to the nineteenth-century Industrial Revolution.

At the beginning of the century, gin was simply flavored whiskey: made in pot stills from barley malt, rye, a few juniper berries, and maybe a couple of other botanicals. When made properly, as the Dutch did, it tasted thick and malty and was good in Hot Toddies. Then came the column still.

The column still fed steam into the bottom and the raw, fermented wash into the top. As the wash made its way down through a series of perforated plates, the rising steam collected the alcohol.

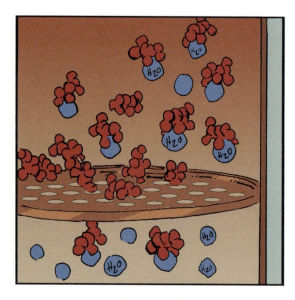

With enough column, the alcohol will rise to a point where it's cool enough for it to condense, with the (heavier) water left several plates below.

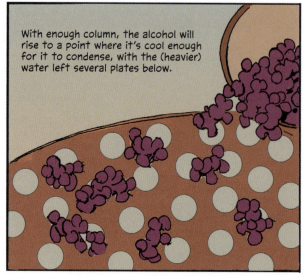

DAMN ME, THAT'S STRONG! BUT METHINKS IT WANTS THE OLD FLAVOR AND BODY.

BODY BE DAMNED! FLAVOR BE DAMNED! THIS, THIS PANJANDRUM MAKES A DAY'S WORTH OF SPIRIT IN AN HOUR! WE'D BE FOOLS NOT TO BUY ONE.

If the new stills left most of the flavor and texture back with the water, English distillers soon found another way to flavor their gin: botanicals.

Supplementing the traditional juniper berries with cornucopian bouquets of herbs, flowers, roots, barks, and peels made a thin spirit taste light, bright, and flavorful.

While one could buy this new gin unsweetened, nobody actually drank it that way. They preferred it as Old Tom or Cream of the Valley (both strong and very lightly sweetened) or especially as the weaker, sweeter, and cheaper cordial gin.

This new style of gin also happened to make delightful mixed drinks: bright, refreshing Punches, crisp Cocktails, light and lively Sours, and of course Pink Gin.

CHAPTER IV

AMERICAN DRINKS IN ENDLESS PROFUSION

New York, Boston, New Orleans, Toronto, Washington, D.C., and so on ~ 1830–1867

What if you didn't want a slug of booze with bitters or a double slug with mint? Fortunately, this burgeoning American art of the bar had you covered. While they were perfecting the Julep and the Cocktail, American bartenders were also creating a whole ecosystem of delightful bar drinks to back them up.

"WHAT'LL YE TAKE, MY FRIEND?"

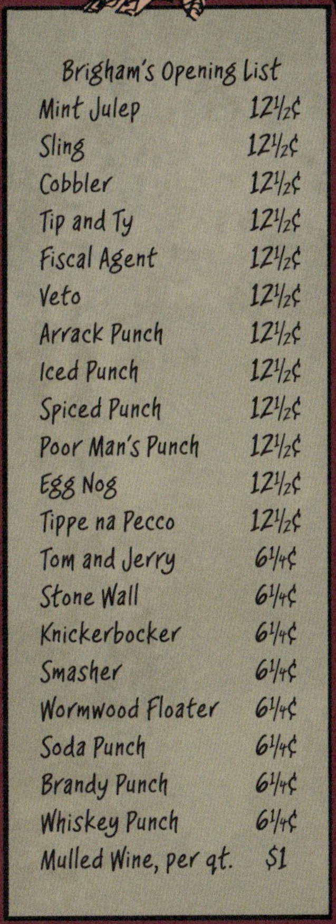

Brigham's Opening List

Mint Julep	12½¢
Sling	12½¢
Cobbler	12½¢
Tip and Ty	12½¢
Fiscal Agent	12½¢
Veto	12½¢
Arrack Punch	12½¢
Iced Punch	12½¢
Spiced Punch	12½¢
Poor Man's Punch	12½¢
Egg Nog	12½¢
Tippe na Pecco	12½¢
Tom and Jerry	6¼¢
Stone Wall	6¼¢
Knickerbocker	6¼¢
Smasher	6¼¢
Wormwood Floater	6¼¢
Soda Punch	6¼¢
Brandy Punch	6¼¢
Whiskey Punch	6¼¢
Mulled Wine, per qt.	$1

You could see this new art on full display at Boston's Concert Hall, where at the end of 1842 a flinty Yankee named Peter Bent Brigham opened a lavishly appointed oyster saloon on the ground floor. Along with the freshest oysters, he offered a printed list of twenty-one mixed drinks plus champagne and Madeira—although within a year the list would more than double in length.

Brigham's Mystery Drinks

Moral Suasion   Tippe na Pecco

Jewett's Fancy   Veto

Ching Ching   Vox Populi

Etc.

Some of Brigham's drinks were familiar, the standards that he had collected and played around with (eventually he offered ten different Juleps, from Mint to Race Horse). Others were purely his own creations. Unfortunately, he left no recipes for those.

The newspapers made hay of Brigham's list, reprinting it far, wide, and often, as if to say, "See what wild fellows we Americans are?" Bartenders picked up on the drinks, making the ones they knew and making up the ones they didn't, as bartenders do, with varying degrees of success.

37

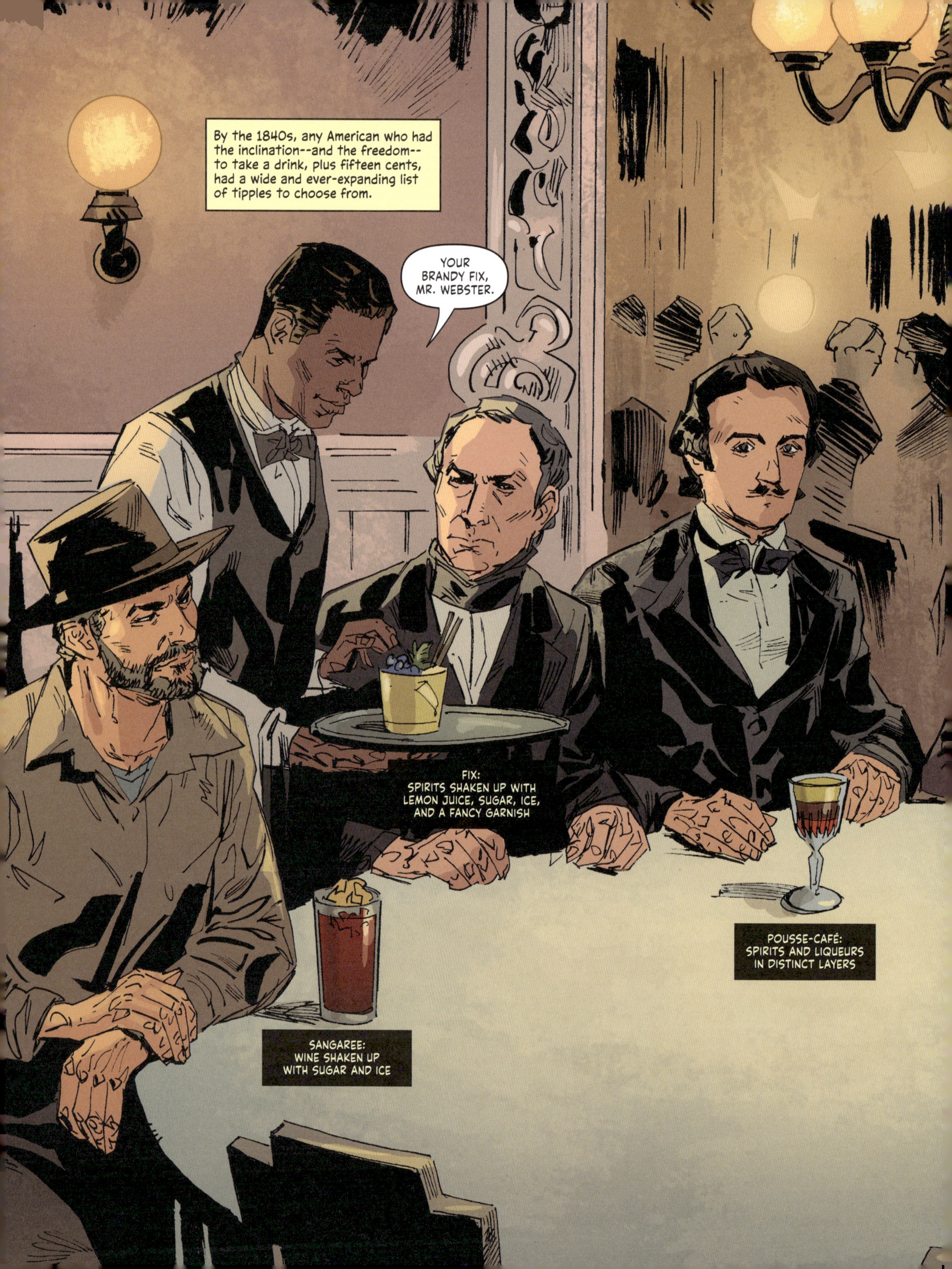
By the 1840s, any American who had the inclination--and the freedom--to take a drink, plus fifteen cents, had a wide and ever-expanding list of tipples to choose from.
YOUR BRANDY FIX, MR. WEBSTER.
FIX: SPIRITS SHAKEN UP WITH LEMON JUICE, SUGAR, ICE, AND A FANCY GARNISH
POUSSE-CAFÉ: SPIRITS AND LIQUEURS IN DISTINCT LAYERS
SANGAREE: WINE SHAKEN UP WITH SUGAR AND ICE

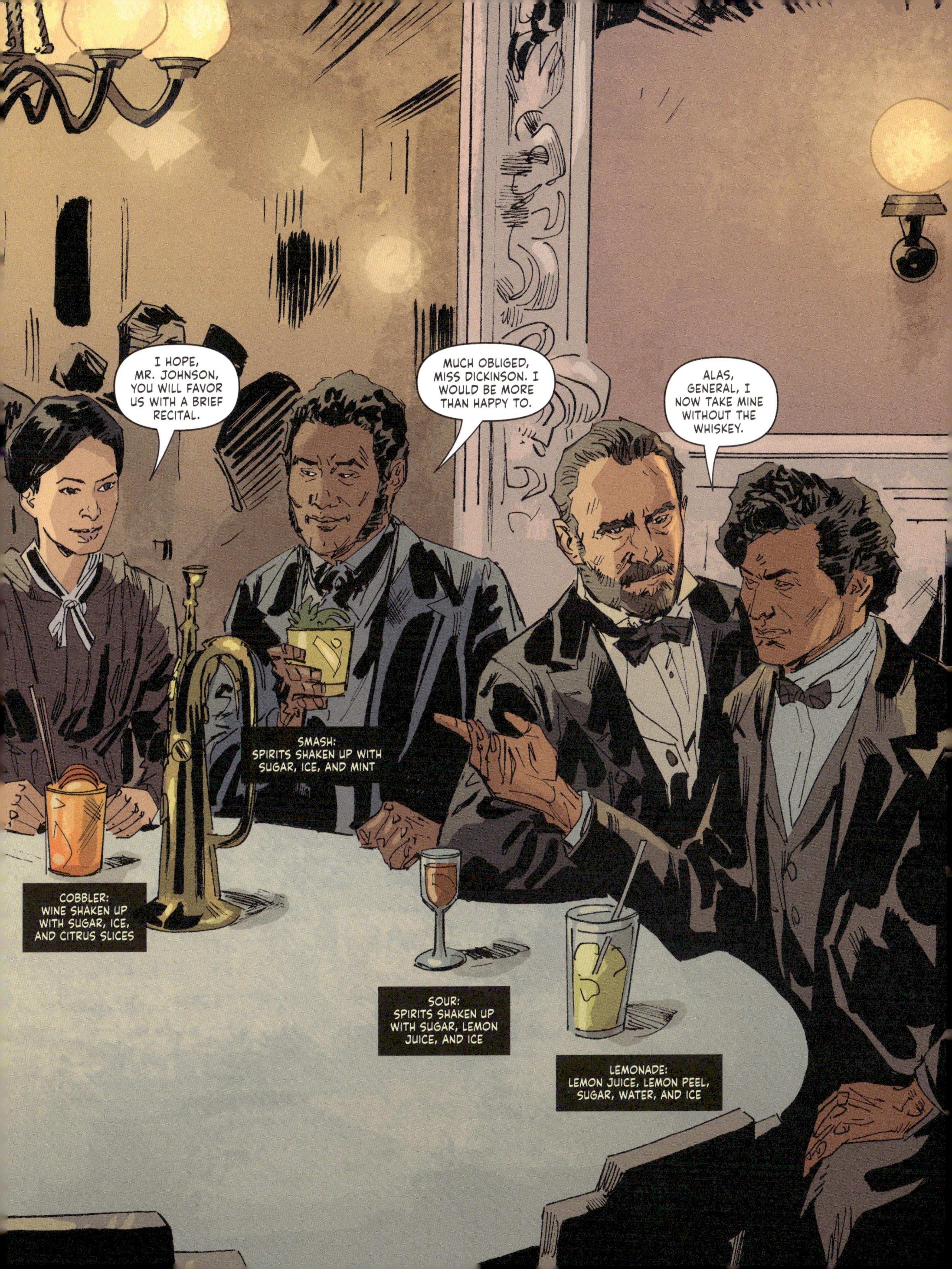
I HOPE, MR. JOHNSON, YOU WILL FAVOR US WITH A BRIEF RECITAL.
MUCH OBLIGED, MISS DICKINSON. I WOULD BE MORE THAN HAPPY TO.
ALAS, GENERAL, I NOW TAKE MINE WITHOUT THE WHISKEY.
SMASH: SPIRITS SHAKEN UP WITH SUGAR, ICE, AND MINT
COBBLER: WINE SHAKEN UP WITH SUGAR, ICE, AND CITRUS SLICES
SOUR: SPIRITS SHAKEN UP WITH SUGAR, LEMON JUICE, AND ICE
LEMONADE: LEMON JUICE, LEMON PEEL, SUGAR, WATER, AND ICE

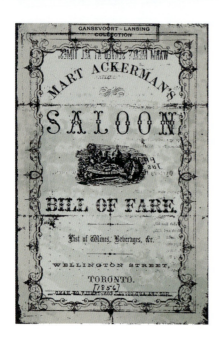

Many bars, not content to plagiarize Brigham, came up with their own lists of fancy drinks.

In 1856, Mart Ackerman's Toronto saloon had 107 of them on offer.

While we can dope out some two-thirds of Ackerman's list from the names of the drinks, that leaves well over thirty head-scratchers, named after celebrities, events of the day, and such--the same things we name cocktails after now.

What's in a Parliament Smash or an Omar Pasha Cocktail? Dunno. The cocktail book won't be invented until chapter 5, and newspapers thought it was unseemly to give too much detail about alcoholic beverages.

Equally creative were the bartenders at John D. Hammack's ornate saloon on Pennsylvania Avenue in Washington, D.C., right across the street from the White House.

Hammack's, too, boasted of thirty undecipherables--but out of only eighty drinks.

While most of the fancy drinks of the mid-nineteenth century were mixed by male hands to go down male gullets, that doesn't mean all of them were. If women weren't generally welcome at the bar itself, many saloons had back rooms that women could share, or even--as Brigham's had--ones created exclusively for them.

While "respectable" women usually stayed away from the boozier drinks--Cocktails, Sours, Slings--they drank plenty of Juleps, and there ain't nothing much boozier than a Julep.

If American men had done everything in their power to take over the job of tending bar, a woman or two still occasionally managed to thrive in it.

For example, Martha King Niblo ran the bar at Niblo's Garden, an indoor-outdoor pleasure garden and music venue that was one of New York's biggest attractions.

If she didn't invent the Sherry Cobbler, which first appeared in print in 1837 and went on to be one of the most popular drinks of the century, Mrs. Niblo can at least be credited with popularizing it. As the veteran actor John Brougham later recalled, "A sherry cobbler from her dainty hand was something specially inviting."

Of course, Martha Niblo wasn't the only woman behind the bar in America.

But while women were common enough in neighborhood joints, country taverns, and urban dives, they were extremely scarce in fancy cocktail bars. Which means that, for their story, you'll need to wait for The Comic Book History of the Dive Bar.

Nor should we forget that the Vermouth Cocktail--ancestor of the Manhattan and the Martini--was first spotted at an 1868 banquet for New York's Sorosis Club, a group of professional women. But we'll get to that part of the story in chapter 7.

With all the fancy drinks in their gaudy splendor, it's easy to lose sight of the fact that, usually, only a couple of the drinks in the American bartender's repertoire were doing most of the work. By the 1860s, those would be the (Gin, Whiskey, or Brandy) Cocktail and the (Whiskey or Brandy) Sour.

(It didn't help that bartenders kept giving fanciful new names to their tiny variations on standard drinks so that, for example, a Brandy Cocktail with a barspoon of orange curaçao became a Merit Rover. Confusing.)

As the Atlanta *Constitution* wrote in 1879, "When American meets American then comes the Whisky Sour."

And no wonder--it was as tasty as it was easy to make. Just as tasty, and even easier to make, was the Cocktail. For many, though, that was still a morning drink--one mid-century Brooklyn barkeeper swore he served more Cocktails at 8:00 a.m. than at 8:00 p.m.--but the rest of the day was catching up fast. In fact, by the end of the Civil War, the Cocktail had displaced the Julep as the American drink.

Proof, of a sort, of the Cocktail's rise is the 1867 international contest between an Anglo-Irish lord and a rich Buffalonian, which took place at the bar of the New-York Hotel.

The challenge?

Who could drink more Whiskey Cocktails in a row.

THE PLAYERS

Antonio "Panama Joe" Fernandez
Born Asturias, Spain, 1832
Bartender, New-York Hotel
152 pounds

Albert Haller Tracy Jr.
Born Buffalo, New York, 1834
Gentleman of Private Means
263 pounds

Randall Percy Otway Plunkett, Lord Louth
Born Louth, Ireland, 1832
Late of Her Majesty's Forces
276 pounds

It started, as extraordinary things so often do, when Louth and Tracy got to drinking together at the bar. But let's let Panama Joe tell it:

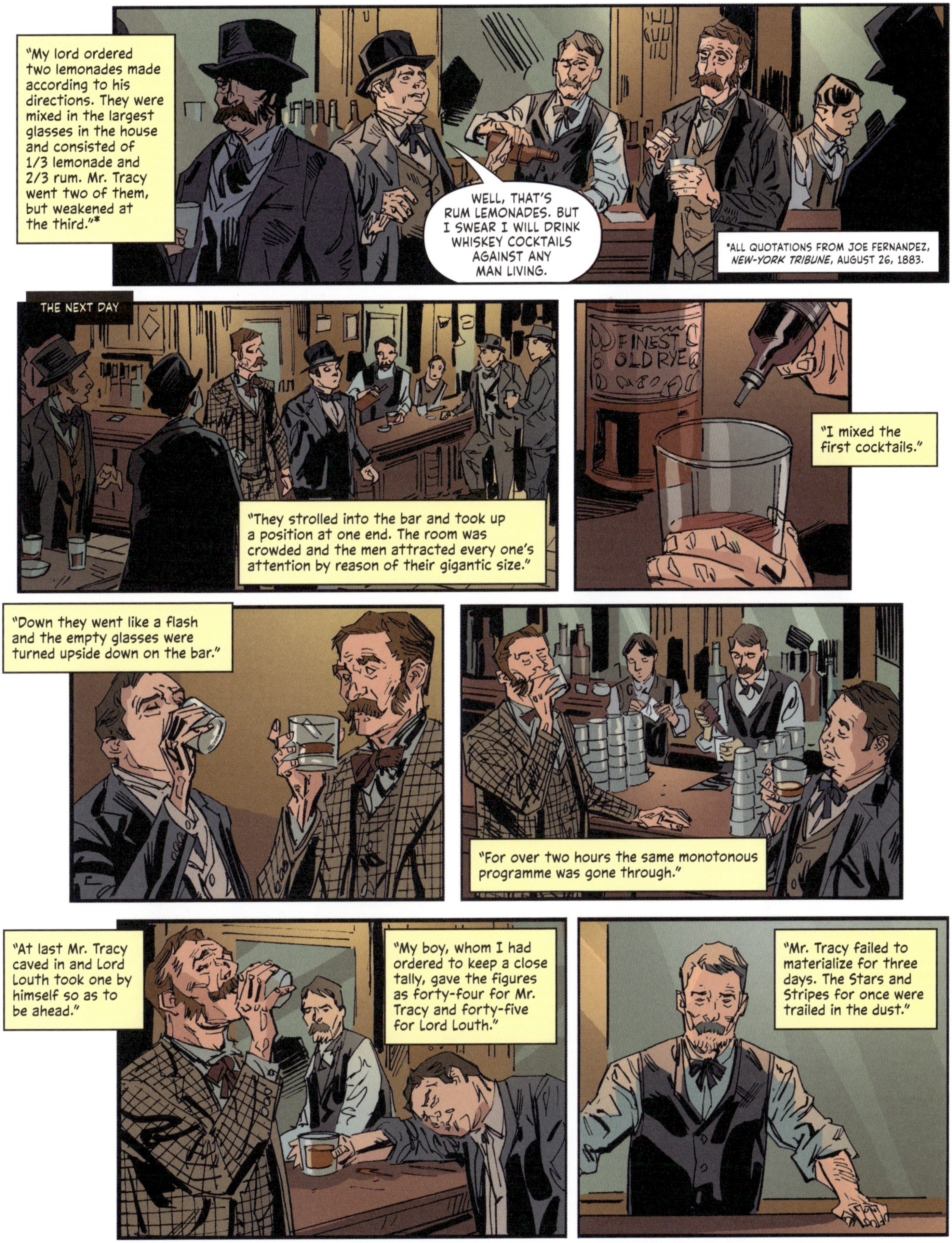

"My lord ordered two lemonades made according to his directions. They were mixed in the largest glasses in the house and consisted of 1/3 lemonade and 2/3 rum. Mr. Tracy went two of them, but weakened at the third."*
WELL, THAT'S RUM LEMONADES. BUT I SWEAR I WILL DRINK WHISKEY COCKTAILS AGAINST ANY MAN LIVING.
*ALL QUOTATIONS FROM JOE FERNANDEZ, *NEW-YORK TRIBUNE*, AUGUST 26, 1883.
THE NEXT DAY
"They strolled into the bar and took up a position at one end. The room was crowded and the men attracted every one's attention by reason of their gigantic size."
FINEST OLD RYE
"I mixed the first cocktails."
"Down they went like a flash and the empty glasses were turned upside down on the bar."
"For over two hours the same monotonous programme was gone through."
"At last Mr. Tracy caved in and Lord Louth took one by himself so as to be ahead."
"My boy, whom I had ordered to keep a close tally, gave the figures as forty-four for Mr. Tracy and forty-five for Lord Louth."
"Mr. Tracy failed to materialize for three days. The Stars and Stripes for once were trailed in the dust."

MIXOLOGY: THE SHERRY COBBLER

MIXOLOGY: THE NEW YORK SOUR

CHAPTER V

THE PROFESSOR: JEREMIAH P. THOMAS

New Haven, New York, New Orleans, and Out West ~ 1830–1885

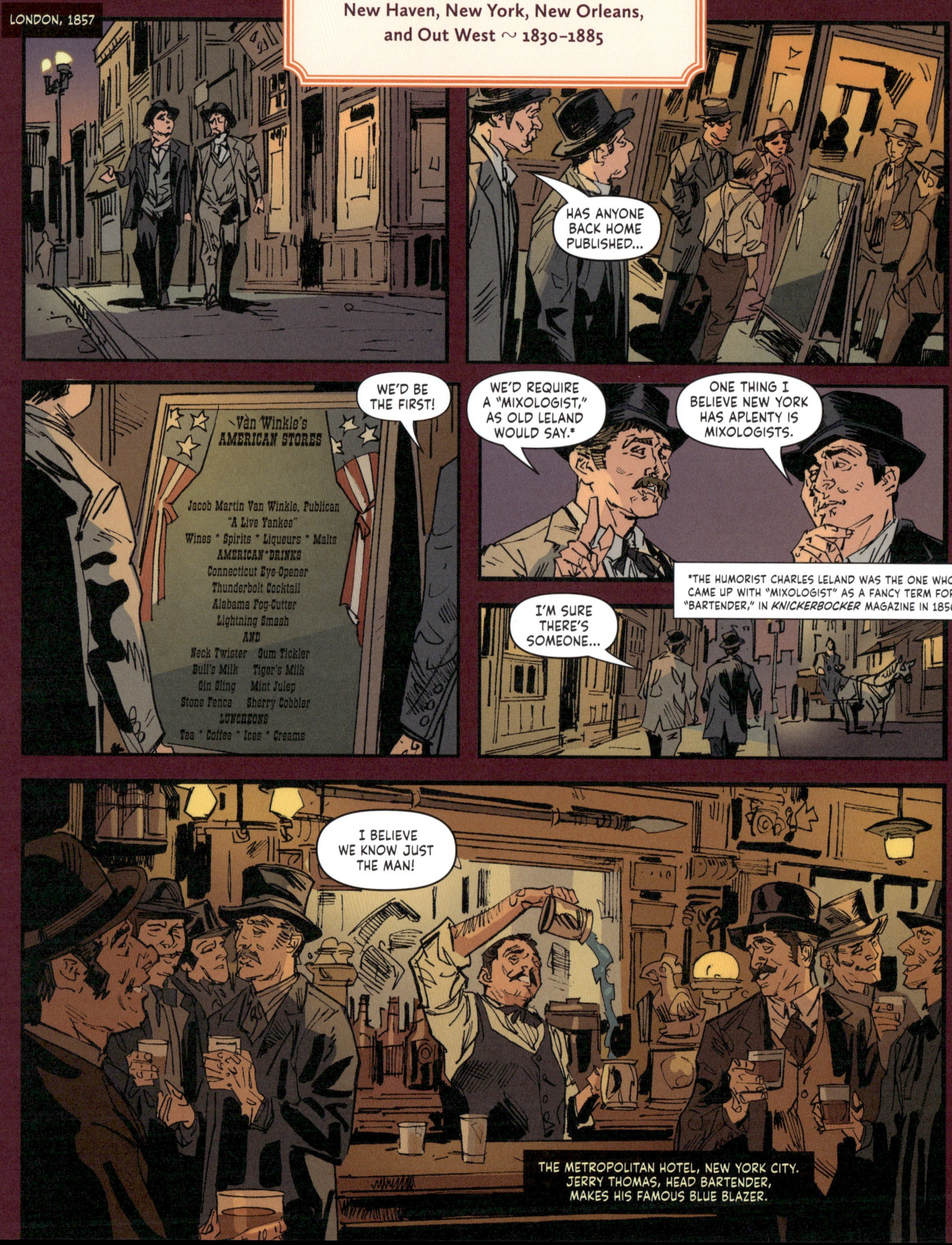
LONDON, 1857
HAS ANYONE BACK HOME PUBLISHED...
Van Winkle's
AMERICAN STORES
Jacob Martin Van Winkle, Publican
"A Live Yankee"
Wines * Spirits * Liqueurs * Malts
AMERICAN*DRINKS
Connecticut Eye-Opener
Thunderbolt Cocktail
Alabama Fog-Cutter
Lightning Smash
AND
Neck Twister Gum Tickler
Bull's Milk Tiger's Milk
Gin Sling Mint Julep
Stone Fence Sherry Cobbler
LUNCHEONS
Tea * Coffee * Ices * Creams
WE'D BE THE FIRST!
WE'D REQUIRE A "MIXOLOGIST," AS OLD LELAND WOULD SAY.*
ONE THING I BELIEVE NEW YORK HAS APLENTY IS MIXOLOGISTS.
*THE HUMORIST CHARLES LELAND WAS THE ONE WHO CAME UP WITH "MIXOLOGIST" AS A FANCY TERM FOR "BARTENDER," IN *KNICKERBOCKER* MAGAZINE IN 1856.
I'M SURE THERE'S SOMEONE...
I BELIEVE WE KNOW JUST THE MAN!
THE METROPOLITAN HOTEL, NEW YORK CITY. JERRY THOMAS, HEAD BARTENDER, MAKES HIS FAMOUS BLUE BLAZER.

"I WAS SUCCESSFULLY LAUNCHED INTO EXISTENCE AS A MEMBER OF THE GREAT AMERICAN NATION AND MADE MYSELF HEARD ON THE THIRTIETH DAY OF OCTOBER 1830 AT SACKETS HARBOR, NEW YORK, ON LAKE ONTARIO'S LONELY EASTERN SHORE.

"MY FAMILY CAME TO AMERICA LONG BEFORE THE REVOLUTION AND WERE ALL GOOD, SOLID TRADESMEN.

"WHEN I WAS YOUNG, MY PARENTS, MY BROTHERS, AND I MOVED TO THE GREAT METROPOLIS OF NEW HAVEN, THEN AS FAMED FOR ITS PORT AS FOR THE ANTICS OF ITS UNDERGRADUATES, AND THERE, AT SIXTEEN, I FIRST STEPPED BEHIND THE BAR, ASSISTING MY BROTHER DAVID H. AT THE PARK HOUSE ON CHURCH STREET.

"ALL THE SWELLS IN TOWN LIKED TO MOISTEN THEIR MORTAL CLAY THERE, AND BEFORE LONG BY CAREFUL ATTENTION TO D.H. AS HE WORKED, I HAD MASTERED ALL THE POPULAR BEVERAGES OF THE DAY--THE COBBLERS, THE SMASHES, THE VARIOUS AND INTRIGUING PUNCHES, THE COCKTAIL.

"THERE CAME A DAY WHEN HE WAS CALLED AWAY ON IMPORTANT BUSINESS, AND WHEN HE RETURNED, HE FOUND I HAD COVERED THE BAR WITH THE WHOLE GAMUT OF DRINKS. BUT YOUNG MEN ARE RESTLESS, AND WHEN THE PARK HOUSE CHANGED MANAGEMENT, WELL, I RAN OFF TO SEA, SAILING ALL AROUND THE WORLD BEFORE THE MAST.

"HOWEVER, AT THE END OF 1849 THE PORT OF CALL WAS SAN FRANCISCO, AND I COULD NO MORE RESIST THE GOLD FEVER THAN A DONKEY COULD A SUNDAY HAT, SO I LEFT THE SEA TO MAKE MY FORTUNE AS A MINER."

"AND SO I DID, ONLY IT WASN'T GOLD I MINED-- I TRIED THAT; I DO NOT RECOMMEND IT.

"RATHER, FROM THE GOLD MINERS THEMSELVES I WAS ABLE TO EXTRACT SIXTEEN THOUSAND DOLLARS IN PURE GOLD DUST BY SEEING TO THEIR DRINKING AND THEIR ENTERTAINMENT.

"INDEED, I COMBINED THE TWO WITH MY 'BLUE BLAZER,' WHICH I FASHIONED FROM AN OLD SAILOR'S DRINK I HAD LEARNED IN MY TRAVELS: A RIVER OF FLAMING WHISKEY, POURED BACK AND FORTH AS THE MINERS GAWPED.

"BUT I WISHED TO SPEND MY EARNINGS WALKING AROUND NEW YORK IN SELECT COMPANY, ALTHOUGH I NEARLY DIED TWICE ON MY WAY THERE.

"THE FIRST TIME, CHOLERA BROKE OUT ON THE BOAT I WAS TAKING DOWN THE SACRAMENTO RIVER TO SAN FRANCISCO; I BARELY SURVIVED AND NO ONE ELSE DID.

"THE SECOND TIME WAS MY OWN DOING, FOR AS I WAS TRAVELING THROUGH MEXICO TO CATCH THE PACKET BOAT, I ALLOWED MYSELF TO DRINK TOO FREELY OF THE SEDUCTIVE AGUAS ARDIENTES OF THE REGION AND THOUGHT I WOULD RIDE MY HORSE INTO THE LOCAL CHURCH TO LIGHT MY CIGAR ON ONE OF THE ALTAR CANDLES--YES, THERE MIGHT HAVE BEEN A WAGER INVOLVED-- AND ONLY THE BRITISH CONSUL COULD HELP ME TO EVADE THE CONSEQUENCES.

"ANYWAY, IN NEW YORK THE MONEY WENT FAST, AND THE LOVELY LITTLE BAR I OPENED BENEATH MR. P.T. BARNUM'S FAMOUS MUSEUM DID NOT LAST LONG.

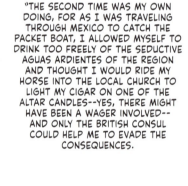

"BY '53, I WAS BACK IN THE ELM CITY--NEW HAVEN--WORKING WITH MY BROTHERS, BUT THAT WOULD NOT DO, AND SO I SET OUT TO SEE THE REST OF AMERICA, FROM BEHIND THE BAR AS IT WERE.

"LET'S SEE, THERE WAS THE MILLS HOUSE, IN CHARLESTON; THEN CHICAGO AND KEOKUK AND A GOOD SPELL AT THE PLANTER'S HOUSE, ST. LOUIS, AND DOWN IN NEW ORLEANS. IN '58, FINALLY, I WENT BACK TO NEW YORK CITY."

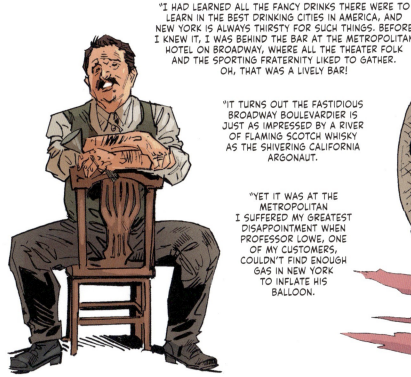

"I HAD LEARNED ALL THE FANCY DRINKS THERE WERE TO LEARN IN THE BEST DRINKING CITIES IN AMERICA, AND NEW YORK IS ALWAYS THIRSTY FOR SUCH THINGS. BEFORE I KNEW IT, I WAS BEHIND THE BAR AT THE METROPOLITAN HOTEL ON BROADWAY, WHERE ALL THE THEATER FOLK AND THE SPORTING FRATERNITY LIKED TO GATHER. OH, THAT WAS A LIVELY BAR!

"IT TURNS OUT THE FASTIDIOUS BROADWAY BOULEVARDIER IS JUST AS IMPRESSED BY A RIVER OF FLAMING SCOTCH WHISKY AS THE SHIVERING CALIFORNIA ARGONAUT.

"YET IT WAS AT THE METROPOLITAN I SUFFERED MY GREATEST DISAPPOINTMENT WHEN PROFESSOR LOWE, ONE OF MY CUSTOMERS, COULDN'T FIND ENOUGH GAS IN NEW YORK TO INFLATE HIS BALLOON.

"YOU SEE, I WAS TO BE A PART OF THE CREW WHEN HE ATTEMPTED THE FIRST TRANSATLANTIC CROSSING BY AIR. I HAD EVEN FURNISHED MYSELF WITH SEALSKIN BOOTS, TROUSERS, AND COAT AGAINST THE COLD AND AN ENORMOUS KNIFE, LEST WE FALL TO THE SHARKS, BUT ALAS THE CROSSING WAS NOT TO BE.

"TO COVER UP MY DISAPPOINTMENT, IN 1860 I OPENED THE MOST BEAUTIFUL BAR YOU EVER DID SEE, ON THE CORNER OF BROADWAY AND WAVERLY PLACE, BUT MY BROTHER GEORGE AND I NEVER COULD GET THE BOOKS TO BALANCE AND I LOST IT. MY, WAS IT FINE! MY NEXT BAR WAS A RATHER MORE HUMBLE ENTERPRISE, AN ALEHOUSE DOWN ON ANN STREET, WHERE ALL THE PUBLISHERS ARE.

"IT SO HAPPENED THAT BILL DICK AND LARRY FITZGERALD, WHO HAD HAD SO MUCH SUCCESS WITH THEIR VARIOUS LITTLE BOOKS TEACHING PEOPLE HOW TO DO WHAT THEY COULDN'T, LIKED TO STOP WITH ME THERE FOR A MUG OF ALE AT THE END OF THE DAY, AND BEFORE LONG I FOUND MYSELF ENLISTED TO APPLY THE SCIENTIFIC METHOD TO THE CLASSIFICATION OF THE VARIOUS MIXTURES, AMERICAN AND OTHERWISE, WITH WHICH I WAS FAMILIAR."

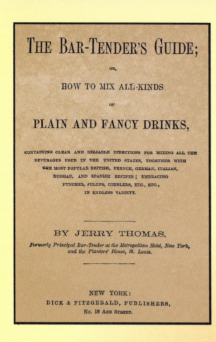

For all his carrying on, Jerry Thomas knew what he was doing, and his book (shown here in its 1876 second edition) was a watershed in the history of the cocktail.

His recipes for popular American drinks weren't the first printed, but they were close, and with the book racking up impressive sales, those recipes were everywhere.

It was no longer necessary for bartenders to take the name and fake the rest. Unfortunately for Thomas, who apparently also provided the illustrations (he was a skilled artist), he got no royalties for the work.

Now the anarchic cloud of American Fancy Drinks had a center. Most important, Thomas assigned the drinks to families that were both user- and bartender-friendly and, fortunately, stable.

Thus a Brandy Cocktail with a spoonful of curaçao was still a Brandy Cocktail, not a "Merit Rover," and if you added a piece of lemon peel and served the drink in a stemmed glass, it was a Fancy Brandy Cocktail, not a "Franklin Peculiar."

In 1863, Thomas was in San Francisco again as head bartender at the new, deluxe Occidental Hotel. There, he self-published a second book: *The Portrait Gallery of Distinguished American Bar Keepers*, with portraits and biographical sketches of America's most prominent bartenders.

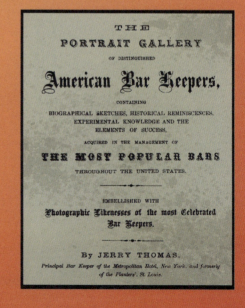

Unfortunately, almost all the print run appears to have burned up in a fire that swept through Virginia City, Nevada, the silver-mining boomtown where Thomas spent 1864. This invaluable work was already scarce by the 1880s, and now all that apparently survives are a draft title page, introductory bits plagiarized from it, and some recipes. If a copy were still available, this history of the cocktail would look very different.

Between 1866 and 1876, the bar that Jerry Thomas ran with his brother George in succeeding locations on Broadway was among New York City's most popular, a grand showcase for the American art of the bar.

Thomas's bars were nothing like our modern temples of mixology: they were brash, even rowdy places, but nonetheless, as the owner of the Metropolitan admitted, "Jerry Thomas was the best barkeeper I ever saw; he had no rival in the city." It wasn't just that he was a genial, sporty, larger-than-life host; he was, as another of his contemporaries recalled, "a genius at mixing drinks" who "knew more about concocting new beverages than any man in America." They called him the Professor.

Weirdly, for a guy who had a statue of himself in his bar, Thomas didn't load his books up with drinks of his own invention. There were some, though. The Japanese Cocktail, commemorating the first Japanese delegation to visit America, combined brandy and bitters with the almond-flavored orgeat syrup.

The Improved Whiskey Cocktail, from 1876, added dashes of maraschino and absinthe to the standard item and put it in a fancy glass. Twenty years later, a couple of tweaks would turn that into the Sazerac.

But Thomas's most famous specialty was the Tom and Jerry, a hot, fluffy Egg Nog variation that he promoted into an American saloon standard.

Until Prohibition stifled the ritual, every November bartenders would ladle out the batter into little shaving mugs, stiffen it with booze, and top it off with hot water or milk and a little grate of nutmeg. (Some bars around the Great Lakes still do it.)

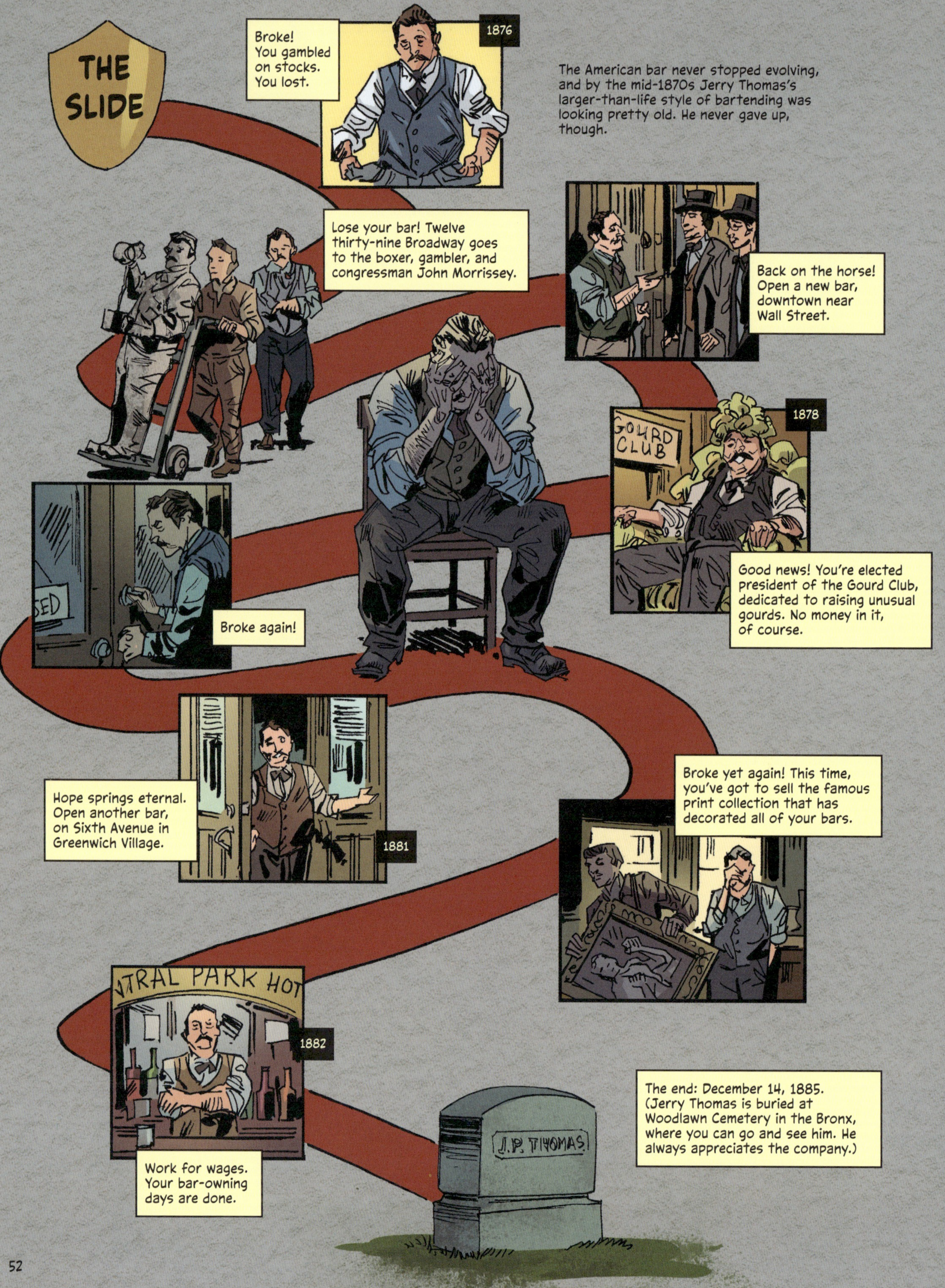
THE SLIDE
The American bar never stopped evolving, and by the mid-1870s Jerry Thomas's larger-than-life style of bartending was looking pretty old. He never gave up, though.
1876
Broke! You gambled on stocks. You lost.
Lose your bar! Twelve thirty-nine Broadway goes to the boxer, gambler, and congressman John Morrissey.
Back on the horse! Open a new bar, downtown near Wall Street.
1878
GOURD CLUB
Good news! You're elected president of the Gourd Club, dedicated to raising unusual gourds. No money in it, of course.
Broke again!
1881
Hope springs eternal. Open another bar, on Sixth Avenue in Greenwich Village.
Broke yet again! This time, you've got to sell the famous print collection that has decorated all of your bars.
NTRAL PARK HOT
1882
Work for wages. Your bar-owning days are done.
J.P. THOMAS
The end: December 14, 1885. (Jerry Thomas is buried at Woodlawn Cemetery in the Bronx, where you can go and see him. He always appreciates the company.)

MIXOLOGY: THE BLUE BLAZER

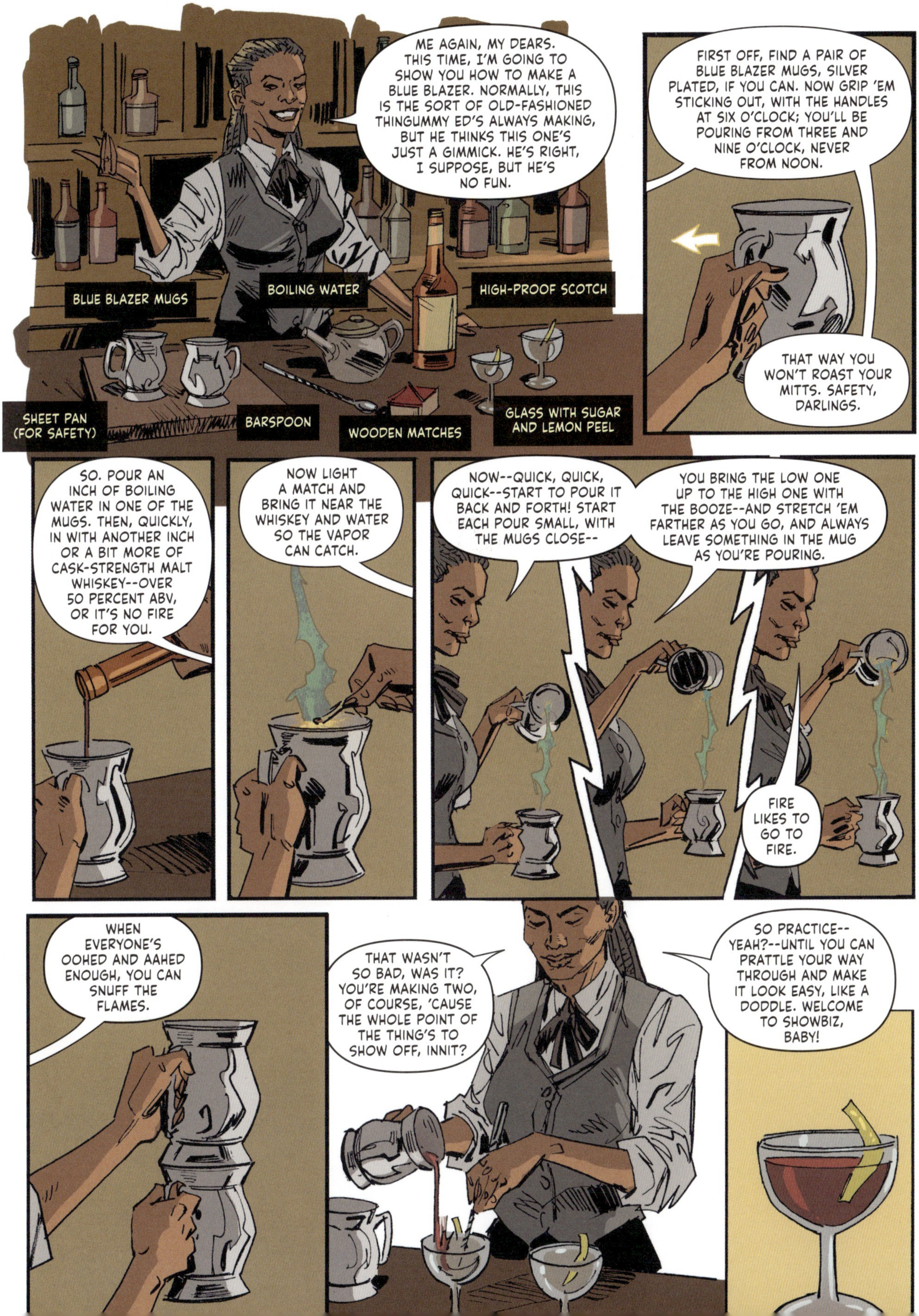

ME AGAIN, MY DEARS. THIS TIME, I'M GOING TO SHOW YOU HOW TO MAKE A BLUE BLAZER. NORMALLY, THIS IS THE SORT OF OLD-FASHIONED THINGUMMY ED'S ALWAYS MAKING, BUT HE THINKS THIS ONE'S JUST A GIMMICK. HE'S RIGHT, I SUPPOSE, BUT HE'S NO FUN.
BLUE BLAZER MUGS
BOILING WATER
HIGH-PROOF SCOTCH
SHEET PAN (FOR SAFETY)
BARSPOON
WOODEN MATCHES
GLASS WITH SUGAR AND LEMON PEEL
FIRST OFF, FIND A PAIR OF BLUE BLAZER MUGS, SILVER PLATED, IF YOU CAN. NOW GRIP 'EM STICKING OUT, WITH THE HANDLES AT SIX O'CLOCK; YOU'LL BE POURING FROM THREE AND NINE O'CLOCK, NEVER FROM NOON.
THAT WAY YOU WON'T ROAST YOUR MITTS. SAFETY, DARLINGS.
SO. POUR AN INCH OF BOILING WATER IN ONE OF THE MUGS. THEN, QUICKLY, IN WITH ANOTHER INCH OR A BIT MORE OF CASK-STRENGTH MALT WHISKEY--OVER 50 PERCENT ABV, OR IT'S NO FIRE FOR YOU.
NOW LIGHT A MATCH AND BRING IT NEAR THE WHISKEY AND WATER SO THE VAPOR CAN CATCH.
NOW--QUICK, QUICK, QUICK--START TO POUR IT BACK AND FORTH! START EACH POUR SMALL, WITH THE MUGS CLOSE--
YOU BRING THE LOW ONE UP TO THE HIGH ONE WITH THE BOOZE--AND STRETCH 'EM FARTHER AS YOU GO, AND ALWAYS LEAVE SOMETHING IN THE MUG AS YOU'RE POURING.
FIRE LIKES TO GO TO FIRE.
WHEN EVERYONE'S OOHED AND AAHED ENOUGH, YOU CAN SNUFF THE FLAMES.
THAT WASN'T SO BAD, WAS IT? YOU'RE MAKING TWO, OF COURSE, 'CAUSE THE WHOLE POINT OF THE THING'S TO SHOW OFF, INNIT?
SO PRACTICE--YEAH?--UNTIL YOU CAN PRATTLE YOUR WAY THROUGH AND MAKE IT LOOK EASY, LIKE A DODDLE. WELCOME TO SHOWBIZ, BABY!

CHASER: RYE AND BOURBON

The Blue Blazer is one of the few common mixed drinks to use Scotch. While there are several kinds of whiskey (or whisky--whatever; it's a tedious modern distinction), the most important one for cocktail use is, of course, American, from the U.S.A. And small wonder--whiskey grew up with the cocktail and was always made with mixing in mind. There are two main kinds: bourbon and its older sibling, rye.

These days, bourbon and rye are made more or less the same way, from barley malt, corn, and rye. Bourbon has at least 50 percent corn (and usually a lot more), and rye has at least 50 percent rye (and a few makers omit the corn entirely). Big brands use column stills; small ones use pot stills.

It didn't use to be like that. Bourbon and rye come from two very different, if intertwined, traditions that didn't fully come together until after World War II.

Rye's roots are with the German farmers who came to Pennsylvania in the early eighteenth century. It was perfected, as Monongahela rye, on the banks of that river, south of Pittsburgh, in the generation after the Revolution.

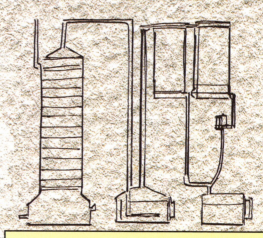

Distillers such as Abraham Overholt (1784-1870) were eager to industrialize their production, turning to the wooden three-chamber still (below), a uniquely American steam-driven gizmo that splits the difference between the pot still and the column still (above).

With an attached doubler (where the vapor partly condensed, purifying itself), it yielded a strong, clean, and flavorful spirit. The last ones weren't scrapped until World War II.

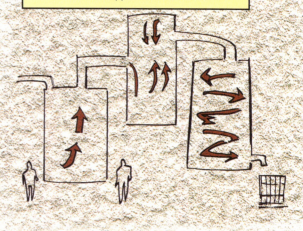

By the 1840s, American rye whiskey was customarily aged for several years in charred oak barrels, making for a rich and pungently spicy dram.

It was the spirit of choice of the industrial East and, generally, the whiskey of choice for mixologists like Jerry Thomas, whose Broadway bar stocked a house-branded rye that was a full eight years old.

The twentieth century wasn't kind to rye. During Prohibition, plenty of corn whiskey got made but not much rye; the grain was sticky and hard to work.

After repeal, rye struggled back, but by the 1950s all but the most stubborn drinkers in the American heartland had moved on to vodka and Canadian whiskey.

Bourbon's roots lie with the Scotch-Irish, Scottish Protestants whom the English had planted in Ireland to insulate themselves from the locals. The Scots got fed up and came to America in large numbers in the mid-eighteenth century; by 1800, they were over the Alleghenies and into Kentucky and Tennessee, where they made a lot of whiskey.

Like Irish whiskey, the whiskey the Scots took to making was a mix of grains: barley malt to turn the starches to sugars, a little rye for spice and flavor, and a whole lot of corn, which grew like crazy where they were and yielded a lot of spirit.

By the 1820s, many western distillers (that is, west of the Alleghenies) began industrializing, often relying on Black workers for labor and expertise. The best bourbon, as their product was known, was made on the "small-tub, sour-mash" principle, where the mash was made in individual batches and each batch was mixed with spent mash from the still instead of hot water.

With "small tub" and "sour mash" came "fire copper," which meant the spirit that went through a three-chamber still or column still was condensed, but then got its final doubling distillation in an open-flame, copper pot still, like the ones used in Scotland and Ireland. All this made a difference.

Prohibition and then World War II almost wiped out rye, while bourbon only survived in part by appealing to crude regionalism. By 1990, the United States had only about a dozen whiskey distilleries left. All of them made a severely streamlined version of bourbon or Tennessee whiskey, which was bourbon filtered through charcoal before aging. Three or four of them also made a little rye. None of them made only rye.

Now, of course, we're the beneficiaries of a revival in distilling and in whiskey. As it was before Prohibition, we've got hundreds of small distilleries coexisting with the big ones, making less mainstream products such as rye. One of them, Leopold Bros. of Denver, even had a three-chamber still made. Now that's progress.

CHAPTER VI

THE AMERICAN BAR VENTURES FORTH

London, Paris, and Points East and West ~ 1840–1890

The Prince of Wales and Lord Louth were not the first Britons to develop a taste for American mixed drinks. Way back in the 1820s, the novelist Frances Trollope had found Americans and their country insufferably crude...

"It would, I truly believe, be utterly impossible for the art of man to administer anything so likely to restore them from the overwhelming effects of heat and fatigue..."

But even she had to admit that a Mint Julep on a hot day "must create a delicious sensation of coolness."

And in 1837, when the English watercolorist Janie Ellice was cornered by an overbearing southern slaveholder as she was crossing Lake George on her way from Canada to New York City, she only wrote down the recipes he kept pushing on her for the Mint Julep and Sherry Cobbler to get rid of him.

A few days later, though, Lady Ellice found that, in fact, the only thing that would help with New York City's stifling August heat was "a large glass of Sherry Cobbler."

Finally, in 1842, Charles Dickens, already an international celebrity, toured America and wrote a book on it, mentioning the "mysteries of Gin-sling, Cocktail" and some of the other staple drinks with more than a little fondness. Britain took note.

Alas, for whatever reason, Dickens—who liked to make an entertaining ritual out of brewing Punch for his friends—never did add American drinks to his repertoire.

Nor was Mr. Van Winkle, whose American bar prompted Dick & Fitzgerald to recruit Jerry Thomas, the first to try selling the Old World on the new "Yankee Sensations." Back in the 1840s, American bartenders had begun to test the waters in cities where numbers of their countrymen could be found. They found those waters to be rather cold, particularly in London.

When a brash young Yankee named Willis Keeney took Peter Brigham's list to Paris's Café Leblond in 1849, the locals were a little more interested than the Brits, but, then again, Paris had always had a large bohemian class that liked to flout traditions.

On the other hand, when American bars reached Italy, such as the one Leopoldo Bomboni opened in Florence in 1869, they found that while Italians really liked the ice and the shaking and the straws, it was with coffee, not booze.

"WHAT'S YOURS, MATE? I FEEL LIKE HAVIN' A GO AT A LOLA MONTEZ."

"FAIR DINKUM, FAIR DINKUM, BUT IT'S A BLEEDIN' SPIDER FOR ME."

A far better terroir for the American way of drinking was found in Australia, where it thrived to the point that by the late 1850s bars in Sydney and Melbourne were offering whole menus of American drinks unknown in America.

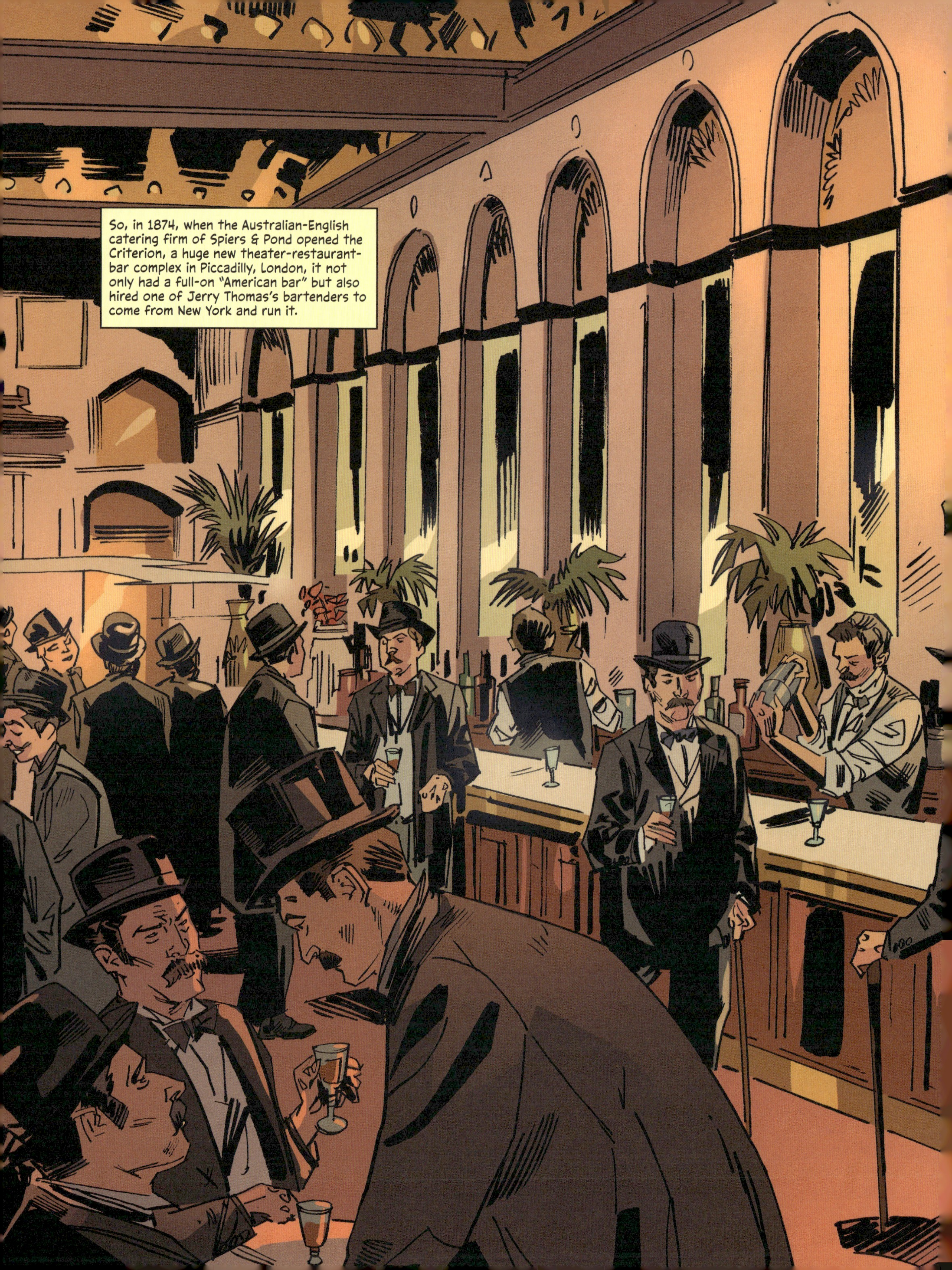
So, in 1874, when the Australian-English catering firm of Spiers & Pond opened the Criterion, a huge new theater-restaurant-bar complex in Piccadilly, London, it not only had a full-on "American bar" but also hired one of Jerry Thomas's bartenders to come from New York and run it.

LEO ENGEL
(1844-1893)

Spiers & Pond had had good success with bars serving American-style drinks at its catering gigs (things in London were changing) and figured it was time to bring in a specialist. It got Leo Engel.

Engel was born in Germany but had learned to pull ale and mix Whiskey Cocktails at Paul Mead's Ridgewood Shades in Brooklyn.

Though his time with Thomas taught him all the standard American drinks, he tended to specialize in making his own creations--elaborate things with odd names in the old style.

In 1878, at the height of his popularity, Engel published a drink book of his own, the first full-scale book of the new American drinks to be published in Europe. Sure, all but a handful of the drinks were swiped from Jerry Thomas, but it still created a toehold for the cocktail and its kin.

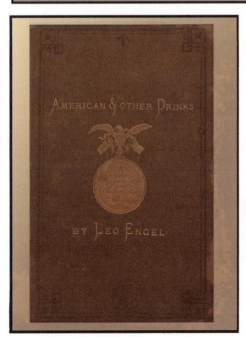

By 1880, Londoners had mostly moved on from the Criterion's American Bar. Engel struck out on his own, went broke, and ended up in France, managing a bar in Paris and, in the winter, the famous and very swank Café de Paris in Monte Carlo, where he died.

Select American Bars in Paris (1849–1940)

(A) Café Leblond
(B) Leo Engel's Bar
(C) Wells & Raymond's American Bar
(D) Delmonico Bar
(E) Frank Meier's Brunswick Bar
(F) Henry's Bar
(G) Hotel Chatham
(H) Ciro's
(J) Johnny's Bar
(K) Ritz Bar

In Paris, things were different. There, the American bar flourished, patronized by the crowds of American expats, to be sure (Americans liked Paris—a lot), but also by the French "sporting" on cards, horses, boxers, and almost anything else. This was rather more

One of the most notable of these bars opened in the summer of 1874 on fancy rue Scribe. Charles B. Wells, a 12-year-old, was the owner, and head bartender Henry J. Raymond was the manager, and Mrs. Wells—Kitty to her friends—was the vivacious hostess.

Lavishly decorated and staffed with handsome young waiters, the bar made an impression, as did Wells, who liked to play the piano when he wasn't behind the bar.

If Champagne Cocktails and Punches failed to hold your attention, you could go and sit in the second-floor lounge or visit Kitty on the third floor, where she hosted a popular and highly illegal gambling salon.

After a while, it must be admitted, some of the swells and sports who patronized the bar began to notice a shifty element hanging around.

Then there were the detectives...

Things came to a head in October 1873, when a London diamond salesman put his satchel down for a moment, only to have it disappear, and with it, a million and a half dollars' worth of diamonds (in today's value).

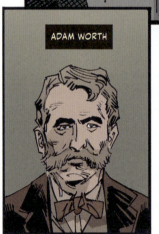

ADAM WORTH

CHARLES BULLARD

KITTY FLYNN

While nothing was ever proven, the episode did reveal the real identities of the trio. Henry Raymond was actually Adam Worth, the notorious bank burglar and international heist planner who was known as the Napoleon of Crime.

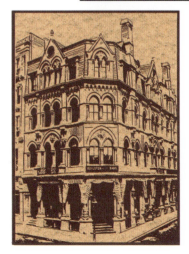

The money that the trio spent tricking out the American Bar had come from the million dollars in cash that Worth and Piano Charley Bullard (aka Charles Wells) had extracted from the safe of the Boylston Bank in Boston in November 1869. They picked up Kitty Wells, née Flynn (who married Bullard but was in love with Worth), in Liverpool, on their meandering path to Paris. By the time the authorities figured this all out, the three had gotten away scot-free.

One thing, though: nobody ever complained about their bar's drinks.

The rest of Paris's American bars were rather less sporty--they would have to be--and their bartenders were known more for their mixology than for their safecracking. Over the years, they would launch a flotilla of new cocktails, some of which would spread around the world (see chapter 8).

The Rose by Johnny Mitta of the Hotel Chatham on Rue Daunou (1910).

French vermouth, kirschwasser, and red-currant syrup. An elegant drink, which, in one version or another, became the drink of Paris.

The Marguerite by Otto Maier of Henry's Bar on Rue Volney (1913).

Gin, lime juice, grenadine, egg white, and a dash of absinthe. A particularly toothsome variation on the Daisy (which means marguerite in French).

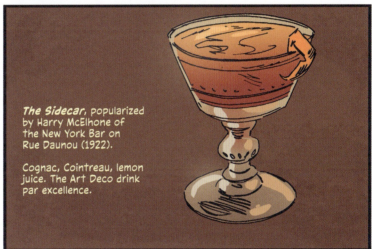

The Sidecar, popularized by Harry McElhone of the New York Bar on Rue Daunou (1922).

Cognac, Cointreau, lemon juice. The Art Deco drink par excellence.

The Bees' Knees by Frank Meier of the Ritz Bar on Rue Cambon (1929).

Gin, lemon juice, and honey syrup. The Ritz was Paris's most famous bar, and Frank, a veteran of the Foreign Legion, its richest and most famous bartender.

The Camparinete by Albert Clavelot, Mitta's successor at the Chatham bar (1929).

An early cousin of the Negroni, with gin, Italian vermouth, and Campari, up. Campari cocktails were everywhere in Paris in the 1920s.

Yet that decade would mark the Paris cocktail scene's peak. With the Great Depression, repeal in America, and the chilling approach of another world war, the 1930s saw the rat-a-tat of the shaker greatly subdued.

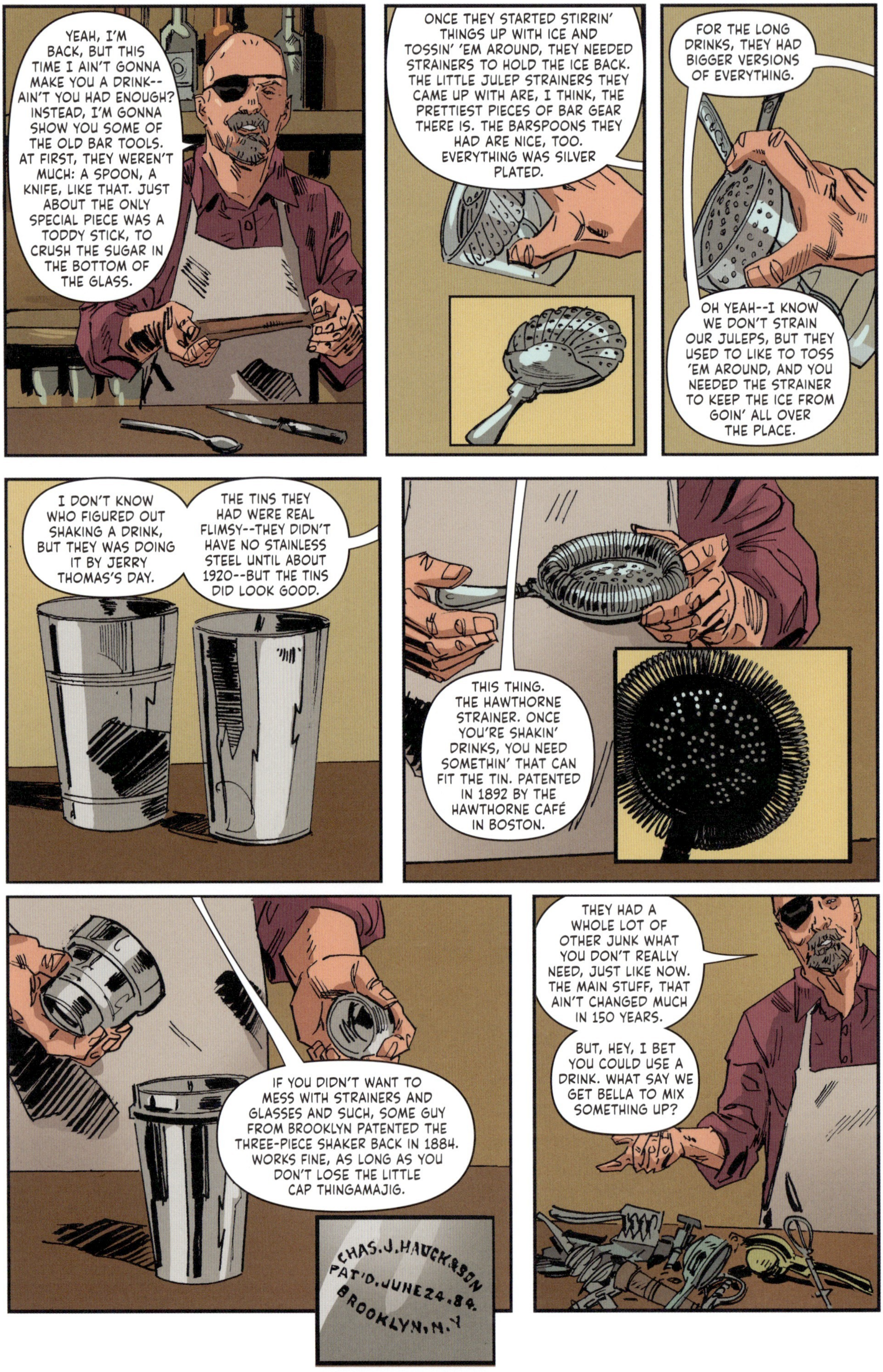
YEAH, I'M BACK, BUT THIS TIME I AIN'T GONNA MAKE YOU A DRINK--AIN'T YOU HAD ENOUGH? INSTEAD, I'M GONNA SHOW YOU SOME OF THE OLD BAR TOOLS. AT FIRST, THEY WEREN'T MUCH: A SPOON, A KNIFE, LIKE THAT. JUST ABOUT THE ONLY SPECIAL PIECE WAS A TODDY STICK, TO CRUSH THE SUGAR IN THE BOTTOM OF THE GLASS.
ONCE THEY STARTED STIRRIN' THINGS UP WITH ICE AND TOSSIN' 'EM AROUND, THEY NEEDED STRAINERS TO HOLD THE ICE BACK. THE LITTLE JULEP STRAINERS THEY CAME UP WITH ARE, I THINK, THE PRETTIEST PIECES OF BAR GEAR THERE IS. THE BARSPOONS THEY HAD ARE NICE, TOO. EVERYTHING WAS SILVER PLATED.
FOR THE LONG DRINKS, THEY HAD BIGGER VERSIONS OF EVERYTHING.
OH YEAH--I KNOW WE DON'T STRAIN OUR JULEPS, BUT THEY USED TO LIKE TO TOSS 'EM AROUND, AND YOU NEEDED THE STRAINER TO KEEP THE ICE FROM GOIN' ALL OVER THE PLACE.
I DON'T KNOW WHO FIGURED OUT SHAKING A DRINK, BUT THEY WAS DOING IT BY JERRY THOMAS'S DAY.
THE TINS THEY HAD WERE REAL FLIMSY--THEY DIDN'T HAVE NO STAINLESS STEEL UNTIL ABOUT 1920--BUT THE TINS DID LOOK GOOD.
THIS THING. THE HAWTHORNE STRAINER. ONCE YOU'RE SHAKIN' DRINKS, YOU NEED SOMETHIN' THAT CAN FIT THE TIN. PATENTED IN 1892 BY THE HAWTHORNE CAFÉ IN BOSTON.
IF YOU DIDN'T WANT TO MESS WITH STRAINERS AND GLASSES AND SUCH, SOME GUY FROM BROOKLYN PATENTED THE THREE-PIECE SHAKER BACK IN 1884. WORKS FINE, AS LONG AS YOU DON'T LOSE THE LITTLE CAP THINGAMAJIG.
CHAS. J. HAUCK & SON
PAT'D. JUNE 24. 84.
BROOKLYN, N.Y
THEY HAD A WHOLE LOT OF OTHER JUNK WHAT YOU DON'T REALLY NEED, JUST LIKE NOW. THE MAIN STUFF, THAT AIN'T CHANGED MUCH IN 150 YEARS.
BUT, HEY, I BET YOU COULD USE A DRINK. WHAT SAY WE GET BELLA TO MIX SOMETHING UP?

MIXOLOGY: THE SHORT DRINK, AKA PRINCE OF WALES

WE BRITS HAVE GOT OUR TOYS, TOO, YOU KNOW. SHINY SILVER SHAKERS AND ALL THE REST. WHY DON'T I USE SOME OF THEM TO MAKE BERTIE, THE PRINCE OF WALES'S SHORT DRINK? HE WAS A HORRIBLE PERSON, HE WAS, BUT HE DID KNOW HIS TIPPLE.

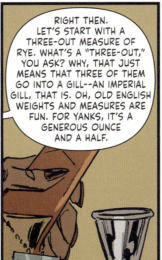

RIGHT THEN. LET'S START WITH A THREE-OUT MEASURE OF RYE. WHAT'S A "THREE-OUT," YOU ASK? WHY, THAT JUST MEANS THAT THREE OF THEM GO INTO A GILL--AN IMPERIAL GILL, THAT IS. OH, OLD ENGLISH WEIGHTS AND MEASURES ARE FUN. FOR YANKS, IT'S A GENEROUS OUNCE AND A HALF.

I'LL USE OUR VERY BRITISH BOSTON SHAKER HERE, AND NO, I DON'T KNOW WHY WE CALL IT THAT; THE YANKS NEVER USED THEM. BUT WE CALL THE OTHER SHAKER, THE SEXY ONE, PARISIAN, EVEN THOUGH IT'S AN AMERICAN DESIGN, SO...

THEN IT'S A SPOONFUL OF MARASCHINO AND NOT A DROP MORE--IT DOES FLAVOR A DRINK. IN FACT, A WEE BIT LESS THAN A SPOONFUL IS BETTER.

AND DON'T FORGET THE BITTERS--THREE DASHES!

AND THEN ICE AND SHAKE IT UP! NORMALLY A HIGHLY SKILLED PROFESSIONAL SUCH AS YOURS TRULY WOULD STIR A DRINK LIKE THIS, BUT SHAKING IS EVER SO MUCH SPORTIER, AND BERTIE WAS A SPORT.

THEN THROUGH OUR LOVELY ASPREY & CO. STRAINER...

...AND TOP IT OFF WITH CHAMPAGNE. NOT ALL THE WAY, BUT DON'T BE STINGY, NEITHER.

NOW HERE'S THE FANCY BIT. YOU STIR IN--QUICKLY!--ABOUT HALF A BARSPOON OF SUGAR, WHICH SWEETENS THE DRINK A BIT AND MAKES THE CHAMPERS FOAM.

WELL, CAN'T LET THIS GO TO WASTE, CAN I? OH YES--GARNISH. CUBE OF PINEAPPLE, LEMON TWIST. SORTED.

CHAPTER VII

THE NEW TESTAMENT, OR THE COCKTAIL 2.0

New York, New Orleans, and Here and There ~ 1880–1920

The bar that New York's Hoffman House hotel maintained from the 1880s until it was remodeled in the mid-1890s has long enjoyed a reputation as the city's all-time best.

It was not--no bar that deliberately excluded more than half of the city's people could be. But if its refusal to serve Black men or women of any color was par for the course for its day, very little else about it was.

Edward S. Stokes, who opened the bar in 1882, saw to that. If Stokes "proceeded upon the theory that you cannot make a saloon too expensive for Americans," as the *Buffalo Commercial Advertiser* noted in 1883, he also spread the pain to his backers on the principle that "the more money a place can be made to cost, the greater will be the prices which can be asked."

Stokes, who had done four years in Sing Sing and Auburn prisons for shooting the robber baron Big Jim Fisk to death on the steps of the Grand Central Hotel (there was a woman involved), was perfectly happy building on his notoriety.

Like, by buying the most scandalous painting of its day--Bouguereau's peerlessly pink, fleshy *Nymphs and Satyr*--and putting it on display in the bar.

When he replaced the hotel's old bar, Stokes also replaced its old bartenders, veteran mixers all, with a young crew headed up by a trio of picture-perfect dudes, as the hipsters of the day were known.

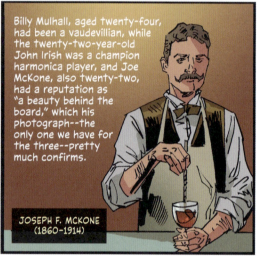

Billy Mulhall, aged twenty-four, had been a vaudevillian, while the twenty-two-year-old John Irish was a champion harmonica player, and Joe McKone, also twenty-two, had a reputation as "a beauty behind the board," which his photograph--the only one we have for the three--pretty much confirms.

JOSEPH F. MCKONE (1860–1914)

Yet the dudes were as skilled as they were good-looking. Stokes was clever enough to keep on Fred Loud, the former head bartender, as bar manager and trainer. Although Loud gave the impression of a "bald-headed snoozer" (as the humor magazine *Texas Siftings* dubbed him), he was a man of great intelligence who created a new kind of bartender, teaching them the art from scratch. "I wanted men," he told *The Evening Telegram*, "who would not talk to their customers." In other words, men who were quick and precise and wouldn't gum up the works with any schmoozing or Jerry Thomas–style holding forth.

There was no time for that: the Hoffman House was the bar to go to in New York--in America--and was always thronged by customers.

What's more, its cocktail list was more than 120 drinks long, with more than half of the recipes invented since Jerry Thomas wrote his book.

In fact, those new drinks included many that would become essentials. Between the bar's local and international clientele, which tended toward the sporty, rich, and popular, and the parade of famous bartenders who apprenticed there, the Hoffman House bar served as a giant megaphone to broadcast these cocktails to the world.

I SAY, HORACE, WHAT DID THE MAN CALL THIS THING?

THE MENHATTAN, I B'LIEVE.

The 1880s saw a revolution in drink mixing. This was connected, in a chicken-or-egg way, to the introduction of a few key new ingredients. The chief of these was vermouth.

This Italian and French fortified and herbalized wine had been imported in a small way since the beginning of the century; only around 1880 did somebody find the best way to fit it into American mixology.

Did it happen like that? Frankly, we have no idea. Theories for the birth of the Manhattan abound, but most are easily disproved and actual evidence is beyond scarce. Sure, it probably came out of the usual barroom sausagefest, yet by the 1880s plenty of women were drinking cocktails and mixing them, too--but we'll get back to that. In any case, this timeless mixture of American whiskey, Italian vermouth, and bitters changed the way the world mixed drinks.

But after 1882, when the Manhattan made it into print and showed America's mixologists how vermouth could stretch out spirits without them tasting watered down, there was a flurry of new vermouth cocktails pairing off the popular spirits of the day--mostly with the sweeter Italian product, though a few used the dry French one.

While vermouth was paired off with everything from cognac to Jamaica rum, its one true love was, of course, English-style gin. First recorded in 1881, even before the Manhattan, the Martini has a pedigree even more obscure. For the Manhattan, we at least know that at the time people thought it came from the bar of the Manhattan Club. We don't have so much as that for the Martini--or Martine, Martinez, Martena, Martigny, and so on; at first, nobody was sure how to even spell the word they were hearing. Likewise, it took a while for its recipe to escape from the Manhattan's intense gravity and reach stable orbit.

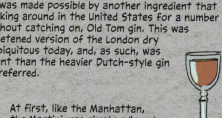

The Martini was made possible by another ingredient that had been kicking around in the United States for a number of years without catching on, Old Tom gin. This was a lightly sweetened version of the London dry gin that's ubiquitous today, and, as such, was quite different than the heavier Dutch-style gin Americans preferred.

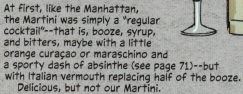

At first, like the Manhattan, the Martini was simply a "regular cocktail"--that is, booze, syrup, and bitters, maybe with a little orange curaçao or maraschino and a sporty dash of absinthe (see page 71)--but with Italian vermouth replacing half of the booze. Delicious, but not our Martini.

It didn't take the drink long to shrug off the syrup and liqueur; by the late 1880s, those additions were rare. The Martini (by then, the name had been settled) was still, however, equal parts Old Tom and vermouth or sometimes even two parts vermouth to one of gin. The absinthe was still pretty common, and there was no set garnish.

The early 1890s saw the absinthe mostly disappear, but the big changes were the switch from Angostura-style aromatic bitters to Dutch-style orange bitters, another new ingredient that made for a lighter, crisper drink, and the introduction of the maraschino cherry as garnish.

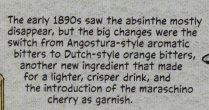

The Dry Martini, with dry French vermouth replacing the Italian and unsweetened London dry or Plymouth gin replacing the Old Tom, began showing up around 1890 and was named in print in 1896. It kept the orange bitters but replaced the cherry with a brined olive or pimola (an olive stuffed with a scrap of roasted red Spanish pepper, as we still use today).

The new century brought the Gibson cocktail, a New York drink perfected in San Francisco: Plymouth (dry) gin, dry vermouth, and no bitters or--at first--garnish of any kind. In the 1920s, when the Dry Martini had also lost its bitters, the Gibson was fitted out with a cocktail onion so you could tell the two drinks apart.

The final word on the pre-Prohibition Martini comes from the Waldorf-Astoria in New York. The Third Degree, as they called it, was seven parts Plymouth gin to one part vermouth, with several dashes of absinthe. It would make anybody talk.

Even the cocktails that didn't take vermouth had evolved from the ones that Jerry Thomas had detailed in 1862. He chronicled the Improved Cocktail in the 1876 second edition of his *Bar-Tender's Guide*.

His "improved" way of mixing one involved dashes of the pungent maraschino liqueur instead of curaçao and a defining dash of absinthe, which was concentrated enough to give the drink a distinct herbal edge.

By the 1880s, the maraschino had company; as the Buffalo barman Patsy McDonough advised in 1883, "keep a line of cordials in your bar" because "a dash...will improve your cocktails in flavor." These began with Bénédictine and Chartreuse and soon included options ranging from the caraway-flavored kümmel and crème de menthe to exotica such as the violet-colored Parfait Amour.

There were even clever "champagne taps" that bartenders could screw through the cork to dispense the wine in floats, dashes, and squirts.

Thus, the Boothby Cocktail, the signature drink of the San Francisco bartender William "Cocktail Bill" Boothby, which was simply a Manhattan with a splash of champagne (and is, by the way, surprisingly tasty).

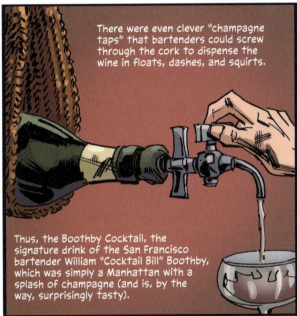

Master bartenders such as the German-born Harry Johnson took advantage of this expanded palette to work their own delightful little variations on the now-venerable cocktail; Johnson's East India (a Brandy Cocktail with raspberry syrup instead of plain, plus dashes of maraschino and curaçao) is a classic example. And to show them off, cocktails now had dedicated glasses, small and stemmed to keep warm fingers away from the cold drink (making a glass pyramid as Johnson was known to do was optional).

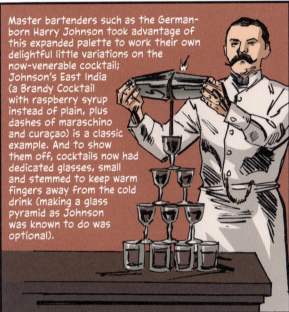

In the late 1880s, Vincent Miret and Billy Wilkinson of the Sazerac House in New Orleans put their own spin on the new-style Improved Cocktail.

Rather than dashing absinthe into the drink, they used it to rinse the glass, and it seems that they might have also begun the now-traditional practice of spiraling the glass up in the air to distribute the absinthe evenly.

THE SAZERAC

According to the handwritten formula retained by the family of one of the bar's owners, the original Sazerac was nearly identical to Jerry Thomas's Improved Whiskey Cocktail, right down to the dash of maraschino. The only differences were that it used two kinds of bitters (Peychaud's and Angostura) rather than one and that business with the absinthe. And yet thanks to Miret and Wilkinson—and New Orleans—the Sazerac still lives (minus the maraschino), while the Improved Whiskey Cocktail is a drink for the history books.

Of course, not everybody was happy about all this... *mixology*.

Editorialists such as the theater critic Leander Richardson, here writing in *Comment* in 1886, and other crusty old poops didn't want any of these newfangled cocktails.

THE COCKTAIL OF TO-DAY

The modern cocktail has come to be so complex a beverage that people are beginning to desert it. A bartender in the habit of whetting their appetites by the use of the friendly cocktail ne̶̶̶̶̶̶w beforehand what they

They wanted theirs made the old way. In fact, like most reactionaries, they rather overdid it, since the style of cocktail they upheld hadn't been current since the 1840s, before most of them were born.

It's probably no coincidence that the Old-Fashioned, as the drink these crotchety old-timers championed became known, got its first foothold in Chicago bars such as the Chapin & Gore saloon on Monroe Street. It was a broad-shouldered, no-nonsense sort of drink. And, it must be noted, an enduringly popular one: a steady favorite from the 1880s through the 1950s, it was also one of the first drinks to be revived in the new millennium.

Of course, it wasn't just the cocktail that was evolving. The old classes of drinks were flirting with new ingredients and techniques, and there were whole new classes--Fizzes, Coolers, Collinses--that spread quickly both by word of mouth and now by newspapers, which in the 1870s began to pay more detailed attention to bartenders and their drinks.

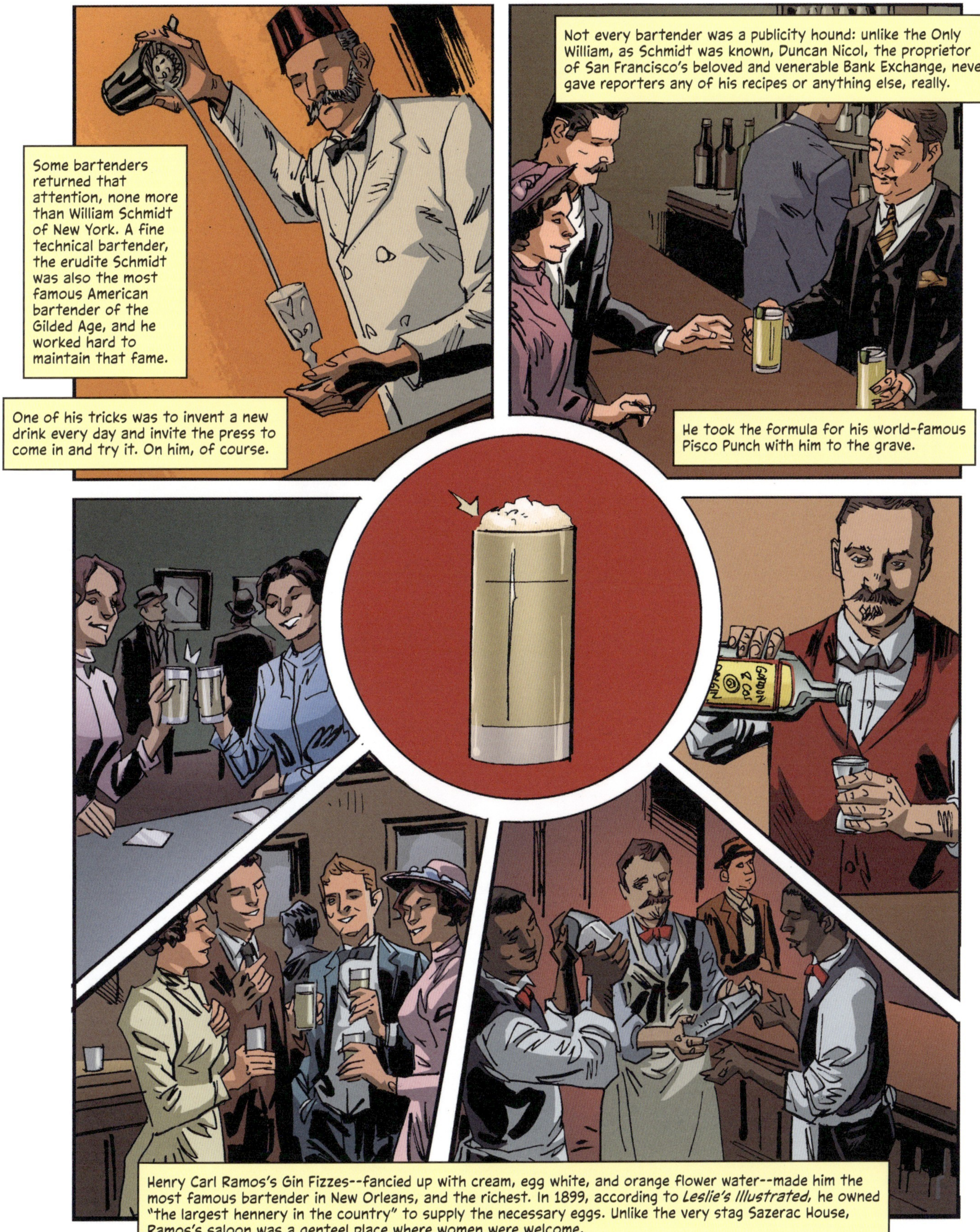

Some bartenders returned that attention, none more than William Schmidt of New York. A fine technical bartender, the erudite Schmidt was also the most famous American bartender of the Gilded Age, and he worked hard to maintain that fame.
One of his tricks was to invent a new drink every day and invite the press to come in and try it. On him, of course.
Not every bartender was a publicity hound: unlike the Only William, as Schmidt was known, Duncan Nicol, the proprietor of San Francisco's beloved and venerable Bank Exchange, never gave reporters any of his recipes or anything else, really.
He took the formula for his world-famous Pisco Punch with him to the grave.
Henry Carl Ramos's Gin Fizzes--fancied up with cream, egg white, and orange flower water--made him the most famous bartender in New Orleans, and the richest. In 1899, according to *Leslie's Illustrated*, he owned "the largest hennery in the country" to supply the necessary eggs. Unlike the very stag Sazerac House, Ramos's saloon was a genteel place where women were welcome.

In 1900, Ramos's bar and Nicol's Bank Exchange were still very much the exception in serving women: most of the high-class saloons where they knew how to mix drinks still refused to serve women at the bar, and many banned them entirely. This was starting to sit poorly with some women.

The Hoffman House and its many imitators had given cocktails cachet, and in places like New York, San Francisco, and Chicago it became increasingly fashionable for women to drink them, too.

(Elsewhere, not so much: "It is not good form for a young woman to drink cocktails"--*St. Louis Post-Dispatch*, 1902.)

In some big cities, fashionable dressmakers, ice cream parlors, tearooms, and other such places that catered largely to women even took to installing actual bars for their patrons.

Another solution for women who weren't welcomed at bars was the cocktail party, an 1890s innovation where men and women could drink together.

Often, women did the drink mixing, and, indeed, the so-called women's pages of newspapers began to print drink recipes among the customary fashion notes and household hints.

Another was to have dedicated, undisguised cocktail bars for women. In 1912, Louis Bustanoby added a ladies' bar to his Café des Beaux Arts in New York, where men were not admitted unless accompanied by a woman. The drinks tended to the pastel, and there were stools (in men's joints, one stood at the bar), but it was otherwise a real cocktail bar and an immediate hit, although its imitators seem to have been confined to New York City.

The best solution, and the eventual way forward, was offered in the 1910s by the lobster palaces, huge establishments that combined eating, drinking, and dancing into a total entertainment experience. There, it wasn't a question of women grudgingly allowed into a male space: these places belonged to both sexes.

The drinking ran largely to champagne, but plenty of cocktails were served, too, including such lobster-palace creations as the Alexander and the Pink Lady.

Meanwhile, behind the bar...

America had lots of women bartenders, but in the nickel-beer joints, not the quarter-cocktail ones. Bartenders and customers saw to it that exceptions were rare.

Despite William's dire predictions, the women quickly mastered the drinks, and business was brisk. Yet after three months Hayward let them go because, as he said, "it grated on [his] nerves to have them hear the thoughtless remarks" made to them by many of the customers.

If one barrier was wobbling, however slightly, another was hardening. The 1890s brought a white backlash to the Black progress of the '70s and '80s. One consequence was that Black bartenders such as Louis Deal of Cincinnati were hounded out of their fancy saloon jobs by boycotts and pickets, or worse, from white bartenders afraid of Black competition.

In 1891, when the Only William's boss, Major W.A. Hayward, joined a local saloonkeepers' scheme to import English barmaids, he wanted William to train his to make cocktails. William quit instead.

Still, it was progress, of a sort.

CINCINNATI, 1893

"THAT'S RIGHT, TWO OF THEM IMPERIAL DAISIES."

"TWO DOLLARS."

Imperial Daisy 25¢

Even despite equal-accommodation policies in places such as New York and Philadelphia, many white bartenders either defiantly refused to serve Black patrons or overcharged them in the hope of either discouraging them or inciting them to make a scene, for which they could be ejected.

Such treatment forced Black bartenders and cocktail drinkers to focus on their own community. In 1898, a group of Washington, D.C., bartenders from the best of the city's bars that catered to the Black community formed a social aid and pleasure club, as such things were known. The Mixologist Club offered education, networking, and mentorship opportunities.

"WASH" WOOD | CHAS. J. EDLINE | EDW. MATTHEWS | JOHN LEWIS | R.R. BOWIE, PRESIDENT

In the couple of years it lasted, the Mixologist Club also held public balls, much as white bartenders' organizations did (it would be decades before such things were integrated). There they gave out awards and reinforced the bonds between bartenders and patrons at a time when even controlled social drinking was very much under attack by the temperance movement.

One place where Black bartenders found jobs that they wouldn't be hounded out of was in (white) clubs, which were immune to the pressure tactics used by white bartenders' unions.

TOM BULLOCK, THE FAMOUS BARTENDER AT THE ST. LOUIS COUNTRY CLUB AND AUTHOR OF *THE IDEAL BARTENDER* (1917), WHICH INCLUDED A PREFACE BY PRESIDENT GEORGE HERBERT WALKER BUSH'S GRANDFATHER

Bullock was probably the creator of the Stone Sour, a sour with a splash of orange juice that hid out in midwestern clubs until having its moment of fame in the 1970s.

Julian Anderson tended bar at the Montana Club in Helena, Montana, from 1893 until 1953 and was an honored local celebrity. He, too, wrote a book: *Julian's Recipes*, published in 1919. He and Bullock were the first African Americans to write cocktail books.

Prince Martin survived Kentucky's most brutal reform school, got a job in the mess hall at Fort Knox, and, once Prohibition took hold, parlayed his experience there into the stewardship of Louisville's most popular private drinking club. As such, he became the city's preferred caterer, a position he gave up only during World War II, when he became the private drink mixer for Secretary of the Navy James Forrestal, the man who integrated that service.

MIXOLOGY: THE DRY MARTINI

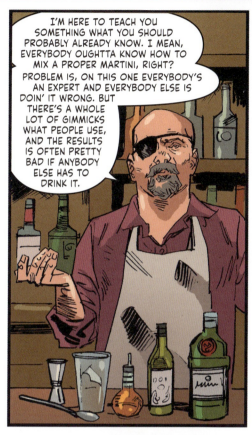

"I'm here to teach you something what you should probably already know. I mean, everybody oughtta know how to mix a proper martini, right? Problem is, on this one everybody's an expert and everybody else is doin' it wrong. But there's a whole lot of gimmicks what people use, and the results is often pretty bad if anybody else has to drink it."

"So, I'm gonna just show you the classic way, how they made it from, like, 1890 to 1950, when people dressed nice and didn't make no big deal about it. That means gin, with enough vermouth to soften it up and make it into a cocktail, not just a big slug of straight booze. So, two ounces gin to one vermouth, or maybe two and a quarter to three-quarters. None of that fifteen-to-one baloney. And stir it in the glass--you can shake it, but it'll look cloudy and won't be as smooth and silky on the tongue."

LONDON DR[Y]
47.4% ABV

"'Cause you're using a lot of vermouth, you'll want a strong gin: 47 percent's the strongest they used to be able to sell in England and is what they sent over here. Still works great."

"Vermouth. They used to always call it French vermouth, and with a reason. In any case, it should be white and dry and fresh--buy the small bottles and keep 'em refrigerated."

"Now, do you wanna go with a lemon twist or an olive? The twist makes for a nice, bright martini, and a couple a dashes orange bitters help it do what it does. But they taste a little weird with the olive, so if I'm goin' olive, I leave 'em out. I ain't, though, so in they go."

"Most of all, a martini's gotta be COLD. So ice straight out of the freezer and crack the cubes, for the most contact with the booze. Hold the cube in your hand--your clean hand--and whack it smart-like with the back of your spoon. Fill the glass three-quarters full."

"Now we stir. Just hold the spoon loose and wrist it around in circles--leave your elbow out of it. A leisurely ten count oughtta do it."

"Strain it with your julep strainer into a chilled glass. You can use one of them V-shaped martini glasses if you want, but I find a coupe-type thing is better at keeping your martini in the glass and not on the bar, the floor, your lap, and wherever else it sloshes."

"'Cause I did the bitters, I'm doin' the twist. Heh. Chubby Checker...you remember that song. But yeah, cut your strip of lemon peel real thin so none of the white stuff is on it (I use a peeler; shhhhh), and just kind of snap it lengthwise, shiny-side down. You can drop it in or throw it away. Folks like to fight over that; I don't. And, oh yeah--cheers!"

CHASER: VERMOUTH

A wine that has been infused with herbs and other botanicals, lightly fortified with neutral spirit, and usually sweetened, vermouth is so much a part of the infrastructure of the cocktail that we tend to take it for granted.

First off, there are three main kinds, not two as old cocktail books and the people who learned from them will generally tell you: the sweet red Italian vermouth; the dry white French vermouth; and, in between, the white but lightly sweet *blanc* or *bianco* style, which is neither fully French nor fully Italian.

Such aromatized wines were a staple of Greek and Roman medicine, but vermouth's immediate roots go back to the eighteenth century and the Duchy of Savoy (now split between Italy and France).

Vermouth takes its name from the German word for wormwood, which used to be the dominant botanical in it. Nowadays, this exceptionally bitter herb is a trace presence at best, buried among ingredients such as rhubarb, cassia bark, bitter orange peel, vanilla beans, mugwort, and hyssop. These are usually combined into a botanical extract that's blended with white wine, neutral spirit, and, for the "red" Italian-style vermouths, sugar and coloring.

The dry French-style vermouth is largely the creation of Joseph Noilly, a Marseille merchant who in the early nineteenth century took wines that had oxidized during shipping, infused them with the herbs of Provence, and aged them in large oak casks stored outdoors by the sea.

Today most producers, wherever they are, make both sweet and dry vermouths, and many also make the unoxidized and uncolored *blanc* or *bianco* style that was a specialty of Chambéry in the French part of Savoy.

In recent years, we've also seen such innovations as orange vermouth, dry red vermouth, and all kinds of styles made far from the wine's heartland using local botanicals that are distinctly nontraditional.

Although, globally, vermouth is primarily a mixer, in its heartland-- northern Italy, southern France, Spain (where it took root in the late nineteenth century)-- much of it is still drunk straight, as a light aperitif, a job it has always done very well.

VERMOUTH LA PLATA

BODEGA LA PLATA, BARCELONA

CHAPTER VIII

THE BLAST AND THE SPARK

Cocktails from Monte Carlo to Singapore ~ 1890–1920

It's 1890. The American art of the bar--the art of mixing individual iced drinks to order--was a mature art. Almost a century old, it had worked out its kinks and been tested abroad.

With the help of its recent infusions of Italian vermouth, French liqueurs, and English gin, it had developed into something coherent yet flexible that could turn almost any spirit into a drink as balanced and toothsome as wine, yet with a far broader palette of flavors. All it needed was a spark to set it off, to send it rocketing all around the world.

Arguably, that spark was struck by one man at a little bar in Monte Carlo.

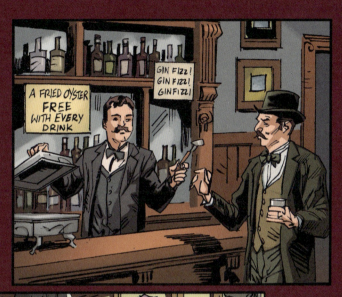

Ciro Capozzi was a sea captain's son from the Bay of Naples who got his bartender training in Philadelphia, where as a teenager he spent a few years in the 1870s at his uncle's saloon. At some point, either then or on a subsequent trip to America in the early 1880s, he worked with Jerry Thomas in New York.

The year 1883 saw the inauguration of France's so-called Blue Train from Calais--where the English Channel ferries docked--to the Côte d'Azur, where it was sunny and warm. Made up only of first-class sleeper cars and a (world-famous) dining car, the train left at midnight, after the last ferry got in, and arrived in the south in the early evening. Rich Londoners never had to suffer through another foggy, damp January--and a great many didn't.

With his excellent English-language and bartending skills, Ciro got a job in the late 1880s at the Café de Paris in Monte Carlo. New, clean, and very expensive, Monte Carlo was the epicenter of Côte d'Azur glamour, and the Blue Train stopped right down the hill from its famous casino.

By 1889, Ciro had his own place,* a small bar in a gallery adjacent to the casino that overlooked the sea. Ciro's Anglo-American Buffet--or Zero's, as his British customers called it--was an instant hit with the marquises and millionaires. Ciro never let their titles or money faze him: he treated everybody like a Philly saloon customer. Polite, but not impressed.

*LEO ENGEL, OUR OLD PAL FROM CHAPTER 6, TOOK OVER CIRO'S POST AT THE CAFÉ DE PARIS, WHERE HE LASTED UNTIL HIS DEATH IN 1893.

"THIS, LORD RANDOLPH, IS WHAT MY FRIENDS IN NEW YORK CALL A DAISY."

The toffs liked that. It probably wouldn't have worked in London, but in Monte Carlo folks such as the Duke of Hamilton, Lord Randolph Churchill (Winston's dad, at right), and, of course, Bertie, the Prince of Wales (left) found it charming. The impeccable English food Ciro's grill turned out didn't hurt, either.

Nor, of course, did Ciro's cocktails, which were American standard. In 1898, he sent the Paris *Herald-Tribune* his thoughts on how the plain Cocktail should be mixed. His recipe was identical to Jerry Thomas's from 1862. Ciro also added some of his thoughts about his competition.

"I'M ASTOUNDED TO READ HOW THEY KEEP PRINTING RECIPES FOR THE COCKTAIL...BY PEOPLE WHO, FRANKLY, KNOW NOTHING ABOUT AMERICAN DRINKS AS THEY REALLY ARE, AND WHO HAVE NEVER MIXED AN AMERICAN-STYLE COCKTAIL BEHIND A BAR OVER THERE...I THINK MANY IN LONDON AND PARIS CALL THEMSELVES BARMEN WHO IN AMERICA WOULDN'T EVEN BE FIT TO WASH GLASSES."

Capozzi's words didn't go down well with his peers up in Paris, as one would imagine. A few Paris barmen, including our other pal from chapter 6, Charlie Paul (he got around), wrote in with their ripostes. One quipped that the only contact Capozzi had with Jerry Thomas was from a book "found in a drawer behind his bar."

That was not true. What was true was that the creative mixology practiced by the Parisian barmen earned them a sometimes-precarious living, while Ciro's conservative cocktails made him money hand over fist (helped, of course, by an affable manner, tight kitchen management, and a canny business sense).

In 1911, Capozzi sold his business to an English syndicate and promptly retired. Paris and London branches soon followed and quickly dominated the high life in those cities. Then came branches and franchises in various French resorts, Berlin, Hollywood, and, briefly, New York.

CIRO'S PARIS (1912)

CIRO'S LONDON (1915)

"...FOURTH DEGREE... TIPPERARY... CHORUS LADY... SWALTER..."

Capozzi was content to watch the world go by from his mansion high on the slopes of Monte Carlo, where he died in 1938. By then, the world knew "Ciro's" as a watchword for luxury, but the man behind the brand was largely forgotten.

HARRY MCELHONE AT CIRO'S LONDON (1915)

Ironically, though Capozzi got the money, those drink inventors got the last word: the drinks at the various new Ciro's were fanciful and creative and not at all like the ones Ciro himself had always mixed, and the style of mixology that set forth to conquer the world had plenty of room for local innovation.

The thing about getting the British gentry to warm up to the cocktail and its kin was that they pretty much ruled the world, directly or indirectly. If they got on board with something, that gave it a sort of global stamp of approval.

And the British had definitely gotten on board, and not just when in Monte Carlo. Ciro's wasn't even the first world-class American bar to open in London. That honor went to the Savoy hotel, which broke down and added an American bar in 1900, then expanded it in 1902.

Following English tradition, the Savoy relied on a pair of highly skilled barmaids to mix the drinks: Ruth "Kitty" Burgess (left) and Ada "Coley" Coleman, a particularly talented mixologist.

(They hated each other.)

The bar's large American clientele testified to the quality of their work.

It did take a while for the young women and the Americans to find common ground on some issues, though. Like loud swearing-- the Yanks reined it in only when the bar made them donate a shilling to charity per cussword.

Not all people in the British Empire got to taste the drinks, of course, or even wanted to. At home, it was the upper classes and those who modeled themselves on them. In most of the rest of the empire, it certainly wasn't the folks whose ancestors' bones lay buried beneath the soil or whose ashes had fertilized it.

THE ROYAL BOMBAY YACHT CLUB

In any case, the empire saw the American bar spread far and wide. The Dry Martinis that the Lost Generation icons Harry and Caresse Crosby guzzled in 1928 on the famous terrace of Shepheard's Hotel, Cairo, were no doubt introduced there in the 1890s by Charlie Paul when he was head bartender there (he really did get around), and had been a specialty ever since.

81

Britain's Southeast Asian colonies were also quick to embrace the cocktail and its tribe, probably quicker than much of Britain itself was.

The Pegu Club in Rangoon, for instance, got a good deal of play out of its eponymous cocktail, a Gin Sour with curaçao and bitters.

Bars in many Asian cities offered bootleg versions of the Shanghai Club's Million Dollar Cocktail, a complex mix of gin, brandy, vermouth, and various juices and syrups.

THE SHANGHAI CLUB

Even more famous was Singapore's version of the Gin Sling, which first surfaced in the 1890s as a raffish little hangover cure.

By 1920, it was everywhere in Singapore and British Asia, though no two bartenders made it the same way--not even at the Raffles Hotel, which would eventually claim to have invented it.

SAY, WHAT MAKESH TH' DAMN THING RED?

CHERRY BRANDY.

CLARET.

SLOE GIN.

ANGOSTURA.

No doubt the basis of the kudzu-like spread of American bars around the world in the 1900s and 1910s isn't so simple as Ciro Capozzi → various British milords (as the French called upper-class Britons) → American bars everywhere.

But it's certainly true that those milords were the world's most visible influencers; they flocked to Monte Carlo, and Ciro's little bar and grill was the focal point of social life there. BC--before Ciro's-- they drank few cocktails. AC, they drank lots.

The boulevardiers of Continental Europe and Latin America followed suit in adopting the cocktail habit. In those places, as in Paris (see page 63), many of the most successful drinks were invented locally.

COUNT NEGRONI ASKS FOR GIN IN HIS.

At Berlin's American bars, such as the popular one at the Hotel Adlon, it was the Ohio Cocktail, a fancy Manhattan topped with champagne that was unknown in the state it was named after.*

*SEE RECIPE ON PAGE 156.

Madrileños preferred the Ginebra Compuesta, which was compounded from vermouth, Angostura bitters, and a splash of gin.

In Milan, it was the Americano--vermouth with a big slug of bitter *aperitivo* or *amaro* and soda. Down in Florence, Count Cammillo Negroni asked his bartender to stiffen up that Americano with a splash of gin, and you know what happened with that.

Like the bar that Victor Morris opened in Lima in 1915, with its famous Pisco Sour, many of these bars adapted Yankee mixology to local tastes and ingredients.

In Argentina and Uruguay, boulevardiers such as the ones who crowded Buenos Aires's Café Tortoni adopted their own red-vermouth Martini, dashed with liqueurs and renamed the San Martin.

No place went further in this kind of adaptation than Havana--but we'll get to Cuba in chapter 10.

MIXOLOGY: THE HANKY PANKY

"RIGHT THEN. HOW ABOUT A LITTLE HANKY PANKY?"

"I KNOW, I KNOW. BUT THERE REALLY IS A HANKY PANKY COCKTAIL, AND IT'S THE ONLY DRINK WE KNOW THAT WAS INVENTED BY MISS ADA COLEMAN OF THE SAVOY AMERICAN BAR, THANK-YOU-VERY-MUCH.

LIKE ANYTHING GOOD, IT STARTS WITH GIN--A GENEROUS OUNCE AND A HALF. LONDON DRY, YEAH?"

"THEN IT'S THE VERMOUTH. RED--THE ITALIAN STUFF. AN OUNCE SHOULD DO."

"BACK IN 1921, WHEN COLEY INVENTED THIS THING, FERNET-BRANCA HAD BEEN AROUND IN LONDON FOR YONKS. BUT USE IT IN A COCKTAIL? WHAT CHEEK! HALF AN OUNCE, AND NO MORE."

"YOU'RE NOT SUPPOSED TO SHAKE A DRINK LIKE THIS, ALL BOOZE AND SUCH, BUT THE SAVOY SAYS TO SHAKE IT, AND IF THAT'S WHAT MISS COLEMAN DID, THAT'S WHAT I'M DOING. IT DOES SOFTEN IT UP A BIT."

CHUKKA CHUKKA CHUKKA

"AND THEN, SURE AS MONDAY FOLLOWS SUNDAY, WE STRAIN. CHILLED GLASS, OF COURSE."

"IF THE SAVOY SAYS AN ORANGE TWIST, THEN AN ORANGE TWIST IT SHALL BE."

"ET VOILÀ. THE HANKY PANKY. DELIGHTFUL, BUT WITH AN EDGE THAT SAYS MIND HOW YOU GO."

CHASER: COCKTAIL BOOKS

Hot on the heels of the boom in cocktails came one in cocktail books, setting a precedent that has held ever since. The 1890s and 1900s saw publishers in the Americas and western Europe churn out stacks of them every year, in English of course, but also in everything from French and Spanish to Swedish and Hungarian. Almost all were simple, nearly characterless compilations of, for the most part, common recipes. Since then, the books have evolved just as much as the drinks have. Now they come in genres.

Those characterless compilations have evolved into what the cocktail evangelist Robert Hess calls the "Wad o' Drinks" book, where the object is to cram in as many recipes as possible. These things have their uses.

PICTURED: KAPPA'S *BARTENDER'S GUIDE TO THE BEST MIXED DRINKS* (TOKYO, 1950s), PAUL E. LOWE'S *DRINKS AS THEY ARE MIXED* (CHICAGO, 1904), AND OSCAR HAIMO'S *COCKTAIL AND WINE DIGEST* (NEW YORK, 1946)

A sort of offshoot of the Wad o' Drinks is the Pocket Guide, meant as a bartender's handy reference to the major drinks of the day--in case they can't remember how to mix a Bronx or a Black Russian.

PICTURED: R. DE FLEURY'S *1700 COCKTAILS FOR THE MAN BEHIND THE BAR* (LONDON, 1934) AND STAN JONES'S *COMPLETE BARGUIDE* (LOS ANGELES, 1977)

Then there's the Hand-Holder, designed to get the amateur mixer through that one big cocktail party. Robert Loeb Jr.'s 1954 *Nip Ahoy* is a particularly fine example. There are scads of modern ones, too.

The Welcome-to-My-Bar book gives one bar's take on drinks, booze, and whatever the hell else they want to talk about. These are beyond common today, but they go back to at least *The Savoy Cocktail Book* in 1930, with stops in between at joints such as the great Boadas in Barcelona and the famous Sardi's in New York.

There are several other popular types, but we'll leave off with the B to B (Bartender to Bartender). Books such as Eddie Woelke's 1936 *Barman's Mentor* are meant for serious professional education, a master bartender's testament.

The rare 1973 *Le Grand Mixology* by James W. Johnson of Panama City Beach, Florida, has to fit in this category since Johnson's recipes, which list ingredients but not how much of each to use, can be interpreted only by a highly experienced mixologist.

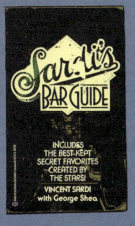

PICTURED: *SARDI'S BAR GUIDE* (NEW YORK, 1988) BY VINCENT SARDI WITH GEORGE SHEA AND *THE PEQUEÑA HISTORIA DEL BAR BOADAS* (BARCELONA, 1993)

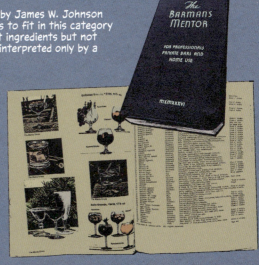

CHAPTER IX

PROHIBITION AND REPEAL
The United States and Its Immediate Neighbors ~ 1919–1941

When Prohibition went into full effect in 1920, it was the culmination of two generations' worth of increasingly bitter political wrestling--rural and small-town America versus the rapidly growing cities. The manufacture, distribution, and sale of alcoholic beverages were now illegal in the United States, its territories, and its ships at sea, and there were federal agents to make sure the law was obeyed.

But it wasn't obeyed. Not at the three-mile limit...*

...not on the back roads...

...and not in the speakeasies, which opened from coast to coast in the tens--hundreds?--of thousands.

Of course, some accommodations had to be made.

THEY'RE HITTIN' THE RYE HARD, DUKE. BETTER MAKE ANOTHER SIX.

I'M ONLY GONNA SHOW YOU THIS ONCE. TWO BOTTLES OF THE GOOD STUFF...

...THEN TWO BOTTLES OF ALCOHOL, RIGHT?

...RIGHT, AND THEN TWO BOTTLES' WORTH OF WATER. STIR IN A COUPLE DROPS BURNT SUGAR FOR COLOR AND YOU GOT SIX BOTTLES BONDED RYE.

...AND LIKE I SAID, YA GOTTA GET THE FOIL RIGHT.

AIN'T NONE OF THESE DRUNKS CAN TELL THIS AIN'T THE REAL MCCOY BY TASTIN' IT, BUT YOU MESS UP THE FOIL AND IT'S ALOHA ON A STEEL GUITAR.

*TO STOP RUMRUNNERS, IN 1922 THE GOVERNMENT TRIED TO UNILATERALLY EXTEND THE LIMIT OF U.S. TERRITORIAL WATERS FROM THREE MILES FROM SHORE TO TWELVE MILES. LITIGATION, AND THREE- AND TWELVE-MILE LIMIT COCKTAILS, ENSUED.

While speakeasies just kept spreading, the great old bars withered and died. Some, such as the Bank Exchange in San Francisco, said to hell with it and closed right off the bat.

Others--Delmonico's, as famous for its bar as its kitchen--tried selling food alone; but no go. A few, like New Orleans's Sazerac House, rebranded as restaurants and sold booze on the sly, but their previous fame made these places raid magnets and they rarely lasted.

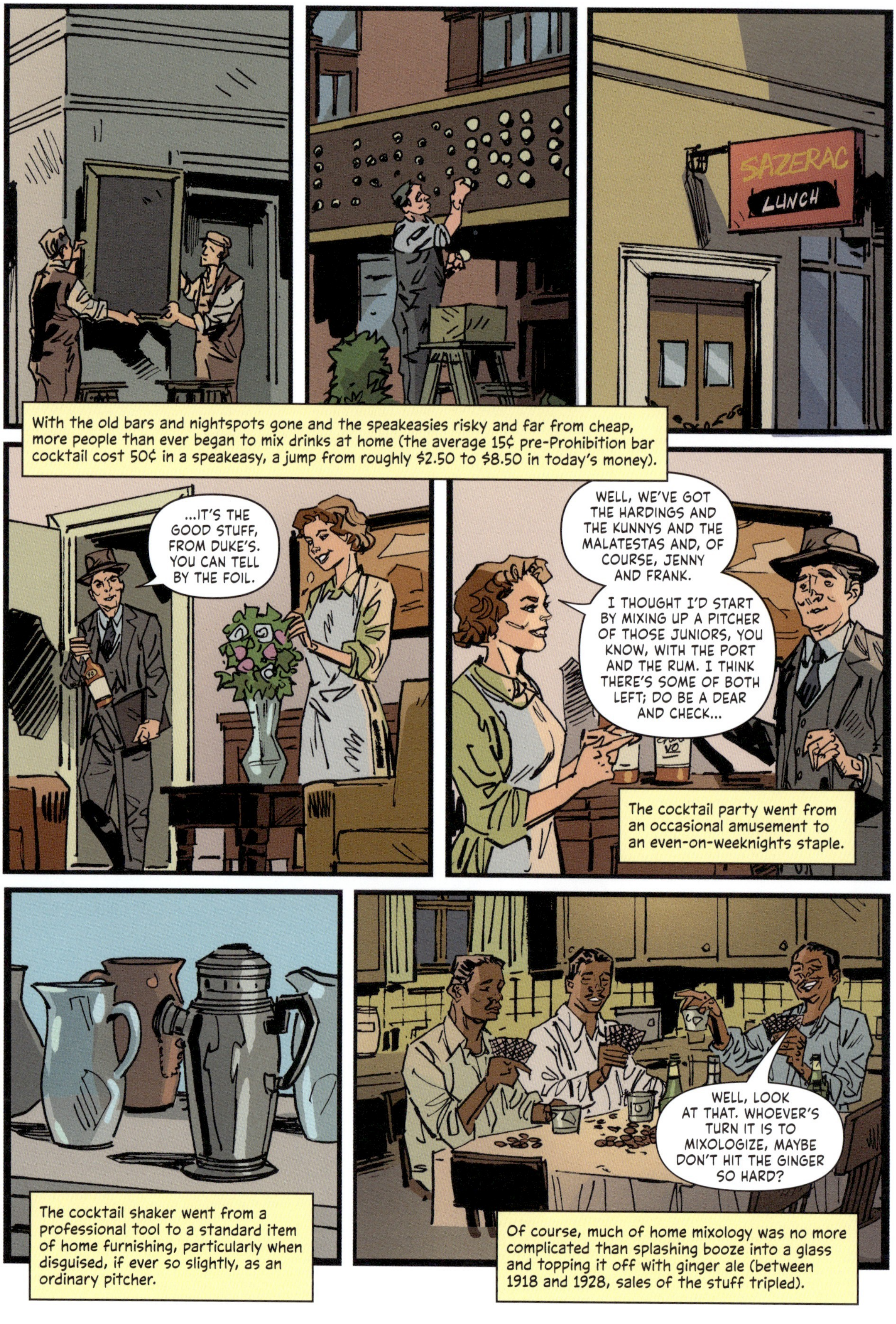

SAZERAC
LUNCH
With the old bars and nightspots gone and the speakeasies risky and far from cheap, more people than ever began to mix drinks at home (the average 15¢ pre-Prohibition bar cocktail cost 50¢ in a speakeasy, a jump from roughly $2.50 to $8.50 in today's money).
...IT'S THE GOOD STUFF, FROM DUKE'S. YOU CAN TELL BY THE FOIL.
WELL, WE'VE GOT THE HARDINGS AND THE KUNNYS AND THE MALATESTAS AND, OF COURSE, JENNY AND FRANK.
I THOUGHT I'D START BY MIXING UP A PITCHER OF THOSE JUNIORS, YOU KNOW, WITH THE PORT AND THE RUM. I THINK THERE'S SOME OF BOTH LEFT; DO BE A DEAR AND CHECK...
The cocktail party went from an occasional amusement to an even-on-weeknights staple.
The cocktail shaker went from a professional tool to a standard item of home furnishing, particularly when disguised, if ever so slightly, as an ordinary pitcher.
WELL, LOOK AT THAT. WHOEVER'S TURN IT IS TO MIXOLOGIZE, MAYBE DON'T HIT THE GINGER SO HARD?
Of course, much of home mixology was no more complicated than splashing booze into a glass and topping it off with ginger ale (between 1918 and 1928, sales of the stuff tripled).

Prohibition has a reputation for having been a golden age for the cocktail, with fancy urban speakeasies serving as temples of the mixologist's art.

SAY, IT'S BEEN A WHILE SINCE I'VE HAD A REAL NEW ORLEANS SAZERAC COCKTAIL. WOULD YOU MIND?

"A REAL NEW ORLEANS SAZERAC." LISTEN, MISTER, YOU'RE LUCKY IF I FIX YOU UP A POP OF REAL NEW JERSEY APPLEJACK.

Actually, the era was anything but. Speakeasies were criminal enterprises and mostly staffed by criminals. By the mid-1920s, most of the old pros were retired, working abroad, or doing something else.

AND DON'T GO TRYIN' TO GIVE ME NO LESSONS. THIS AIN'T BARTENDER COLLEGE.

Still, Americans did manage to produce a bunch of new drinks during the thirteen-year drought, most of them pretty uninspiring. Indeed, very few lasted beyond repeal. See the ingredients in the endnotes (page 164).

CORN POPPER
WHITE CARGO
EARTHQUAKE
BARBARY COAST
MAIDEN'S PRAYER
PALM BEACH

There were, however, two cocktails born during Prohibition that managed to survive and even thrive: the French 75--a Tom Collins with champagne instead of soda (see page 96)--and the Bloody Mary.

1928 *Tomato Juice Cocktail*: Strain the contents of a No. 3 can of tomatoes (16 ounces of strained juice), one teaspoon salt, one and one-half teaspoons malt vinegar, one and one-half teaspoons lemon juice, two-fifths teaspoon Worcestershire sauce and six drops of tobasco sauce. Shake, or mix thoroughly and serve ice cold. This recipe will serve eight persons.

Ironically, the Bloody Mary came from another wing of mixology that saw a lot of play during Prohibition: the nonalcoholic or temperance drink. But tomato juice already had a reputation as a hangover cure, and people had ideas...

SAY, THAT REALLY DOES BEAT THE BROOKLYN BOYS* BACK INTO THEIR CAGE.

*TO HAVE THE "BROOKLYN BOYS" WAS TO BE SEVERELY HUNGOVER.

In general, if you were sick of ginger ale highballs or bad booze, there was only one thing to do.

If you wanted to drink well, your best bet was to cross a border. Okay, maybe not to Canada, which had its own patchy, passive-aggressive Prohibition going on, but to anywhere else.

By the mid-1930s, the Tequila Daisy, Henry Madden's mistake, was all over the Southwest. Then, with Cointreau in place of the original grenadine and "daisy" translated into Spanish,* the cocktail took over the world (see page 114).

*DAISY = MARGARITA

If you drank too many Daisies, the next morning the "scientists" who manned the Gold Bar at Tijuana's ritzy Agua Caliente resort could make you their famous Tequila Sunrise (with lime, grenadine, cassis, and soda; our tequila-OJ-grenadine version is a 1970s make-do).

90

Soon every bar within two days of an American port was packed. Dirty Dick's, in Nassau, the Bahamas, was typical.

Mostly, the booze cruisers stuck to their whiskey and gin, though rum drinks such as the Planter's Punch (old rum with lime, sugar, and ice) had their converts.

Some of these bars became legends. If you were longing for an Old-Fashioned in an old-fashioned saloon, it was worth a trip to Panama and the joint Max Bilgray, a former Chicago speakeasy keeper, ran in Colón.

If you preferred a more strenuous nightlife, across the isthmus in Panama City lay Kelley's Ritz, where anything went--until it didn't. And then Mamie Kelley--five feet ten and brawny--would toss you out herself.

Most people, however, only went as far as Havana, Cuba, the undisputed capital of fancy drinking in the Americas during the Prohibition years--

--but we'll get to that in chapter 10.

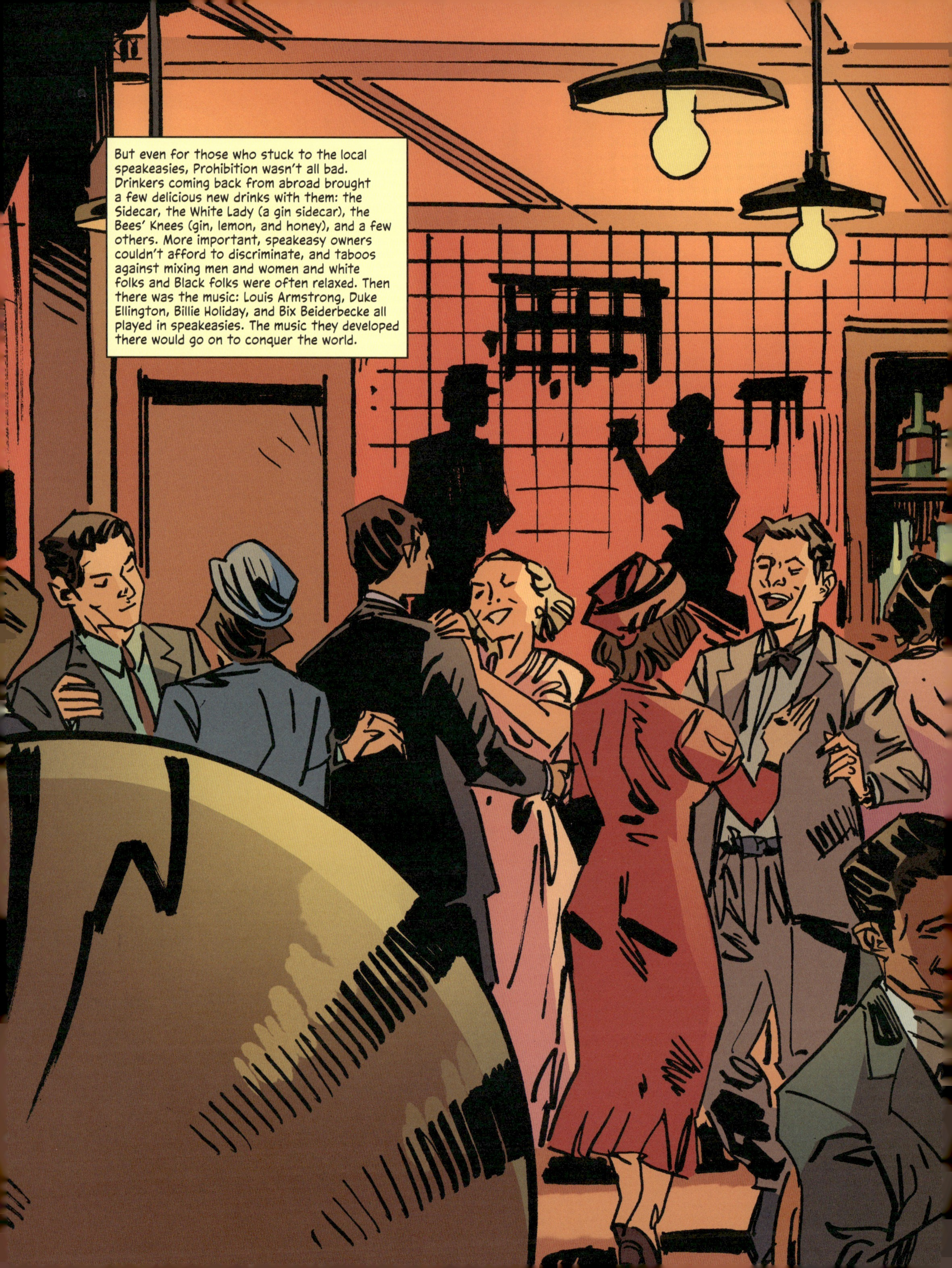
But even for those who stuck to the local speakeasies, Prohibition wasn't all bad. Drinkers coming back from abroad brought a few delicious new drinks with them: the Sidecar, the White Lady (a gin sidecar), the Bees' Knees (gin, lemon, and honey), and a few others. More important, speakeasy owners couldn't afford to discriminate, and taboos against mixing men and women and white folks and Black folks were often relaxed. Then there was the music: Louis Armstrong, Duke Ellington, Billie Holiday, and Bix Beiderbecke all played in speakeasies. The music they developed there would go on to conquer the world.

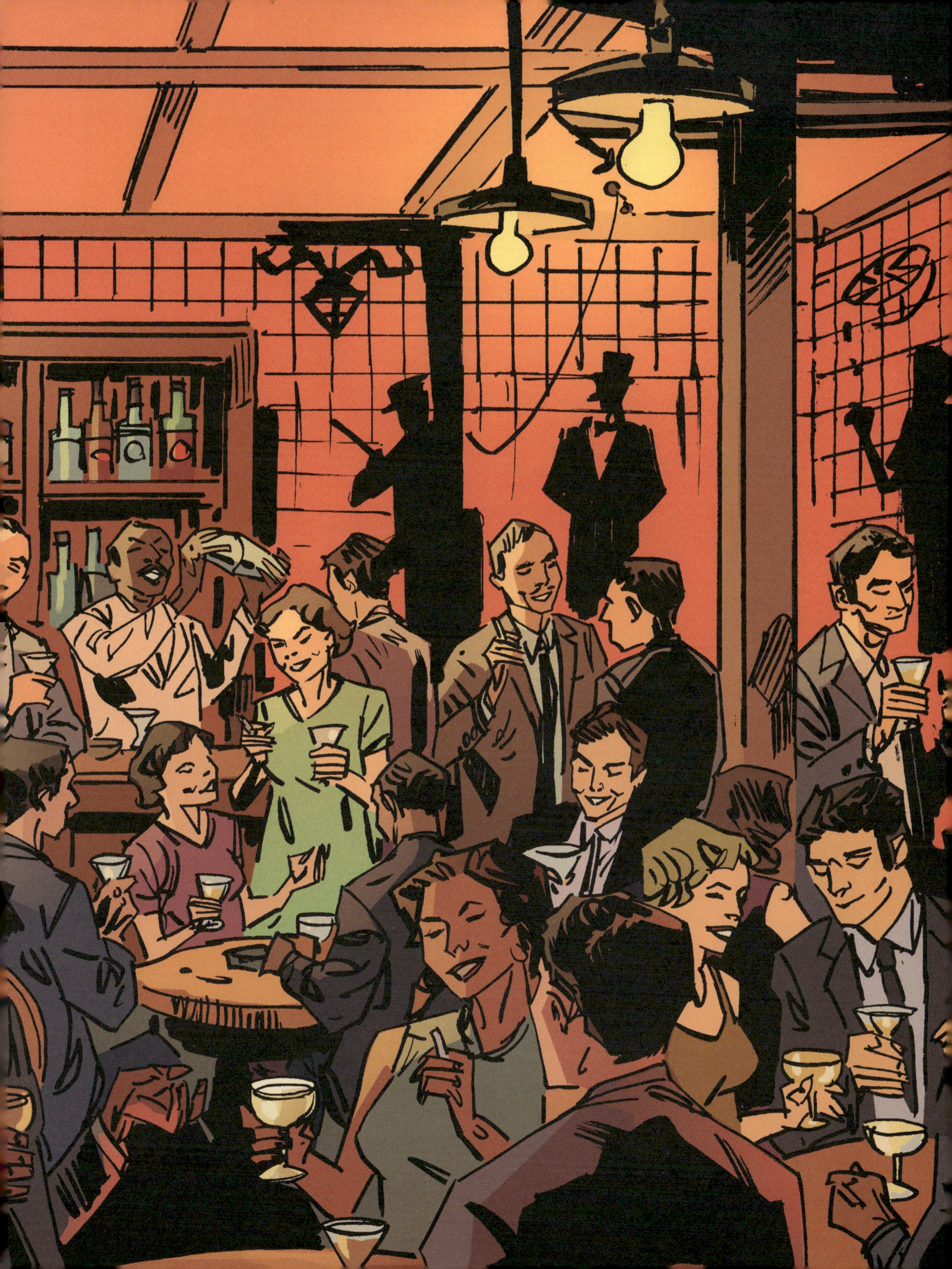

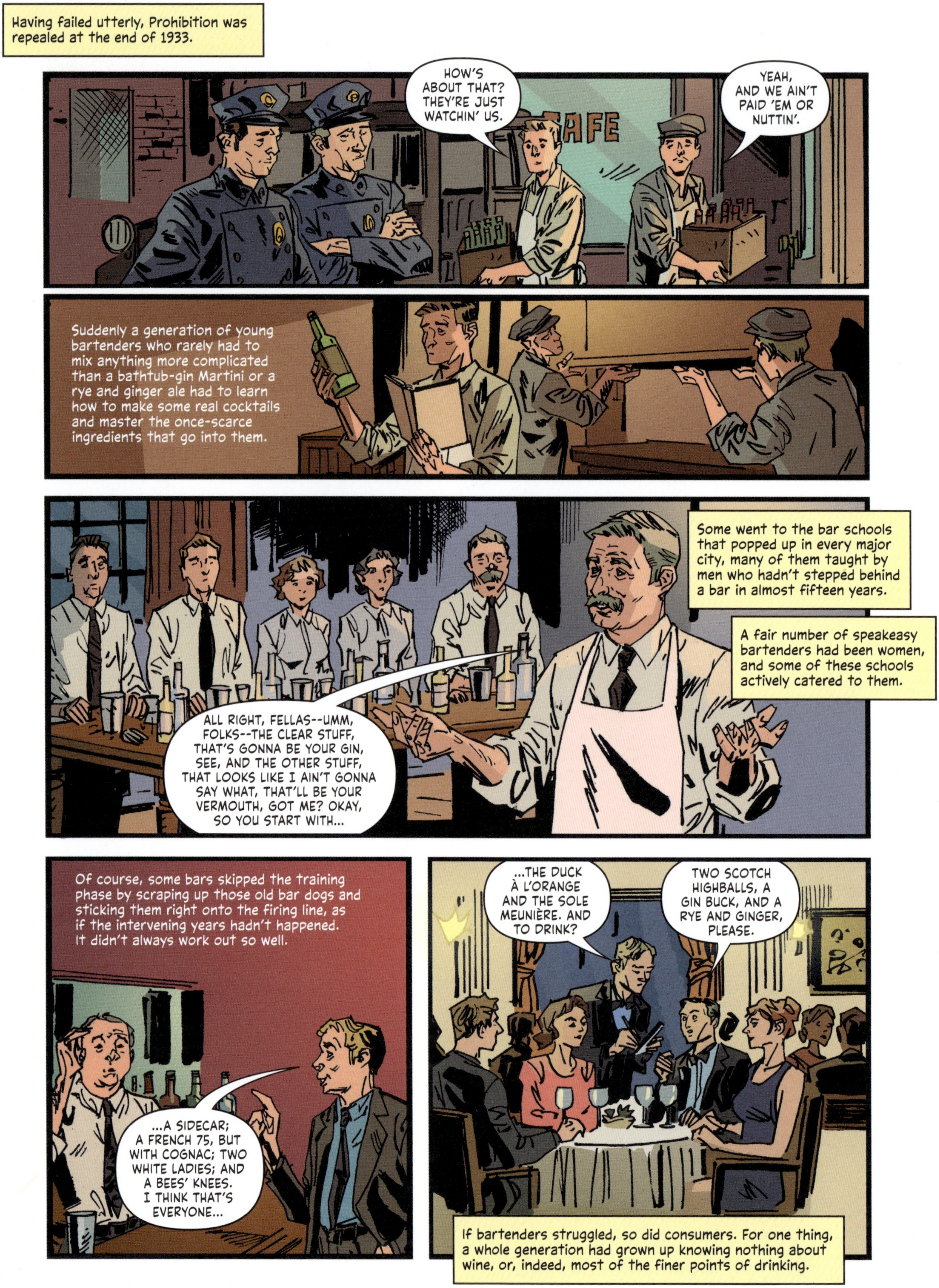
Having failed utterly, Prohibition was repealed at the end of 1933.
HOW'S ABOUT THAT? THEY'RE JUST WATCHIN' US.
YEAH, AND WE AIN'T PAID 'EM OR NUTTIN'.
Suddenly a generation of young bartenders who rarely had to mix anything more complicated than a bathtub-gin Martini or a rye and ginger ale had to learn how to make some real cocktails and master the once-scarce ingredients that go into them.
Some went to the bar schools that popped up in every major city, many of them taught by men who hadn't stepped behind a bar in almost fifteen years.
A fair number of speakeasy bartenders had been women, and some of these schools actively catered to them.
ALL RIGHT, FELLAS--UMM, FOLKS--THE CLEAR STUFF, THAT'S GONNA BE YOUR GIN, SEE, AND THE OTHER STUFF, THAT LOOKS LIKE I AIN'T GONNA SAY WHAT, THAT'LL BE YOUR VERMOUTH, GOT ME? OKAY, SO YOU START WITH...
Of course, some bars skipped the training phase by scraping up those old bar dogs and sticking them right onto the firing line, as if the intervening years hadn't happened. It didn't always work out so well.
...A SIDECAR; A FRENCH 75, BUT WITH COGNAC; TWO WHITE LADIES; AND A BEES' KNEES. I THINK THAT'S EVERYONE...
...THE DUCK À L'ORANGE AND THE SOLE MEUNIÈRE. AND TO DRINK?
TWO SCOTCH HIGHBALLS, A GIN BUCK, AND A RYE AND GINGER, PLEASE.
If bartenders struggled, so did consumers. For one thing, a whole generation had grown up knowing nothing about wine, or, indeed, most of the finer points of drinking.

By the mid-1930s, a new kind of bar began to appear: the cocktail lounge. Rather than trying to re-create the old saloon, these establishments leaped boldly into the future with distinctive, ultramodern designs based on an often-over-the-top interpretation of the new European Art Deco style. For the first time, barstools and carpeting became regular additions to the American cocktail bar.

More important, so did women, usually in front of the bar but sometimes also behind it, despite a good deal of male resistance. Take Elsie Gelli, a Dutch-Italian former vaudeville dancer and speakeasy bartender, who headed the bar at New York's sporty Hotel Gorham.

In 1935, when she was the only woman to compete in a New York cocktail contest, Gelli was also the only competitor to bring her own ingredients, in little cosmetics bottles. She didn't win, but neither did the master bartender Eddie Woelke, and it's a good bet that her drink was more interesting than the winning one, a mix of gin, Bénédictine, and lime with a dash of curaçao.

That winning drink was typical of Repeal-era mixology. Drinks featuring citrus, some European liqueur, and one of the lighter spirits--gin, white rum, Canadian blended whiskey, vodka (a newcomer in American bars)--ruled the day, in part because reborn American whiskeys had yet to reach maturity.

WHITE LADY — JUNIOR — GYPSY QUEEN

The 1930s did see the establishment of one enduring icon when American drinkers started misusing the distinctive champagne glass that architect Oswald Haerdtl designed for the Austrian Lobmeyr company in 1925, for the Paris decorative arts exhibition that would give Art Deco its name, but see page 97 for that.

MIXOLOGY: THE FRENCH 75

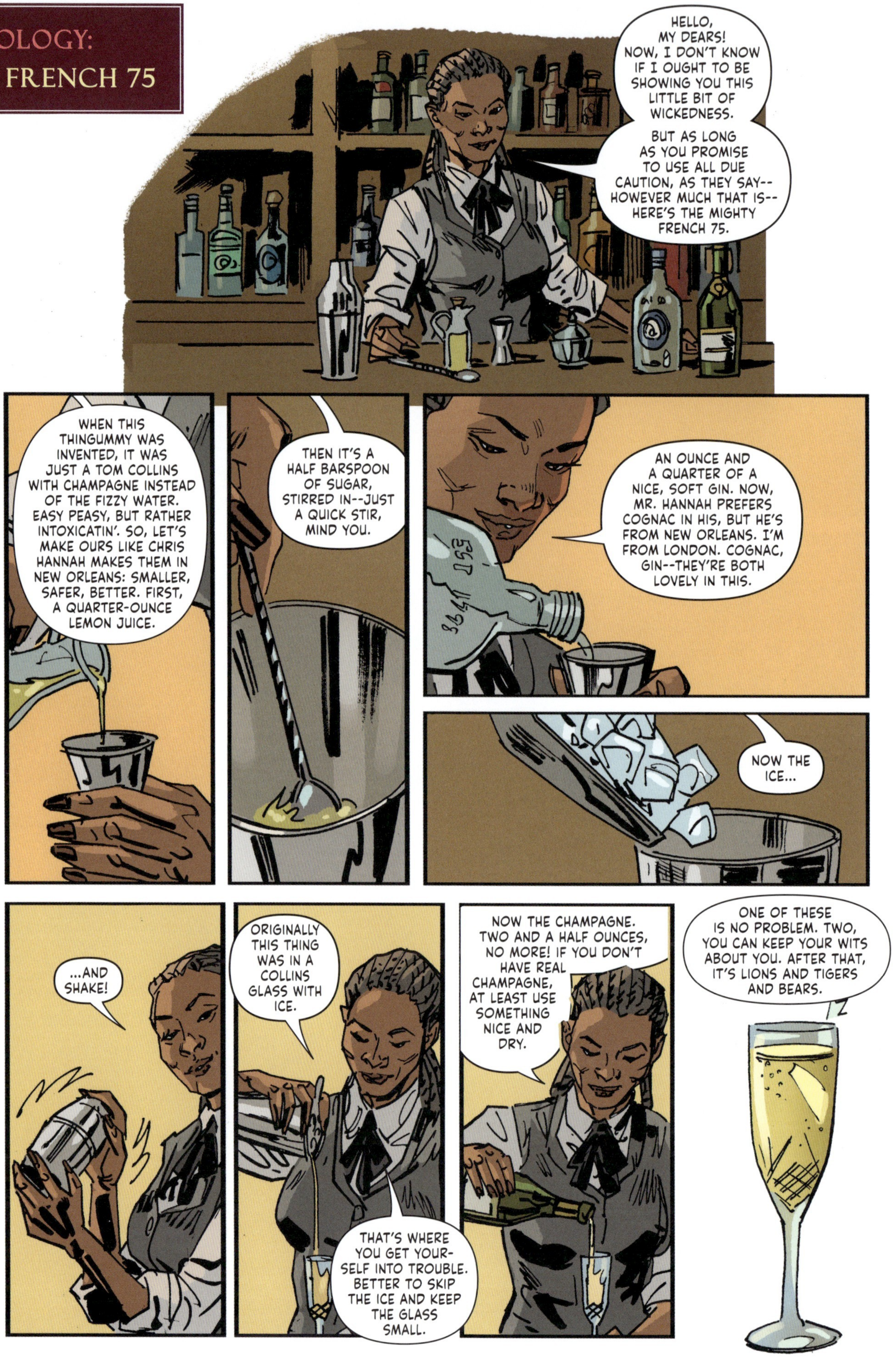

HELLO, MY DEARS! NOW, I DON'T KNOW IF I OUGHT TO BE SHOWING YOU THIS LITTLE BIT OF WICKEDNESS.
BUT AS LONG AS YOU PROMISE TO USE ALL DUE CAUTION, AS THEY SAY--HOWEVER MUCH THAT IS--HERE'S THE MIGHTY FRENCH 75.
WHEN THIS THINGUMMY WAS INVENTED, IT WAS JUST A TOM COLLINS WITH CHAMPAGNE INSTEAD OF THE FIZZY WATER. EASY PEASY, BUT RATHER INTOXICATIN'. SO, LET'S MAKE OURS LIKE CHRIS HANNAH MAKES THEM IN NEW ORLEANS: SMALLER, SAFER, BETTER. FIRST, A QUARTER-OUNCE LEMON JUICE.
THEN IT'S A HALF BARSPOON OF SUGAR, STIRRED IN--JUST A QUICK STIR, MIND YOU.
AN OUNCE AND A QUARTER OF A NICE, SOFT GIN. NOW, MR. HANNAH PREFERS COGNAC IN HIS, BUT HE'S FROM NEW ORLEANS. I'M FROM LONDON. COGNAC, GIN--THEY'RE BOTH LOVELY IN THIS.
NOW THE ICE...
...AND SHAKE!
ORIGINALLY THIS THING WAS IN A COLLINS GLASS WITH ICE.
THAT'S WHERE YOU GET YOURSELF INTO TROUBLE. BETTER TO SKIP THE ICE AND KEEP THE GLASS SMALL.
NOW THE CHAMPAGNE. TWO AND A HALF OUNCES, NO MORE! IF YOU DON'T HAVE REAL CHAMPAGNE, AT LEAST USE SOMETHING NICE AND DRY.
ONE OF THESE IS NO PROBLEM. TWO, YOU CAN KEEP YOUR WITS ABOUT YOU. AFTER THAT, IT'S LIONS AND TIGERS AND BEARS.

CHASER: HOLLYWOOD DISCOVERS THE COCKTAIL

During the 1920s and 1930s, Hollywood turned the cocktail into an American cultural icon.

In early silent films, as in the Broadway plays of the time, the cocktail and its mixing were mostly a chance for some comic business, as in Charlie Chaplin's incomparable take on bartending in the movie *The Rink* (1916).

SCOTCH--VERMOUTH--BITTERS--ICE--A WHOLE EGG, SHELL AND ALL--A CARNATION

By the early 1930s, a decade-plus of Prohibition had made cocktail drinking a mark of sophistication, not dissipation.

Hollywood seized on this concept, as in the famous scene in the 1934 movie *The Thin Man*, where Nora Charles (Myrna Loy) sets out to catch up with the half a dozen Martinis that Nick Charles (William Powell) has drunk. Now cocktails were *stylish*.

Hollywood specialized in stereotypes, archetypes, and visual shortcuts. One such shortcut was created when production designers took to using Lobmeyr's elegant, V-shaped champagne glass not for the wine (as it was used in Buster Keaton's 1929 movie *Spite Marriage*) but rather for a cocktail glass, as in the 1932 movie *One Way Passage*, where William Powell and Kay Francis drink from them in one of the pivotal scenes where they bond over Paradise Cocktails.

By the end of the decade, the V-shaped glass exclusively meant "cocktails" and all they stood for--and not just in the movies. Abstracted and rendered in bent, neon-filled glass tubing, it became a real-world icon.

BUT THAT'S HOW IT WENT. FROM THE 1930S ON, WHEN IT CAME TO WHO DRANK WHAT, THE GREATEST INFLUENCERS WERE IMAGES SEEN ON A SCREEN: RICK BLAINE AND ILSA LUND; CARRIE BRADSHAW; BRIAN FLANAGAN; JAMES BOND; THE DUDE.

CIRO'S OF HOLLYWOOD, 1950

Of course, it wasn't just the flickering images that were influential. The men and women of California's so-called film colony saw their doings chronicled obsessively in the press, and what they drank often became what America drank.

THE TAIL O' THE COCK

In 1941, the owners of Smirnoff vodka and the Cock'n Bull pub in Hollywood, which made its own ginger beer, tasked Wes Price, the pub's head bartender, with finding a drink to sell their products. Price tested out the Moscow Mule (as it was called) on the tough-guy actor Broderick Crawford. He liked it, and soon all of Hollywood did, too; after the war, the rest of America followed suit.

When America began drinking tequila in earnest in the late 1950s it was because of the Margarita, a Mexican-border formula from the 1930s that finally got named and discovered.

That was in 1953 at the Tail o' the Cock, a Hollywood film colony hangout.

MIXOLOGY: THE MOSCOW MULE

"WES PRICE'S MOSCOW MULE IS WHY YOU GET A PROFESSIONAL TO DO THIS SORT OF THING. HE SKINNED IT DOWN TO THE BONE, BUT IT'S STILL DAMN TASTY. IT'S THREE INGREDIENTS: VODKA, LIME JUICE, AND GINGER BEER (NOT GINGER ALE; YOU WANT THE SPICY STUFF)."

"SO, YOU SQUEEZE HALF A LIME INTO YER COPPER MUG, IF YOU GOT ONE, OR WHATEVER YOU'RE USIN', AND THEN DROP IN THE SQUEEZED-OUT SHELL."

"THEN IT'S A COUPLE OUNCES OF VODKA, WHATEVER KIND, AND FILL THE MUG WITH CRACKED ICE."

"TOP IT OFF WITH THE GINGER BEER-- YOU WANT, LIKE, FOUR OUNCES, GIVE OR TAKE--AND DRINK 'ER DOWN."

CHAPTER X

CUBA AND THE TROPICAL COCKTAIL

Santiago, Havana, and Cuba's Far-Flung Outposts ~ 1897–1941

After Prohibition, America's cocktail culture took inspiration from a lot of different places as it was rebuilding itself: from the hazily remembered saloons of the past, Paris and London and their famous "American" bars, Hollywood and its Art Deco cocktail reveries. Yet no place was more influential than Cuba, and in particular Havana.

In the 1920s, Havana was anything but a sleepy tropical backwater. By far the largest settlement in the Caribbean, it was all trolleys and tall buildings, cocktails and chorus girls, with more than enough bustle, hustle, and--if you took the hustle wrong--muscle to make even a New Yorker hold onto his hat. It was Broadway, in the key of rum.

Back before 1898, when Cuba was still part of Spain, its people drank in the Spanish style: at any hour they pleased, without taboo, but lightly.

Nonalcoholic drinks abounded, many based on the fruits grown on the island in such profusion. Light Spanish wines were popular, and Spanish brandy and the local rum were enjoyed--at least by all but the roughest people--in small doses, well diluted.

By the 1890s, there was even the occasional Havana bartender who could make a Yanqui (Yankee) cocktail--usually accompanied by a flashy display of old-fashioned drink throwing, a skill by then all but forgotten in the United States itself.

Then, in 1898, the American battleship *Maine* blew up in Havana Harbor, bringing the United States into the long-simmering Cuban War of Independence. The subsequent Spanish-American War ended with American troops occupying Cuba, and they would stick around, on and off, until 1922.

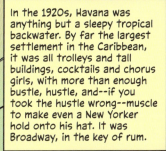

Cuban bartenders quickly picked up on the new ingredients, techniques, and recipes that accompanied the raft of American bartenders who followed the troops. Those opportunists, in turn, learned to handle tropical fruits and cater to tropical tastes.

Ironically, what may be the most popular drink to come out of this encounter was the simplest: Cuban rum, Coca-Cola, a squeeze of lime, and ice. It was called the Cuba Libre, or "Free Cuba," although now most people simply call it a Rum and Coke.

Cuba's greatest contribution to the art of the cocktail, however, came just before the war, among the (mostly American and Canadian) engineers who ran the giant iron mine at Daiquiri in Cuba's southeast, not far from the city of Santiago.

I HAVE TO SAY, BOYS, I WOULD GIVE MY EYETEETH FOR A GIN RICKEY.

THEY DID TELL ME DOWN AT THE VILLAGE THAT THE GRUB BOAT OFF-LOADED A COUPLE OF CAKES OF ICE THIS MORNING.

NOW IF WE COULD JUST GET THE GIN BOAT TO...

I'VE GOT A BOTTLE OF BACARDI I PICKED UP IN SANTIAGO. IT'S NOT GIN, BUT...

HEY, LYMAN-- DIDN'T YOU SAY YOU BROUGHT A COCKTAIL SHAKER?

THAT'S IT, BOB! THAT'S THE OL' ENTHUSIASALUM!

The drink that Jennings Cox and his engineers devised was shaken up with lime, sugar, Bacardi rum, and mineral water and served unstrained, with the ice it was shaken with in the glass. No doubt it was very refreshing, but it was just a rough draft of the Daiquiri as we know it.

"...AND ABOUT HALF A GLASS OF MINERAL WATER, AND THEN YOU SHAKE IT UP AND POUR IT ALL INTO A GLASS--A TALL ONE, BUT NOT TOO TALL. DOWN AT THE MINE, WE CALL IT THE DAIQUIRI."

It wasn't until Cox's crew brought the drink to Havana that it was perfected. Credit for that generally goes to Emilio "Maragato" González at the Café Telegrafo.

While Maragato's early role is poorly documented, in later years he was widely hailed as the patriarch of the city's Daiquiri mixers.

"YES. ES MUY SIMPLE."

"YOU START--LIME JUICE. Y PUES SUGAR-- ONE SPOON; STIR IT GOOD."

"RUM--CARTA BLANCA--TWO OUNCES. SHAKE IT MUCH, WITH ICE."

In any case, by 1908, Bacardi rum, aged and then, uniquely, filtered for smoothness and clarity, had made it to the United States, and with it the improved Daiquiri. The cocktail's first conquest was the Army and Navy Club in Washington, D.C., in 1909. By 1914, it was included in all the new drinks books.

With Prohibition, Americans poured into Havana like thirsty locusts and brought their bartenders with them. Mostly, they drank, and mixed, the same drinks they always had, plus Daiquiris.

Some of the Yankee barmen at least experimented with Cuban ingredients. Eddie Woelke, once of Paris and New York, gave it a try and ended up with the Mary Pickford, a delightful mix of Bacardi, fresh pineapple juice, and a dash of grenadine that became one of the most popular drinks of the 1930s.

Meanwhile, Cuban bartenders were coming up with drinks of their own.

Around 1910, the forgotten genius behind the bar at one of the snooty clubs on Havana's Playa de la Concha muddled some mint in lime juice and sugar, splashed in a little rum, and topped it off with soda water. The Mojito was all Cuban: light, refreshing, delicious.

The subtle, intriguing El Presidente, a sort of Cuban rum Manhattan, soon followed. It was the most popular of the Cuban cocktails among actual Cubans.

We don't know who invented the El Presidente, which first turned up in a 1915 Cuban cocktail book, but it was later attributed to Constante Ribalaigua y Vert, of the Bar Florida, aka Floridita, in central Havana. He's certainly a good candidate.

Born outside Barcelona in 1888, Constante began working at the Floridita as a young man. By 1916, he was already getting his picture in the paper as the "general en jefe" of the Floridita's bartenders. His claim to fame wasn't an exuberant personality. It was the William Schmidt-like attention he paid to the fine art of mixing drinks, from fine-tuning the recipe of every classic to squeezing limes only with his fingers to avoid expressing the bitter oil from the skin.

By the 1920s, while bars such as the one at the Sevilla-Biltmore hotel, where Eddie Woelke worked, drew most of the tourist trade, the Floridita was the most popular cocktail bar among the city's natives, and was already becoming known among mixology-curious Americans.

The 1930s saw the bar become a destination for American and other traveling celebrities, drawn by the worldwide reputation of Constante's drinks. In 1938, when Ernest Hemingway and Martha Gellhorn were living outside Havana, they drove into the city every week to drink there; Hemingway would be a regular on and off until his death.

Few of Constante's elegant, unfussy recipes became standards, but his approach to mixing drinks, with its unusual combinations of standard ingredients, was hugely influential.

The bar gave out a booklet with all of his recipes in it, which helped.

DAIQUIRI NO. 3—ERNEST HEMINGWAY (WHITE RUM, LIME JUICE, AND SUGAR; DASHES OF GRAPEFRUIT AND MARASCHINO)

For all of his attention to detail, Constante wasn't stuck in the past: in fact, the Floridita was one of the first bars to use electric cocktail mixers, capable of making a Daiquiri slushy with ice.

Ultimately, Constante's greatest skill was his ability to seamlessly weave non-Cuban ingredients in with the island's characteristic rums and tropical fruits. His clever juxtapositions of common flavors created surprise and delight and marked him as the greatest mixologist of the twentieth century.

Of course, Havana drinking wasn't only the genteel Floridita kind. Three blocks from there, Sloppy Joe's Bar, Spanish owned and tourist centered, packed 'em in every day and night with its evocation of a pre-Prohibition American businessman's saloon.

"The Mecca of every American or foreigner who visits Havana," as *The Galveston Daily News* dubbed it in 1924, Sloppy Joe's made as much profit on beer and Whiskey Highballs as it did on Daiquiris and other Cuban drinks.

You'd find the same sort of saloon in Panama or along the Mexican border. What you wouldn't find is the Club de Cantineros, an elite, invitation-only bartenders' union founded in 1924 to help Cubans compete with all the foreign barmen there. By 1931, it had Constante and other stars sharing their knowledge through classes in cocktail making and history.

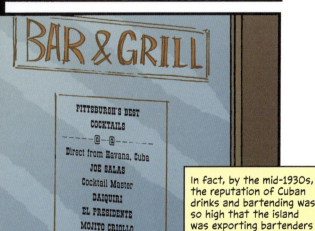

In fact, by the mid-1930s, the reputation of Cuban drinks and bartending was so high that the island was exporting bartenders to the United States and elsewhere.

Cuba and Cuban drinks supplied a good deal of the fabric that American bars were stitching together to make a new cocktail culture. Mostly, it showed in the Daiquiri on the menu and the stools at the bar--long a feature of the finer Cuban joints.

Then there was Don the Beachcomber (aka Donn Beach) on McCadden Place in the heart of Hollywood, where Donn would spray water on the awnings to make his customers feel that they were in some monsoon-beset tropical rum shack.

Donn Beach, or Ernest Raymond Beaumont Gantt (as he was born), was a Texan who had kicked around the South Seas some, drunk his way through the Caribbean, bootlegged, and tended bar. At repeal, he opened a tiny twelve-stool bamboo bar decorated with objects he had picked up in his travels.

Donn's "perfect burlesque of a South Seas dive" (as columnist Mollie Merrick dubbed it) thrived, its popularity driven by stars such as Carole Lombard, a fixture there.

People came for the bamboo--Hollywood was in the middle of a South Pacific craze--and stayed for the drinks, which were inventive and delicious. Donn had clearly spent his time watching Constante.

Take his Zombie, the ancestor of the whole gnarly tiki-drink tribe. His secret 1934 recipe, as uncovered by the tiki historian extraordinaire Jeff "Beachbum" Berry, reveals it to be a classic Barbados Green Swizzle, as Donn would have encountered at the Ice House in Bridgetown, with a couple of Constante-style twists and one or two that were pure Donn.

ANGOSTURA	151 RUM
ABSINTHE	ABSINTHE SUB.*
SODA WATER	ANGOSTURA
	GRENADINE
SUGAR	DONN'S MIX #3**
LIME JUICE	LIME JUICE
FALERNUM	FALERNUM
BARBADOS RUM	RUMS***
GREEN SWIZZLE	ZOMBIE

*PERNOD
**GRAPEFRUIT JUICE AND CINNAMON SYRUP
***PUERTO RICAN AND JAMAICAN

The grapefruit juice–lime juice combo and use of grenadine instead of sugar are straight out of the Floridita playbook, though the cinnamon syrup and multiple, overlapping rums are purely Donn's own, as was the way he flash-blended it with ice--and his two-to-a-customer limit.

The Zombie might have been the most famous of Beach's "rum rhapsodies," as he called them, but he had a whole range of prismatic versions of basic Caribbean punches, where each element--the sweet, sour, strong, weak, and spice--was split among several ingredients.

When it came to naming his drinks, Beach leaned more toward the Pacific than the Caribbean, though his version of the Pacific was derived as much from movies and the South Seas tales by Robert Louis Stevenson and Somerset Maugham as from the actual islands of Polynesia.

PEARL DIVER · MISSIONARY'S DOWNFALL · NAVY GROG · SHARK'S TOOTH · VICIOUS VIRGIN

Even though Beach tried to keep his recipes secret, as the Great Depression wore on, the mix of Constante-style mixology and faux-tropical escapism that he had brewed became too potent to keep under wraps. By the time the United States joined World War II, artificial island paradises were materializing from coast to coast.

They ranged from the perfunctory to the plagiaristic, from the Hawaiian Room at New York's Hotel Lexington, the usual ballroom with a few fake palm trees and a couple of pineapple drinks, to Monte Proser's Beachcomber, over on Broadway, which took everything—drinks, decor, even its very name—from its Hollywood model.

HAWAIIA HOTEL LEX · TE PROSER'S CHCOMBER

Donn Beach had Constante's mixological bent and Harry McElhone's talent for branding, but he wasn't much of a businessman (he left that to his ex-wife, Cora "Queen Sunakora" Sund). Most of his imitators and disciples were trend chasers who lacked one or two of those qualities. Victor Bergeron had all three, in spades.

Trader Vic, as Bergeron took to calling himself, was certainly a trend chaser. In 1938 he went on a fact-finding mission to Don the Beachcomber, but unlike most of Donn's other disciples, he went on to various bars in New Orleans and the Caribbean.

When he got back home to Oakland, California, he fitted out his bar, Hinky Dinks, with a new "Bamboo Room." That was a little odd, since the bar was patterned after a Quebec trapper's shack (Vic's father was Quebecois), but no matter.

Although he started with a mix of international oddities—like the Pisco Sour, Bloody Mary (then new), Mojito, and Tequila Cooler—and a few drinks lifted from the Beachcomber, before long Bergeron was adding drinks of his own, and good ones. People noticed.

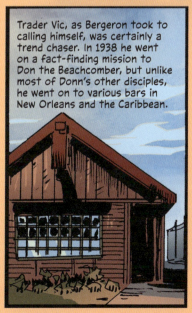

By 1940, Hinky Dinks had become Trader Vic's, with a full redo in the Beachcomber style.

TRADER VIC'S

By 1940, Donn Beach and Trader Vic (whose menus gave Beach full credit for pioneering the tropical-ish rum-drink trade) were both opening branches in various cities and laying the foundations for commercial empires. What they weren't doing, however, was tending bar. They were hosts, impresarios, figureheads.

Meanwhile, the actual bartending was generally done by anonymous young men whose roots were in the Philippines or the Pacific's various overseas Chinese communities, such as Philippine-born Ray Buhen (left) or Honolulu-born, Hong Kong–educated Robert Ching (right), two of Beach's first bartenders. Beach, at least, had friends in the Filipino community from his scuffling days, but there was still a strong and nasty element of Hollywood stage setting involved, particularly among his imitators.

Ching turned the theatricality to his advantage when he moved as host, manager, and chief Zombie mixer to Monte Proser's Beachcomber rip-off in New York. Smart and charming, Ching seemed to amuse himself there by uttering Charlie Chan–style fake-Confucian aphorisms, acting mysterious, and insisting that he came from Tahiti, land of the Zombies (Tahiti, Haiti--it's the same letters, right?). His act was a huge hit with the public and the press, and the bar sold Zombies by the tens of thousands, spawning a whole new wave of imitators.

"DONN'S SPICES NO. 2? YEAH, EASY. JUST VANILLA SYRUP AND THAT PIMENTO DRAM STUFF THERE; SAY, HALF AND HALF."

SIDECAR
1 jigger ~~Cognac~~ California Brandy
3/4 jigger ~~Cointreau~~ triple sec
3/4 jigger or little less lemon juice

Mostly, the Filipino bartenders left the front bar, where the customers were, to the owners and to show-offs like "Mr. Ching," as he was billed. Donn and Vic and their imitators had learned to tuck them out of sight at service bars, where nobody could copy down their recipes. There, they kept their heads down and mixed and mixed and mixed. Along the way, however, they built a tight-knit brotherhood of men who knew the recipes for some of the most popular drinks in America, at a time when their creators treated them as state secrets. This would eventually come in handy.

It's no coincidence that during the twenty-seven months between the outbreak of World War II and the bombing of Pearl Harbor, while Poland and France fell, London burned, Moscow was imperiled, and the Japanese were raging through China, Americans escaped to bright, boldly colorful cocktail lounges and the often crudely artificial visions of distant, serene tropical paradises, drinking round after round of sweet anesthesia to hold the darkness at bay.

MIXOLOGY: THE BENJAMIN MENÉNDEZ SPECIAL

WELL, HELLO THERE! I HOPE YOU'RE IN THE PINK--WHAT'S THAT YOU SAY? OH, I SEE. WELL, I'VE GOT JUST THE THING FOR THAT, AND FROM OLD CONSTANTE, OF THE FLORIDITA, NO LESS. THE BENJAMIN MENÉNDEZ SPECIAL, IT'S CALLED--AND NO, I DON'T KNOW WHO HE WAS. BUT HE LIKED SCOTCH WHISKEY!

THIS STARTS, ANYWAY, LIKE YOU'D EXPECT FROM A CUBAN DRINK--HALF A LIME, SQUEEZED INTO YOUR SHAKER (I'M USING MY FINGERS LIKE HIMSELF DID)...OH, AND SAVE THE SHELL, RIGHT?

NOW STIR IN A BARSPOON OF SUGAR...

...AND TOSS IN THE LIME SHELL; IT'LL GIVE EVERYTHING A NICE, BITTER LITTLE EDGE-- YOU'LL SEE.

TWO OUNCES OF SCOTCH, NOW, AND INTO THE SHAKER. YOU WANT A BLEND, BUT A NICE ONE, YEAH? OH, AND ADD A BARSPOON OF ORANGE CURAÇAO WHILE YOU'RE AT IT.

FOUR OR FIVE NICE MINT LEAVES AND DROP 'EM RIGHT IN.

NOW ICE IN THE SHAKER, AND YOU JUST WANT TO ROCK IT BACK AND FORTH, REALLY-- GENTLY-GENTLY, SO THAT THE ICE DOESN'T CUT UP THE MINT. MOVE YOUR WRISTS, NOT YOUR ARMS.

STRAIN NOW--IF YOU GOT A BIT OVEREXCITED IN YOUR SHAKE, YOU MAY NEED TO HOLD A LITTLE TEA STRAINER OVER THE GLASS TO CATCH THE MINT BITS.

HE REALLY WAS A GENIUS AT THIS-- CONSTANTE, THAT IS. SUCH A SIMPLE DRINK, AND YET WITH LAYERS. OH, AND DO FLOAT A MINT LEAF ON IT, JUST 'CAUSE IT'S PRETTY.

MIXOLOGY: MR. CHING'S ZOMBIE

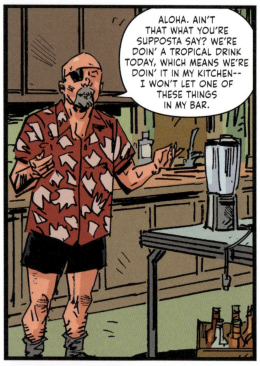

CHASER: THE COCKTAIL AND THE TWO WORLD WARS, 1914–1918 AND 1939–1945

The great world wars of the twentieth century might have left a few human institutions unaffected, but the cocktail wasn't one of them. As the American columnist Robert Ruark wrote in 1950, recalling "World War Twice," as he called it, "It is a matter of uncut fact that in times of stress people are apt to crave a snifter or something to lighten the pain of fear and boredom and death and taxes." The wars were as stressful as events can be, on institutions as much as on individuals, and to keep those snifters coming took ingenuity and flexibility.

Normally, military drinking tends to leave little room for subtleties such as fresh juices or a splash of vermouth. Certainly, the rum ration that helped World War I British soldiers cope with the horrors of trench warfare was usually gulped straight.

But not everyone fought in the trenches. Those who were accustomed to drinking cocktails before the war saw no reason to stop during the war if they could get them.

Pilots and aircrew, for example, could be in a desperate struggle for their lives one minute and—if lucky—drinking an ice-cold cocktail at their officers' club ten minutes later.

Mostly, those cocktails were the same as before the war, though there were exceptions: Harry McElhone included a number of novelties among the thirty-five cocktails on his 1915 opening list at Ciro's in London (see page 80)...

...and Angelo at the New York Bar in Paris introduced a calvados- and gin-based "75" Cocktail that same year that was as popular as it was potent (it was different from the French 75, although named after the same iconic cannon).

But if the first world war had little fundamental effect on the fine art of mixing drinks, the second one was a different story.

For one thing, after a wild flirtation with abstract, bizarre "Futurist Mixology" in the 1920s, the Italian Fascists turned against cocktail drinking as a foreign and corrupt practice. They even banned the very word "cocktail." The Nazis followed suit in 1941.

Elvezio Grassi's 1936 book, *1000 Cocktails*, had to be published with a cover where the Italian word "Misture," or "Mixtures," was crudely stamped over the English "Cocktails" in the title.

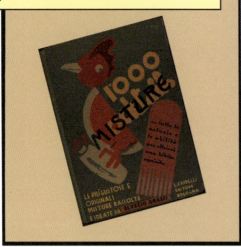

Britain and America thought different. In London, joints like the Savoy bar stayed open until they were bombed out. In New York, well, according to *Esquire*, on one typical summer evening in 1944 the Hotel Commodore's bar served more than one thousand Tom Collinses alone.

THE "COMMUTER'S BAR" AT THE HOTEL COMMODORE

Still, the war brought down many famous bars. Harry's in Paris closed, its owner fled to London (where he survived two close calls with German bombs). The Raffles in Singapore became a Japanese headquarters and the Pegu Club in Rangoon a Japanese officers' club.

Don the Beachcomber didn't close, but in 1942 it lost Donn to the Air Corps, which used him to set up officers' clubs.

In North Africa, France, and Italy, he did that with such style that the Air Corps made him a colonel and he gave Joseph Heller the inspiration for Milo Minderbender, the hyperactive mess officer in *Catch-22*.

Meanwhile, Shepheard's in Egypt (see page 81) almost suffered the same fate as the Raffles when the Germans closed in on Cairo in July 1942.

According to legend, the head bartender, Joe Scialom, saved the day when he whipped up eight gallons of a gin- and bourbon-based hangover cure, dubbed it the Suffering Bastard, and sent it to the front to rally a badly hungover British unit that was being rushed into battle.

Thanks to this vital stimulant, of course, the British stopped Rommel at El Alamein. Good story, huh?*

*PARTS OF THIS ARE TRUE, ANYWAY: THE AFRIKA KORPS ALMOST MADE IT TO CAIRO, BUT WAS HALTED AT EL ALAMEIN. THE SUFFERING BASTARD IS A FINE HANGOVER CURE THAT WAS INVENTED BY JOE SCIALOM AT SHEPHEARD'S. UNFORTUNATELY, HE SEEMS TO HAVE DONE SO IN 1947, FIVE YEARS AFTER THE BATTLE OF EL ALAMEIN.

One documented field expedient was the Screwdriver, created by American oil workers in the Middle East who mixed canned orange juice and Turkish or Iranian vodka.

Meanwhile, up in the Aleutians--it really was a global war--American troops were mixing medical alcohol and canned grapefruit juice to make the Aleutian Solution (later known as the Greyhound).

On the home front, even in America (by far the best supplied of the combatants), enemy occupation, submarine warfare, and rationing made severe dents in the supply chain. Sure, you could get a drink, but maybe not your regular one.

For one thing, the U.S. government required all whiskey distilleries that had modern column stills to make neutral spirits for munitions use. Those that had older pot or three-chamber stills could replace them or shut down entirely.

This made whiskey quite scarce, needless to say.

"HIYA, POPS! WHAT'S SHAKIN'?"

There was also a good chance you wouldn't get your regular bartender, what with men volunteering or getting drafted literally by the millions. Mixing a fine Manhattan was no protection from the draft. As with many jobs, women stepped in to fill the gaps. Some bartenders were okay with that; others, including the New York City bartenders' union, fought it tooth and nail.

"WHOO-EE, FELLAS, I DON'T KNOW WHAT IT IS, BUT IT SURE AIN'T WEAK!"

Americans sent abroad--bartenders and customers alike--often got an education in obscure foreign drinks. Calvados in Normandy, grappa and vermouth in Italy, schnapps and körn in Germany, sake on islands liberated from the Japanese...

In March 1945, when American troops relieved the Germans of a cave full of looted French booze, a couple of intelligence officers turned to tactical mixology to find a fair way to share the spoils.

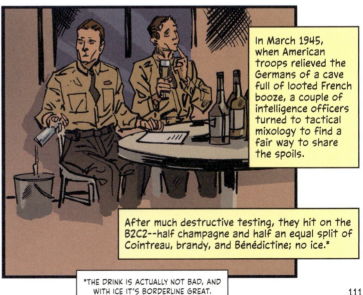

After much destructive testing, they hit on the B2C2--half champagne and half an equal split of Cointreau, brandy, and Bénédictine; no ice.*

*THE DRINK IS ACTUALLY NOT BAD, AND WITH ICE IT'S BORDERLINE GREAT.

The Americans didn't invent military mixology. Before World War I, every last regiment of the kaiser's army had its own mixed shot and its own regimental punch, to be assembled in the field.

The tradition was one of many that died in the trenches. The Germans did not revive it for the next war.

During World War II, it was the Americans who kept up the tradition best. When a paratrooper was promoted from the ranks to officer, for instance, it was customary to toast him with a "Prop Blast," a potent, communal Brandy Sour with vermouth and champagne, drunk from an artillery shell.

And as commander of the Second Armored Division, George S. Patton liked to travel with a portable bar so he could serve the "Armored Diesel" to his guests, another Sour variant (blended, with whiskey and bitters) that was drunk from special cups made from cut-up long-spouted oil cans and dashed with maraschino cherry juice from an intact one.

The navy got into some mixology of its own. Though its ships were officially dry, the officers of the Pacific Fleet, at least, liked to irrigate their shore parties with a special Old-Fashioned (Scotch based, with a splash of rum and sweetened with honey) devised by Admiral Charles McMorris, the fleet's widely respected chief of staff.

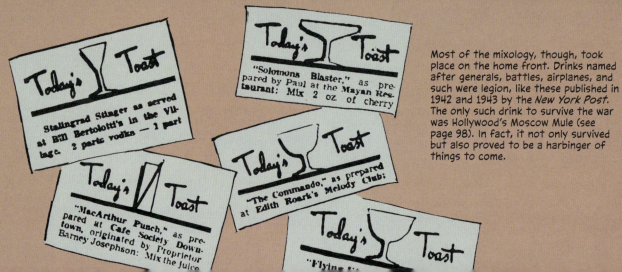

Most of the mixology, though, took place on the home front. Drinks named after generals, battles, airplanes, and such were legion, like these published in 1942 and 1943 by the *New York Post*. The only such drink to survive the war was Hollywood's Moscow Mule (see page 98). In fact, it not only survived but also proved to be a harbinger of things to come.

CHAPTER XI

DOPOGUERRA

Trying to put the world back together ~ 1945–1965

In 1945, when the guns stopped their unbearable barking and the tank engines finally coughed to silence, the world was shattered, and with it many of the cocktail's most loyal outposts. Even those that had been spared the bombing and shelling had nonetheless been stripped of so many things—bartenders and regulars, ingredients, the frills and subtleties that generate delight—that they were often barely recognizable.

Yet there were still many who believed that a proper cocktail could make things better. Slowly, Europe's cocktail route began to be rebuilt, if not the way it was before, which was impossible, then at least in a way that somehow worked.

> Just as American bars had drawn on Europe after repeal, in the immediate postwar years European bars looked to America.

In the dopoguerra, the "afterwar" (as the Italians called it), the first breakthrough drink surfaced on the isle of Capri in the summer of 1947, when crowds of young hipsters gathered to celebrate the collapse of the old order and the rise of the new.

Their drink: Count Negroni's simple old mixture of gin, vermouth, and Campari, the brand that led the recovery of the Italian drinks industry (see page 83). With the war over and the Fascists gone, there was nothing to stop the Negroni from spreading.

ORSON WELLES AT CAFÉ DONEY, 1947

By 1948, the Negroni had jumped to the Via Veneto in Rome, where the new, international leisure class—eventually, it would be dubbed the jet set—gathered. This was the perfect drink for that crowd: stronger than a typical Italian drink, sweeter and more bitter than a typical American one. A new drink for a new world.

The Negroni wasn't the only iconic drink to come out of postwar Italy. In 1949, Giuseppe Cipriani, owner of the tiny, exclusive Harry's Bar in Venice, muddled some fresh white peaches and topped the puree off with cold prosecco.

He called it a Bellini, after the Venetian artist who was the subject of a huge retrospective in his hometown that year.

Unfortunately, the Bellini didn't travel well. It was too weak for postwar America's tastes, and the ingredients were too exotic. But once Campari's export operation was up and running again, the Negroni began to make serious inroads among America's bohemians, and the world's, as this 1956 *New Yorker* ad suggests.

Another country at the periphery of the old cocktail culture contributed the next postwar classic, the Irish Coffee. The chef Joe Sheridan, a son of county Tyrone, came up with it in 1944 or (more likely) 1945 when tasked with making something special for some VIPs touring the international seaplane port where he worked.

By simply layering some lightly whipped cream on top of the Irish whiskey-stiffened coffee he took for his (frequent) hangovers, Sheridan created an instant classic.

DELAPLANE, YOU SON OF A BITCH, LOOK WHAT YOU DID!

By 1947, Ireland's new airport at Shannon, which all American air travelers to and from Europe had to pass through, had made the Irish Coffee its official welcome drink. The San Francisco travel columnist Stanton Delaplane was one of those air travelers. In 1953,* he and Jack Koeppler, owner of the Buena Vista café (Delaplane's local), reverse engineered the drink. By mid-1955, Koeppler was selling the things at the rate of 250,000 a year. His sales would only go up as the drink caught on nationwide.

Another drink from the periphery hit in 1953, when the old tequila-lime-Cointreau mixture that had been floating around since the 1930s (see page 90) caught on in the low-key resort town of Ensenada, a few miles south of Tijuana on the coast. From there, the Margarita made it to the Tail o' the Cock in Hollywood, where the bartender Johnny Durlesser shaped it into a nationwide hit (see page 98).

*THOUGH THE POPULAR STORY CLAIMS THIS HAPPENED IN 1952, EVIDENCE FROM THE TIME SAYS DIFFERENT.

Yet the biggest outsider to hit in the postwar years was the Beast from the East, aka vodka.

A little-known immigrant's drink before Prohibition, vodka became something of a hip nightclub drink in 1930s New York and Hollywood (and pretty much nowhere else).

During World War II, when whiskey was scarce, vodka, along with rum and tequila, was one of the spirits that tried to take its place. Russia was an ally, after all. In 1946, Smirnoff--by far the leading brand since its launch in 1934--sold 108,000 bottles. Not much, but not nothing.

In the late 1940s, though, Smirnoff really began to take off. At the time, people claimed that the rise was because vodka "leaves you breathless"--that is, you didn't smell like whiskey or gin after drinking it. Of course, you still smelled like alcohol, but no matter.

The real reason for its popularity was that vodka fit the age. It was clean, efficient, streamlined. It got you from A to Z just as effectively as gin or whiskey, but without any flounces or frills. It was as sleek and modern as an F-86 Sabre jet.

Plus, it was easy to mix. Simple vodka cocktails such as the Bloody Mary (see page 89), Moscow Mule (page 98), and Screwdriver (page 111) began to break out, helping to drive fussy old classics such as the Sherry Flip and the Clover Club off drinks lists.

In 1957, Smirnoff sold twenty-five million bottles--more than 230 times what it was selling a decade before--and its many new competitors added another forty-seven million bottles on top of that. Before long, vodka would blow past such previously dominant spirits as gin and blended whiskey and come in second only to whiskey in general. America became a vodka-drinking country.

The new minimalism went far beyond vodka. Just look at what happened to the Martini, the King of Cocktails in the postwar years.

Before the war, a Dry Martini was made two to one gin-vermouth. Strong, but not too strong. During the war, the ratio quickly increased to five or seven to one. After the war, the drink just got drier, to the point that some even considered fifteen to one too wet.

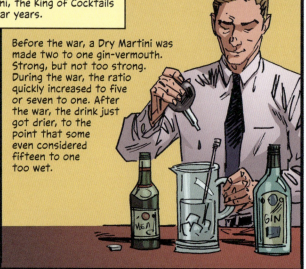

The Dry Martini had become almost a cult, with drinkers competing to show their devotion by finding ways to put as little vermouth as physically possible in the drink without abandoning it entirely for pure gin--or, as was increasingly popular, the even more minimalist vodka.

In 1950, the critic Bernard DeVoto could write that there were only two cocktails worth drinking-- a Dry Martini and a "slug of whiskey," served cold--and meet with general approval.

But even he was too broad-minded for some. As the madam-turned saloonkeeper "Dirty Helen" Cromell wrote in her autobiography, if someone tried to order a Daiquiri or even a Dry Martini at her famous Sun Flower Inn in Milwaukee, he or she would "get cursed out for a fare-thee-well." Cromell served only one thing: whiskey. Ice, if you wanted it.

At urban and suburban cocktail parties, such as this "cocktail sip" (as they were called in Harlem), gone were the Sidecars, Champagne Cocktails, and Bronxes of the 1930s. Now the cocktail was generally reduced to the (very) Dry Martini, the Highball, and--in some parts of the country--the Old-Fashioned, with a whiskey-rocks back. What the drinks lacked in variety they made up in repetition.

Of course, this streaking-into-the-future, streamlined minimalism generated some pushback. It was particularly strong among those who wanted their drinks to be an off-ramp: a path to a world without freeways, executive rat races, or nuclear warheads. A lush, tropical world.

The 1950s were the glory days of tiki.

The fuse Donn Beach had lit in 1934 set off an impressive blast in the postwar years, particularly in the new suburbs, where land was cheap. Huge, purpose-built tiki bars (as they were becoming known) sprang up nationwide, including such iconic places as the Mai-Kai in Fort Lauderdale, Florida. Like the original Beachcomber, its look was Polynesian, its food Chinese, and its drinks...

BALI HAI, SAN DIEGO

THE ISLANDS, PHOENIX

KOWLOON, SAUGUS, MASSACHUSETTS

THE KAHIKI, COLUMBUS, OHIO

...well, the drinks were the same old Caribbean-inspired rum rhapsodies, but now with ever more elaborate presentation.

When he got back from the war, Donn Beach sold most of his interest in the Beachcomber to Cora Sund and, in 1947, lit out for his place in Hawaii, for which he had kept exclusive rights.

Sund built the Hollywood restaurant into a nationwide chain, and Beach built an intricate bar-restaurant compound in Waikiki that was as authentically Polynesian as he could make it. They both seemed happy.

Meanwhile, Victor Bergeron kept building his restaurants--Trader Vic's, of course, with some sixteen locations by 1965, but also the Outrigger (more tiki) and Señor Pico's (Mexican; two locations)--and wrote bartender's guides and cookbooks. But he still mixed drinks.

Eventually, he hit on the Mai Tai: rum, lime juice, curaçao, and orgeat syrup. When he introduced it at the Outrigger in Seattle in 1952, it sank without a trace.

When he brought it to the Royal Hawaiian in Waikiki, though, it became the drink of the islands--whether as his version or in some rum and random juices knockoff. Now it's tiki's most enduring classic.

In the postwar years, many of the Asian and Pacific Islander bartenders who were generally stuck behind the scenes mixing tropical drinks in service bars got the chance to step out of the shadow.

They still faced stinging prejudice in daily life, but at work--well, they were the men who knew the recipes. With the tiki boom, such men were scarce and could write their own tickets. Here are four who made it into the limelight.

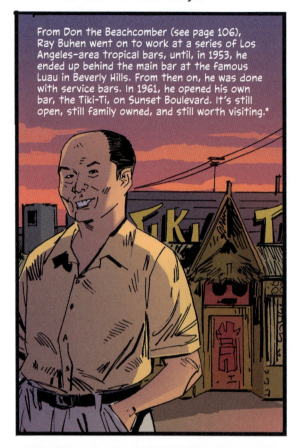

From Don the Beachcomber (see page 106), Ray Buhen went on to work at a series of Los Angeles-area tropical bars, until, in 1953, he ended up behind the main bar at the famous Luau in Beverly Hills. From then on, he was done with service bars. In 1961, he opened his own bar, the Tiki-Ti, on Sunset Boulevard. It's still open, still family owned, and still worth visiting.*

Manila-born Mariano Licudine was another Don the Beachcomber veteran, having worked at the Hollywood spot until 1939, when he went to help set up the bar at the new Chicago branch. There, he ended up as second-in-command of the bar, a job from which he was poached in 1956 by the Mai-Kai in Florida, then under construction. Licudine headed the renowned bar there with style and creativity almost until his death.*

When Trader Vic brought the Mai Tai to the Royal Hawaiian, one of the bartenders he would have taught the recipe to was Takao "Taka" Yamaguchi, a barman there from the late 1930s through the 1970s. Honolulu-born of Japanese parents, Yamaguchi took time off from the Royal Hawaiian only to fight in World War II. By 1960, he was head bartender of the hotel's famous Surf Room and its Mai Tai evangelist.

Harry Yee, another son of Honolulu, only started bartending after the war, which he spent in China as a fighter pilot in Chiang Kai-shek's air force. A reserved and deliberate man, he went from the Honolulu Trader Vic's to heading up the bar at the Hawaiian Village resort in Waikiki. In his twenty-plus years there, he came up with the orchid as a drink garnish and invented the ever-popular Blue Hawaii, among a slew of other drinks.

*FOR MORE ON BUHEN AND LICUDINE, SEE JEFF BERRY'S SEMINAL 2007 BOOK, *SIPPIN' SAFARI*.

By the late 1950s, the tiki bar was one of the last bastions of traditional, full-spectrum American mixology, with its dedication to balance, embrace of complexity, and openness to new ingredients. The men who had juiced limes and mixed Zombies behind bamboo screens were now pillars of the art--and none more so than José Valencia "Popo" Galsini.

CURRICULUM VITAE
JOSÉ VALENCIA GALSINI
1924–1928. Schoolteacher, Philippines
1932–1934. Ship's bartender
1936. The Tropics, Beverly Hills
1939–1942. The Tropics, Hollywood
1947–1949. Palm Springs Tennis Club
1948. Beach House, San Clemente
1950–1951. Little Harbor Club, Harbor Springs, Michigan
1952–1957. Kelbo's Hawaiian BBQ, Hollywood
1958. The Islands, Phoenix
1959. La Cuisine, Fullerton
1960. Hukilau Polynesian Lounge, Long Beach
1961–1962. The Outrigger, Laguna Beach
1963–1964. The Palms, Anaheim
1965–1968. The Kona Kai, Huntington Beach
1969. The Fisherman, Huntington Beach
1970. Sailmaker's Den, Disneyland
1971. Disneyland Hotel
1973. The Ninth Wave, Huntington Beach Ambrosia, Newport Beach
1979–1982. The Saloon, Laguna Beach

Born in the Philippines in 1900, Galsini was a mainstay of the Southern California tiki world, having headed up most of the major bars, and a bunch of not-so-major ones, during his long career. More than that, though, he was an important member of the California Bartenders Guild, a talented mixologist, and a fierce competitor, finishing in the money in a record nine of the guild's annual contests and three international contests. Three of those wins were first places.

Popo's 1967 prizewinner, the Saturn, is now acknowledged as a tiki classic.

Its creator outlived tiki's heyday, but whatever kind of bar you had, Popo could work it. In fact, patrons still talk about him at the (very casual) Saloon in Laguna Beach, where he was working when he died, in 1982.

Most of Galsini's contest wins were in events sponsored by the International Bartenders Association (IBA) or its California affiliate. Founded in Torquay, England, in 1951 by a slew of fancy-hotel bartenders from France, Italy, the Netherlands, Sweden, Switzerland, Denmark, and Britain, the IBA was conceived as a way to rebuild the hospitality industry in Europe. It was a classic European craft guild dedicated to promoting what were considered best practices.

IBA bartenders were expected to be precise, know their classics (there was a list, with recipes and a test), and understand formal service. They twisted their lemon twists with tongs. If the style of mixology they upheld had as much Leo Engel in it as it did Ciro Capozzi--classic, sure, but maybe a little stiff--at least those contests were frequent, giving lots of chances for the ambitious to make a mark.

Of course, not all the European master bartenders were stiff; the spirit of Ciro Capozzi lived on in Valentino Clementi of the Café Rosati in Rome, the dean of dolce vita barmen, and Eddie Clarke in London, who for a time held Ada Coleman's and Harry Craddock's old post at the Savoy, or...

...Maria Dolores Boadas in Barcelona, who worked in the bar founded there in 1933 by her father, Miguel (a former bartender with Constante Ribalaigua at the Floridita), following the finest traditions of Cuban mixology--right down to "throwing" her Martinis.

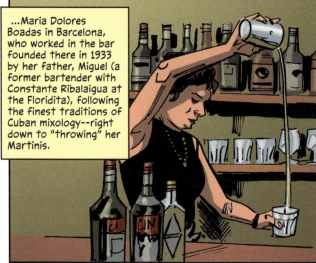

Yet not even the top European professionals were immune to transatlantic trends. You can see that in the widespread popularity of the Black Russian, a mix of vodka and coffee liqueur on the rocks.

Ironically, Gustave "Gus" Tops, who invented the drink when he was at the luxurious Grand Hotel Brasseur in Luxembourg, was very much a barman of the old school, with experience in New York and Asia and ships at sea. His drink, however, was as modern American as a tube of Pillsbury biscuits, and even simpler to prepare. Your dog could mix one.

In America, things worked out differently. Limited to a hundred members, the IBA's California affiliate was too exclusive to have a wide influence, and its East Coast one did no better. IBA-style bartending was fine when the only cocktail bars in town were in fancy hotels. But Americans expected properly made cocktails from the bar where such formal service would go over like a case of cholera.

Besides, American bartenders had other worries. Prewar, bartending had been a working-class job, but a good one. It rewarded intelligence and generated respect. Postwar, things were different. In part, that was due to the public's thirst for simple vodka, no-vermouth martinis and such, which took the skill out of skilled labor.

SO YOU'RE STUDYIN' WHAT--

ENGLISH LIT. AND YOU?

'LECTRICAL ENGINEERING. LOOK AT US, RIGHT?

HEH.

Yet there were deeper issues. With the 1944 GI Bill, scads of quick-minded young Americans who couldn't afford college or vocational school suddenly could. Bartending looked a lot less attractive. It didn't help when, in 1948, the Veterans Administration declared courses in bartending and mixology "avocational or recreational" rather than professional and stopped covering them (courses in cooking were still covered).

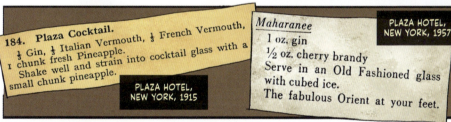

184. Plaza Cocktail.
⅓ Gin, ⅓ Italian Vermouth, ⅓ French Vermouth, 1 chunk fresh Pineapple. Shake well and strain into cocktail glass with a small chunk pineapple.

PLAZA HOTEL, NEW YORK, 1915

Maharanee
1 oz. gin
½ oz. cherry brandy
Serve in an Old Fashioned glass with cubed ice.
The fabulous Orient at your feet.

PLAZA HOTEL, NEW YORK, 1957

Until the 1950s, cocktail mixing in America had mostly been left to the skilled and experienced, to the trained bartender. But now sour mix, vodka, and other bland spirits; bottled mixers; and two-ingredient formulas--or even one, in the case of the extra-dry Martini--meant that anyone could balance a drink. People seemed to like the results just the same, so why bother?

In any case, by the late 1950s, cocktail lists were shrinking drastically, even in the big hotels that had been such bastions of American fancy drinking. And what drinks there were, were getting cruder, with simpler recipes and cheaper ingredients.

1939

1959

"THE ART OF MIXING DRINKS IS A LOST CAUSE IN MOST BARS. NOT ONE LOCAL TAVERN IN FIFTY SERVES A MARTINI OR A MANHATTAN IN A PROPERLY CHILLED GLASS. NOT ONE IN FIFTY ASKS THE CUSTOMER IF HE LIKES BITTERS [...]."

It's easy to see why an old-timer like Frank Kane, a newspaperman, booze-industry PR guy, and detective book author (sample title: *Trigger Mortis*) might yield just a bit to despair, as he did in 1965.

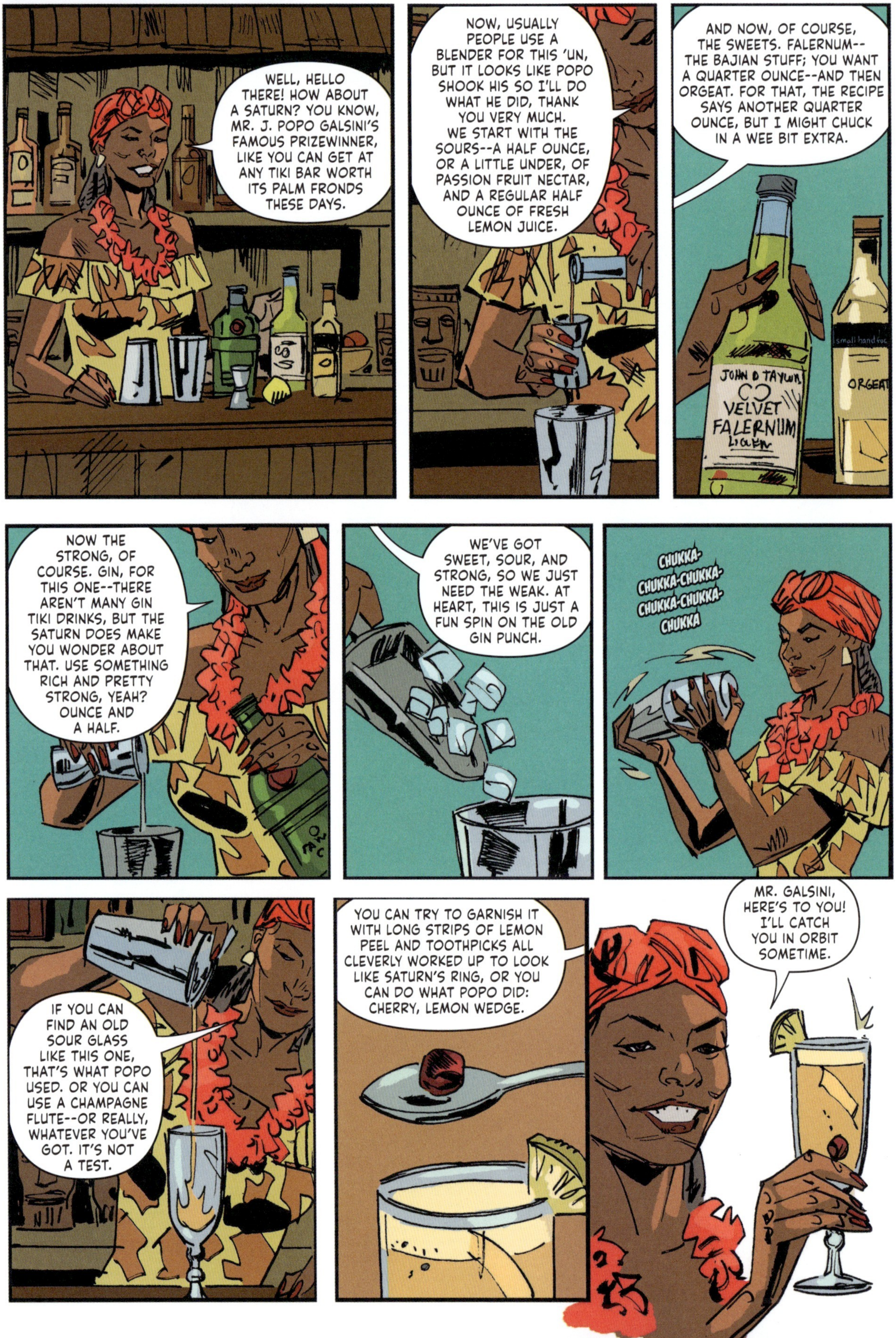
WELL, HELLO THERE! HOW ABOUT A SATURN? YOU KNOW, MR. J. POPO GALSINI'S FAMOUS PRIZEWINNER, LIKE YOU CAN GET AT ANY TIKI BAR WORTH ITS PALM FRONDS THESE DAYS.
NOW, USUALLY PEOPLE USE A BLENDER FOR THIS 'UN, BUT IT LOOKS LIKE POPO SHOOK HIS SO I'LL DO WHAT HE DID, THANK YOU VERY MUCH. WE START WITH THE SOURS--A HALF OUNCE, OR A LITTLE UNDER, OF PASSION FRUIT NECTAR, AND A REGULAR HALF OUNCE OF FRESH LEMON JUICE.
AND NOW, OF COURSE, THE SWEETS. FALERNUM--THE BAJIAN STUFF; YOU WANT A QUARTER OUNCE--AND THEN ORGEAT. FOR THAT, THE RECIPE SAYS ANOTHER QUARTER OUNCE, BUT I MIGHT CHUCK IN A WEE BIT EXTRA.
VELVET FALERNUM
ORGEAT
NOW THE STRONG, OF COURSE. GIN, FOR THIS ONE--THERE AREN'T MANY GIN TIKI DRINKS, BUT THE SATURN DOES MAKE YOU WONDER ABOUT THAT. USE SOMETHING RICH AND PRETTY STRONG, YEAH? OUNCE AND A HALF.
WE'VE GOT SWEET, SOUR, AND STRONG, SO WE JUST NEED THE WEAK. AT HEART, THIS IS JUST A FUN SPIN ON THE OLD GIN PUNCH.
CHUKKA-CHUKKA-CHUKKA-CHUKKA-CHUKKA-CHUKKA
IF YOU CAN FIND AN OLD SOUR GLASS LIKE THIS ONE, THAT'S WHAT POPO USED. OR YOU CAN USE A CHAMPAGNE FLUTE--OR REALLY, WHATEVER YOU'VE GOT. IT'S NOT A TEST.
YOU CAN TRY TO GARNISH IT WITH LONG STRIPS OF LEMON PEEL AND TOOTHPICKS ALL CLEVERLY WORKED UP TO LOOK LIKE SATURN'S RING, OR YOU CAN DO WHAT POPO DID: CHERRY, LEMON WEDGE.
MR. GALSINI, HERE'S TO YOU! I'LL CATCH YOU IN ORBIT SOMETIME.

CHASER: CAMPARI

If la dolce vita has a theme color, it's a vivid, slashing red. Campari red. Bitter, sweet, lightly--but not too lightly--alcoholic, and startlingly, sinfully red, "Bitter Campari" was one of the great success stories of the dopoguerra, becoming, along with vermouth and prosecco, one of the pillars of postwar Italian mixology. In 1950, it sold a million bottles, more than twice what it sold in 1946, and it was only up from there.

The Milanese *distillatore-liquorista*--"distiller-liqueur maker"--Gaspare Campari came up with his Bitter Campari in the 1860s when shooting for a then-standard apothecary's formula: Stoughton's bitters, Dutch-style. Like every known formula for Stoughton's bitters, this has little connection to the original (see page 27), but at least Campari was able to make his version taste good.

In 1865, Campari's distillery-café was one of the businesses torn down to build a huge, modern shopping gallery in the heart of Milan. When the Galleria Vittorio Emanuele opened, Campari got one of the choicest spots. It was a great place to promote his Bitter, which thrived.

CIRCA 1920

Led by Gaspare's son Davide, who took over in 1888, the Campari company developed from a local business into an international one, with exports to the United States and branches in France and Argentina. A strong believer in advertising, Davide commissioned some of the most striking commercial images of his day, such as this iconic 1921 poster by Leonetto Cappiello.

If by the 1930s the introduction of such products as the premixed Campari Soda in its little conical bottle had driven the brand to new heights of visibility, it wasn't until the dopoguerra that it became truly integrated into the fine (or fine-ish) art of mixing drinks.

JEFFREY ONG OF THE KUALA LUMPUR HILTON WITH HIS CAMPARI-SPIKED JUNGLE BIRD, 1973

It would take the modern cocktail revolution--with the rise of the Negroni, a wider appreciation for bitter flavors, and Campari's increasingly sophisticated marketing--to make the scarlet bitter indispensable, and increasingly imitated by distillers large and small. Today, it's more than a brand; it's essentially a category.

CHASER: VODKA

The history of vodka begins with the great wave of grain distilling that swept through northern Europe from the mid-fifteenth to the mid-sixteenth century and also gave us gin, whiskey, aquavit, and schnapps. Like them, vodka was at first nothing more than a raw, pot-stilled grain spirit, in this case made mostly from rye.

Originally, in eighteenth- and nineteenth-century Russia, "vodka" was the good stuff, a double-distilled, charcoal-filtered version of the raw, lower-proof swill--vino--the ordinary folk got. Like barrel aging does, filtration cleaned up some of the nastiest impurities in the spirit and sanded off the rough edges.

The late nineteenth century, however, saw distillers such as Pyotr Smirnov, the purveyor to the tsar's court, invest heavily in column stills and ever more sophisticated filtration. The old vino was gone; now all vodka was distilled to high proof and filtered.

After initially prohibiting vodka, the Soviets came to embrace it, devoting considerable resources to incrementally improving its quality with fine-tuned column distillation and equipment such as catalyst filters.

The liquid is pumped under pressure through ultrafine screens of silver or even platinum to help break down impurities and make a demonstrably smoother product.

Wherever it's made, a good-quality modern vodka will be almost (but not quite) flavorless, clean, and quaffable, particularly when chilled to below zero in the traditional eastern European manner. In fact, a carafe of freezer-cold vodka shared among friends over a table of *zakuski*--the traditional small plates that go with it--is about as good as drinking gets.

Today, vodka can be made anywhere, from anything: if it's distilled to near neutrality, it can be vodka. Wheat and rye are the old-timers, followed by potatoes, which came in the nineteenth century. After that--well, whatcha got? We'll make vodka from it.

CHAPTER XII

THE SO-CALLED DARK AGES

Mostly the United States ~ 1965–1995

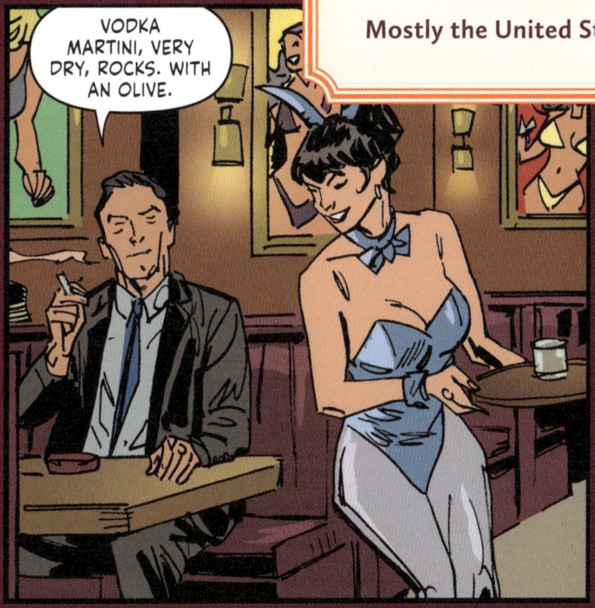
VODKA MARTINI, VERY DRY, ROCKS. WITH AN OLIVE.

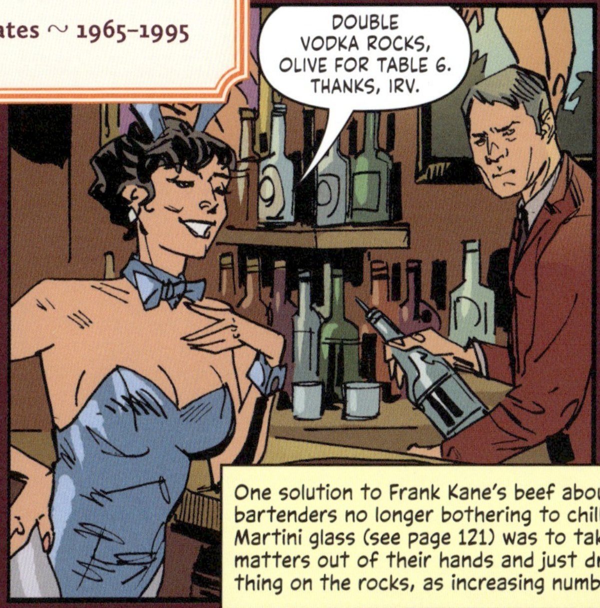
DOUBLE VODKA ROCKS, OLIVE FOR TABLE 6. THANKS, IRV.
One solution to Frank Kane's beef about bartenders no longer bothering to chill the Martini glass (see page 121) was to take matters out of their hands and just drink the thing on the rocks, as increasing numbers did.

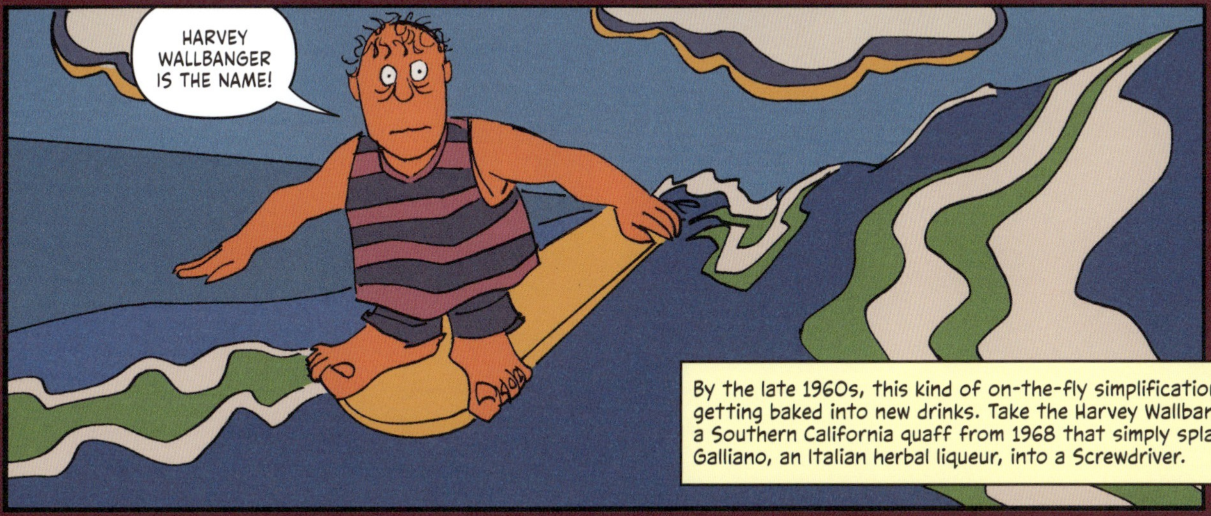
HARVEY WALLBANGER IS THE NAME!
By the late 1960s, this kind of on-the-fly simplification was getting baked into new drinks. Take the Harvey Wallbanger, a Southern California quaff from 1968 that simply splashed Galliano, an Italian herbal liqueur, into a Screwdriver.

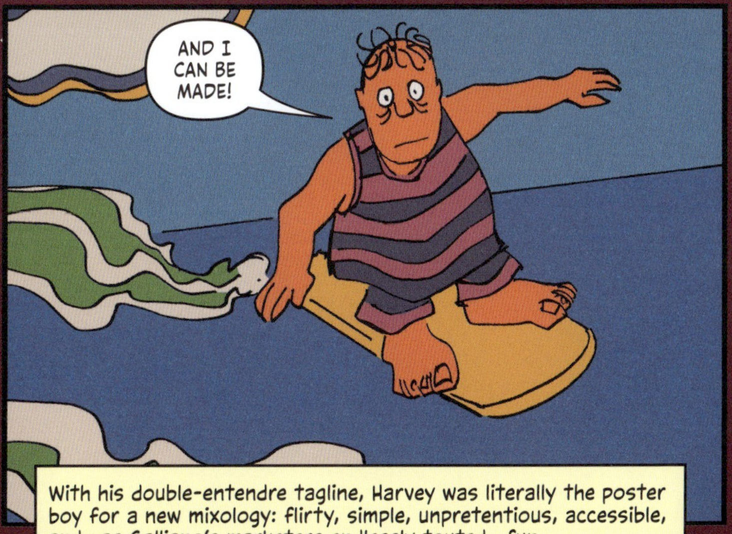
AND I CAN BE MADE!
With his double-entendre tagline, Harvey was literally the poster boy for a new mixology: flirty, simple, unpretentious, accessible, and--as Galliano's marketers endlessly touted--fun.

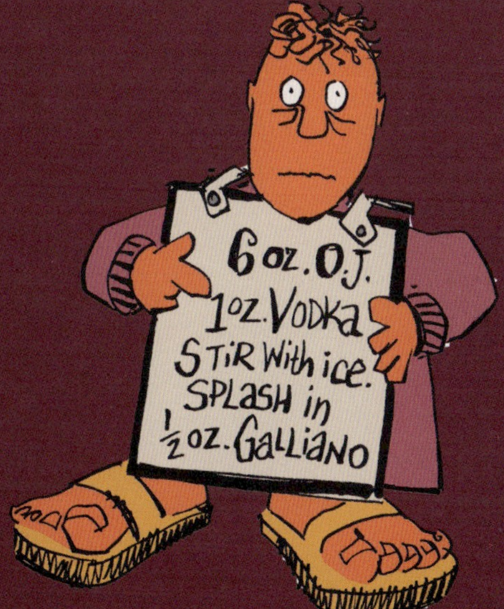
6 oz. O.J.
1 oz. Vodka
STIR With ice.
SPLASH in
1/2 oz. Galliano

Not everybody went full Wallbanger. But even in the more conservative bars--the ones that still stocked Martini glasses--the new, streamlined mixology crept in.

GODFATHER (SCOTCH & AMARETTO; 1972)

RUSTY NAIL (SCOTCH & DRAMBUIE; 1961)

Nor were tiki bars immune, as they introduced drinks with fewer ingredients and less complex flavors. Here, Harry Yee (see page 118) was a pioneer with his late-1950s Blue Hawaiian, with pineapple juice, sour mix, blue curaçao, and vodka.

At Kelbo's in Los Angeles, where Popo Galsini had once held forth, the bar manager Hank Riddle (born in the Philippines to an American father and Filipina mother) introduced a whole series of "Tropkols," based on vodka or gin rather than the complex, pungent rums favored by tiki tradition.

It didn't help that Cuba, the great generator of real tropical drinks, had joined the Eastern Bloc. The last pre-Castro innovation had been the (blended) Banana Daiquiri. Now everyone was broke--even the tourists, who were now from Russia and East Germany--and the latest in Cuban drinks was a cheap rum Highball the locals dubbed *matarratas*, or "rat poison."

That left the field open for Puerto Rico and its update of the traditional Caribbean Piña Colada: rum with pineapple juice and the "jelly" from green coconuts. Simple--if you could get the green coconuts, which didn't travel well. That problem was solved in 1947 when Ramón López of the University of Puerto Rico patented a way to preserve coconut meat by emulsifying it with sugar.

At some point around 1960, the bar of the large and modern Caribe Hilton in San Juan switched its blended Piña Colada from fresh coconut to Coco López, the ultra-sweet, thick coconut cream López had quit his job to market. In 1968, the new Piña Colada jumped to the mainland and jumped hard, making López a very rich man.

The classic American mixology, going back to Jerry Thomas, Cato Alexander, and even old James Ashley in London, was based on balancing sweet and sour, strong and weak, and smooth and spicy to make a harmonious whole. That wasn't always easy, which is why it was left to professionals, at least, until the New American mixology pretty much took it off the table.

Instead, industry stepped in to balance everything for you. For the home mixer, that meant premade mixes--just add booze. There were different ones, or at least differently labeled ones, for each of the major surviving sours. The mixes came in frozen, bottled, or powdered form, ranging from almost homemade to chemistry experiment.

Bars kept things simple with one premade, all-purpose (and often artificial) "sweet and sour mixture," which served for lemon drinks and lime drinks alike.

Eventually, it ended up in the gun (another innovation) with soda, cola, and tonic water.*

Some of the most popular new drinks didn't bother with juices at all: the Rusty Nail, the Black Russian, and the Godfather, to name three of many, were all elemental booze-liqueur combinations, built on the rocks.

*OH, YOU NEED GINGER ALE? JUST HIT COLA AND TONIC WATER TOGETHER. NOBODY WILL NOTICE THE DIFFERENCE.

Functionally, though, these drinks (at right) were simply glasses of spiced booze, just like the venerable Old-Fashioned. Only here all the work was already done: the sugar, spice, and even some of the water and booze were built into the liqueur. And since that was perfectly palatable on its own, there was no real way to screw the drink up: a bit more of this, a bit less of that, so what?

Others (far right) bypassed sour mix entirely by mixing the booze with pineapple or orange juice, which already offset their acidity with an innate sweetness (so no need to measure carefully).

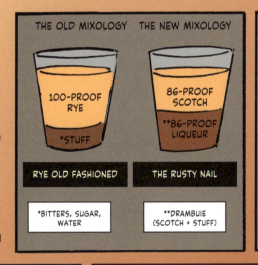

THE OLD MIXOLOGY — 100-PROOF RYE, *STUFF — RYE OLD FASHIONED
THE NEW MIXOLOGY — 86-PROOF SCOTCH, **86-PROOF LIQUEUR — THE RUSTY NAIL
*BITTERS, SUGAR, WATER
**DRAMBUIE (SCOTCH + STUFF)

And lest people still found the drinks too tart, better splash in something sweet--coconut cream for the Piña Colada and grenadine for the Tequila Sunrise, a 1970 makeover of the 1920s tequila, lime, and crème de cassis classic (see page 90).

PINEAPPLE JUICE / WHITE RUM / COCO LÓPEZ
ORANGE JUICE / TEQUILA / GRENADINE

	% Alcohol by Volume		
	1940	1970	1980
Hennessy cognac	42%	40%	40%
Myers's Jamaica rum	48.5%	42%	40%
Bacardi white rum	44.5%	40%	40%
Gordon's gin	47.2%	45%	40%
Smirnoff vodka	50% & 40%	40%	40%
Jim Beam bourbon	45% & 43%	43%	40%
Old Overholt rye	50%	43%	43%
Jack Daniel No. 7	45%	45%	45%

Not only was the booze weaker, but also there was less of it: between 1940 and the 1970s, the average bar jigger, for those who still bothered to use one, went from one and a half or two ounces to one and a quarter or one and a half ounces.

Of course, not everyone cared.

The balance of these drinks was helped along by the fact that the liquor in them was usually weaker than in years past. Postwar taxes meant the higher the proof, the higher the price, and with vodka--most of which was sold at the legal minimum of 40 percent--setting the pace, the other categories had to sink to its level or get run over. At a proof higher than 43 percent, even a good spirit can make a drink harsh and boozy if not carefully mixed; at 40 percent, most spirits are quite sippable no matter what you do to them, and particularly if that's cutting them with some pleasant liqueur, as was increasingly popular.

Plus, there was much more dilution from the ice. In the 1960s, the introduction of affordable, quick-freezing ice machines meant that bars made their own ice rather than buying it, but the ice they made filled more of the glass and was much quicker to melt.

MARIJUANA IS A BENEVOLENT NARCOTIC, BUT J. EDGAR HOOVER PREFERS HIS DEATHLY SCOTCH.

ALLEN GINSBERG, *DEATH TO VAN GOGH'S EAR*, 1957

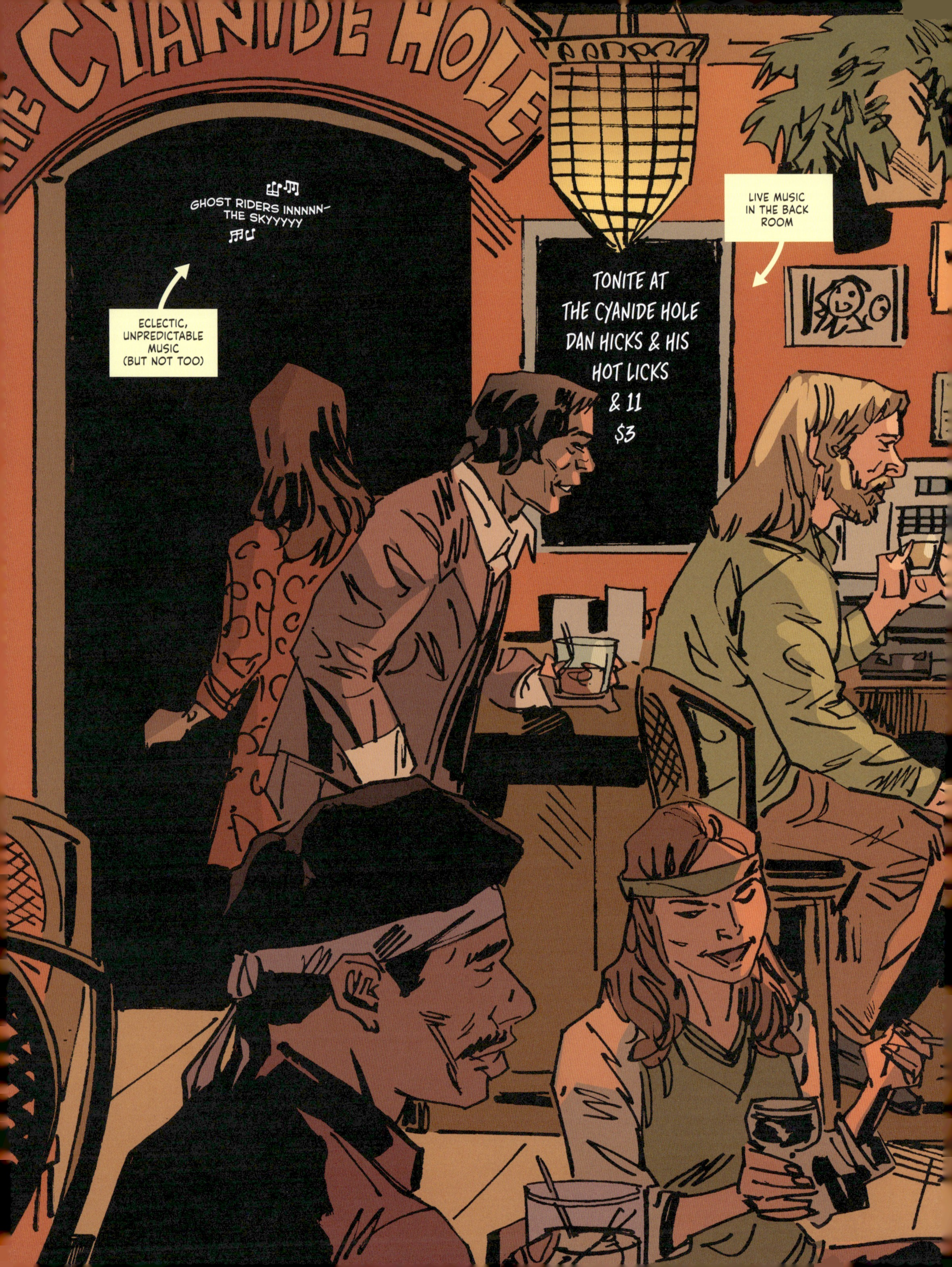
THE CYANIDE HOLE
GHOST RIDERS INNNNN- THE SKYYYYY
ECLECTIC, UNPREDICTABLE MUSIC (BUT NOT TOO)
TONITE AT THE CYANIDE HOLE DAN HICKS & HIS HOT LICKS & 11 $3
LIVE MUSIC IN THE BACK ROOM

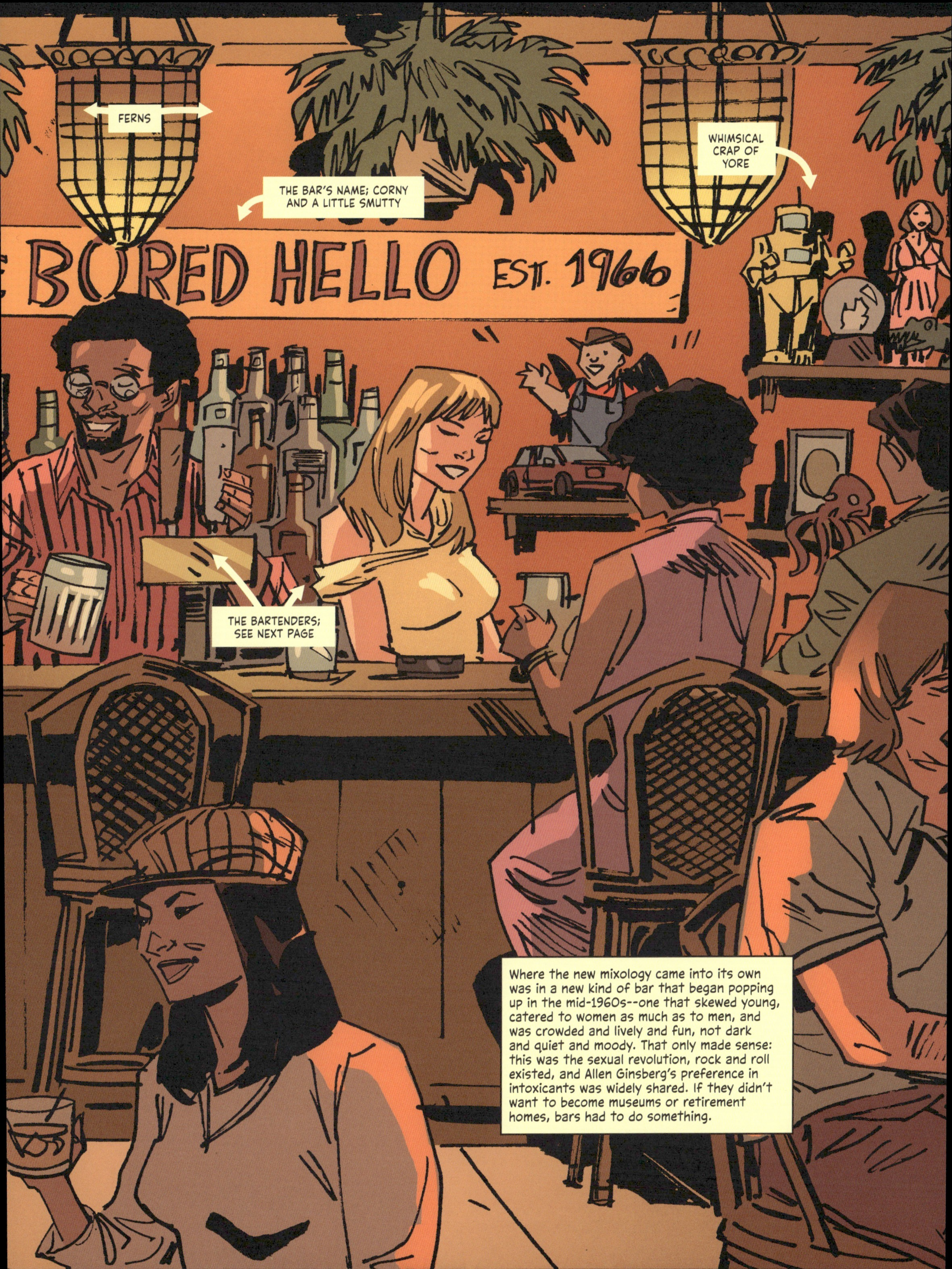
FERNS
THE BAR'S NAME; CORNY AND A LITTLE SMUTTY
WHIMSICAL CRAP OF YORE
BORED HELLO EST. 1966
THE BARTENDERS; SEE NEXT PAGE
Where the new mixology came into its own was in a new kind of bar that began popping up in the mid-1960s--one that skewed young, catered to women as much as to men, and was crowded and lively and fun, not dark and quiet and moody. That only made sense: this was the sexual revolution, rock and roll existed, and Allen Ginsberg's preference in intoxicants was widely shared. If they didn't want to become museums or retirement homes, bars had to do something.

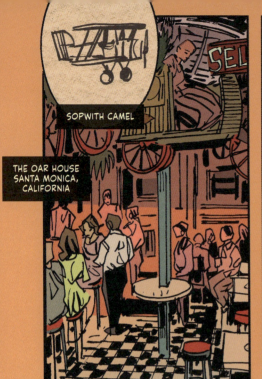

SOPWITH CAMEL

THE OAR HOUSE
SANTA MONICA,
CALIFORNIA

T.G.I. FRIDAY'S
NEW YORK

HENRY AFRICA'S
SAN FRANCISCO

F-104
STARFIGHTER

If jet-age cocktail lounges were F-104 Starfighters, sleek and supersonic, these bars were Sopwith Camels: proudly old-fashioned, fusty, and a bit weird. Yet the people who pioneered them were not those things.

Al Ehringer, the airline pilot who opened the Oar House in 1964, was a tough and smart businessman, as was Alan Stillman, the jewelry salesman who opened T.G.I. Friday's a year later.

Norman Hobday, whose enormously popular Henry Africa's (1969) was the first fern bar, well--he was a little weird (he pretended he'd been in the French Foreign Legion, and dressed like it). But he, too, could run a business and knew just what the times demanded from a bar and its bartenders.

It's traditional to blame the 1960s–1970s penchant for sweet, simple drinks on the influx of young women into the space of the bar, still widely considered a male bastion. But, of course, plenty of men drank those drinks, too.

It was less about gender and more about age: the Baby Boom meant that young people need not try to fit into a world their elders had made. They could make their own.

That had its good points. The 1960s and 1970s saw unprecedented numbers of women working behind the bar and the return of Black bartenders to public, white-oriented bars for the first time since the 1890s.

BARTENDERS--Due to promotion Henry's Africa is losing 3 Legionnaires. Need 3 short-haired, 21-25 yrs., well proportioned 5'10"+ replacements. College degree required, experience not. Apply in person only, 11-2, Thurs. & Fri. 2101 Polk.

Then there was Norman. Hobday's was far from the first bar to prefer presentation to skill (see the Hoffman House, page 68). But he read the times well. In these bars, mixology was the least important part of the bartender's job; bartenders were party facilitators, referees, brokers of introductions. For that to work, they had to basically be their customers, only better.

But nothing stands still. By the mid-1970s, the streamlined drinks of the previous decade began to seem pretty stodgy. An easy solution was to splash in a little cream: it made everything smoother, sweeter, younger.

And so the Godmother (vodka and Amaretto) became the Godchild, and Gustave Tops's old Black Russian became the White Russian (a better drink, to be honest).

Eventually, the new collegiate-type, short-term bartenders began passing the time waiting to be cast or published or whatever by inventing drinks of their own. The punk-themed drinks bartender-about-town David Smith created in 1976 for the infamous Max's Kansas City in New York capture the zeitgeist well.

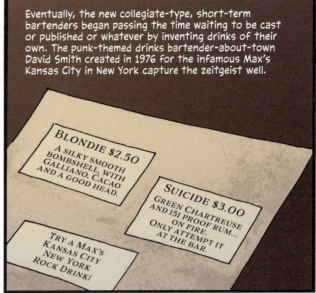

Naturally, the consultants and marketers got into the act, too, inventing all kinds of improbable things. Case in point, the Swampwater: 110-proof Green Chartreuse (a popular ingredient at the time; see above) and pineapple juice with a hint of lime, on the rocks.

When questioned about the venerable liqueur's use in such a drink, Paul Goiffon, president of the liqueur's French manufacturer, noted with unusual candor, "Years ago, Chartreuse would have been ashamed...but now we're promoting it."

The late 1970s saw the introduction of a drink that bartenders, marketers, and tipsy barflies alike could really agree on: the shooter. Spirits, liqueurs, and whatever (sour mix? Seven Up? half-and-half? a raw oyster?), shaken, strained into a shot glass, and knocked back on the spot. By then, the new-style, exciting bars of the 1960s had spawned a vast horde of low-imagination, hokey imitations—perfect shooter country.

These punky little palate bombs, created on the fly, named outrageously, and sold for cheap, at least got bartenders dusting off bottles and just maybe thinking about flavor combinations. Some, like Smith and Cutsail, even rode them to the edge of fame.

Considered purely from a mixological perspective, Cutsail's Training Bra—with three of its four ingredients being sweet and orange flavored—would have given, say, William Schmidt an aneurysm.

But if shooters were cavalier and anarchic, at least they weren't minimalist.

Yet, there was still farther to fall. Case in point, the Upside-Down Margarita, mixed directly in the drinker's mouth--for those who didn't need a stinkin' shot glass.

Invented at the Jolly Jester in Aspen in the late 1970s, the thing spread like a skin rash. By 1980 it was everywhere. Bad as it was, though, it wasn't the worst the age had to offer.

That honor went to drinks like the Chocolate Snow Bear, as served at Lettuce, in Wichita, Kansas: splashes of amaretto and crème de cacao and dashes of chocolate syrup and vanilla extract, all blended up with eight ounces of vanilla ice cream and globbed into a snifter.

Such weak, thick, and diabetic-shock-inducing drinks became more or less inevitable once bars made blenders a fixture, spurred by the popularity of the Piña Colada, the Frozen Margarita (introduced by the Dallas restaurateur Mariano Martinez in 1971), and such.

Factor in the trendiness of cream drinks, and the ice cream cocktail is a given.

"MA CHE VUOL DIRE 'STO "SLOW COMFORTABLE SCREW"?"

"SLOW COMFORTABLE SCREW SAREBBE, NON LO SO, "CHIAVATA LENTA E COMMODA.""

"MINCHIA!"

Very little of this stuff got out of North America; it was an American solution to American conditions. In the rest of the world's cocktail bars, the buttoned-down IBA standards tended to prevail (by 1980, the association had thirty-one member countries worldwide).

Of course, in the rest of the world, cocktail mixing was still considered an actual profession. Italy even published a thick register of the country's bartenders, *Il Barman e i suoi cocktails*, divided into masters, journeymen, and apprentices, with a photo and signature drink for each. (All of the drinks were right side up.)

On the other hand, the most successful non-U.S. trend of the age was the spread throughout the Hispanic world of drinks cutting a local spirit with Coca-Cola or some other soda. Easy to make and surprisingly tasty, these drinks came from the barrios, not the fancy bars, and caught the streamlined spirit of the age without going overboard. for the drinks, see the endnotes.

Back in the United States, some American drinkers were getting fed up with the all-fun-all-the-time mixology freak show and the goofy culture that went with it. As the 1980s wore on, such people began sorting themselves into loose groups.

"...BUT MCINERNEY'S JUST SO... STAGED."

"RIGHT? I MEAN..."

CAPE CODDER

MADRAS

The preppies, for example, dressed as if it were 1957 and favored simple, unshowy concoctions such as the Gin and Tonic, the Cape Codder (vodka and cranberry juice), or the Madras (vodka, cranberry, and orange).

The "fitness freaks" preferred the White Wine Spritzer (wine and soda water), a drink going back to the old Austro-Hungarian Empire, or the old French favorite, Kir or Kir Royale (a glass of white wine or--for the Royale--champagne with a little splash of crème de cassis).

Low alcohol, low sugar, not so fun.

Then there were the Martini people, would-be traditionalists who believed the Martini was the only drink that mattered. Pulling in yuppie bankers, downtown artists, WASPs, and curmudgeons of all ages, this group was loose to the point of no one agreeing on what went into a Martini. The curmudgeons and the WASPs usually insisted on gin, while the others skewed vodka. Most of them at least nodded to the past by drinking theirs straight up in the classic Lobmeyr-style glass.

MARTINI, VERY DRY

DIRTY MARTINI

MUDDLED MARTINI

CAJUN MARTINI

Yet the 1980s Martini was only loosely tied to the Martini of old. Mostly it was vodka with mere drops of dry vermouth, if any, but variations abounded. In the Muddled Martini (by John Tourtellotte of Birmingham's Highlands Bar & Grill), the ice was pounded to bits during mixing. The Dirty Martini used a spoonful of olive brine, an old trick that finally got a name in 1988. And the Cajun Martini...

...that was from K-Paul's, the pathbreaking restaurant that Paul Prudhomme and his wife, Kay "K" Hinrichs opened in New Orleans in 1979. They inherited a liquor license, but didn't want to deal with a full bar.

Instead, Hinrichs came up with one drink: jalapeño-infused vodka with drops of vermouth, served straight from the freezer with Cajun pickles.

It was surprisingly tasty, but like the others, it was still miles from the traditional Martini. To get back there would take a revolution.

MIXOLOGY: THE AMARETTO SOUR (NO. 2)

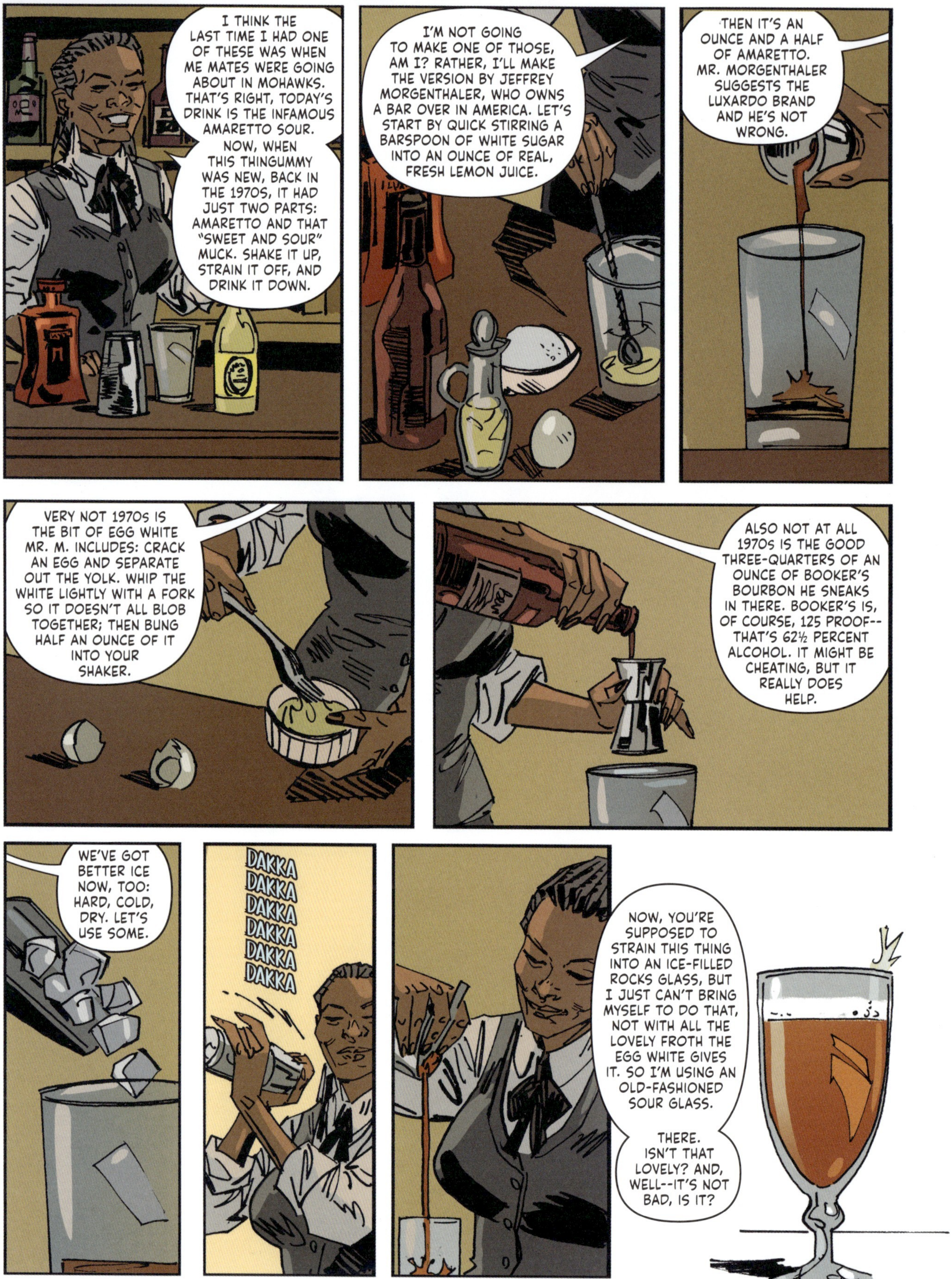
I THINK THE LAST TIME I HAD ONE OF THESE WAS WHEN ME MATES WERE GOING ABOUT IN MOHAWKS. THAT'S RIGHT, TODAY'S DRINK IS THE INFAMOUS AMARETTO SOUR.
NOW, WHEN THIS THINGUMMY WAS NEW, BACK IN THE 1970S, IT HAD JUST TWO PARTS: AMARETTO AND THAT "SWEET AND SOUR" MUCK. SHAKE IT UP, STRAIN IT OFF, AND DRINK IT DOWN.
I'M NOT GOING TO MAKE ONE OF THOSE, AM I? RATHER, I'LL MAKE THE VERSION BY JEFFREY MORGENTHALER, WHO OWNS A BAR OVER IN AMERICA. LET'S START BY QUICK STIRRING A BARSPOON OF WHITE SUGAR INTO AN OUNCE OF REAL, FRESH LEMON JUICE.
THEN IT'S AN OUNCE AND A HALF OF AMARETTO. MR. MORGENTHALER SUGGESTS THE LUXARDO BRAND AND HE'S NOT WRONG.
VERY NOT 1970S IS THE BIT OF EGG WHITE MR. M. INCLUDES: CRACK AN EGG AND SEPARATE OUT THE YOLK. WHIP THE WHITE LIGHTLY WITH A FORK SO IT DOESN'T ALL BLOB TOGETHER; THEN BUNG HALF AN OUNCE OF IT INTO YOUR SHAKER.
ALSO NOT AT ALL 1970S IS THE GOOD THREE-QUARTERS OF AN OUNCE OF BOOKER'S BOURBON HE SNEAKS IN THERE. BOOKER'S IS, OF COURSE, 125 PROOF--THAT'S 62½ PERCENT ALCOHOL. IT MIGHT BE CHEATING, BUT IT REALLY DOES HELP.
WE'VE GOT BETTER ICE NOW, TOO: HARD, COLD, DRY. LET'S USE SOME.
DAKKA DAKKA DAKKA DAKKA DAKKA DAKKA
NOW, YOU'RE SUPPOSED TO STRAIN THIS THING INTO AN ICE-FILLED ROCKS GLASS, BUT I JUST CAN'T BRING MYSELF TO DO THAT, NOT WITH ALL THE LOVELY FROTH THE EGG WHITE GIVES IT. SO I'M USING AN OLD-FASHIONED SOUR GLASS.
THERE. ISN'T THAT LOVELY? AND, WELL--IT'S NOT BAD, IS IT?

CHAPTER XIII

A BOOZY RENAISSANCE

New York, London, and Everywhere ~ 1988–Present

FIRST STIRRINGS, 1988–1999

ALICE WATERS (CHEZ PANISSE, BERKELEY) AND LARRY FORGIONE (AN AMERICAN PLACE, NEW YORK)

The late 1980s saw a loose-knit little band of American chefs, devoted to reconnecting American cooking to its old traditions and agrarian roots, become not only successful but sometimes even famous, or nearly so.

Meanwhile, bartenders had their own shot at fame, only theirs was thrust upon them unexpectedly with the popularity of *Cocktail*, the 1988 movie based on Heywood Gould's considerably darker and more cynical novel about the New York bar business.

Unfortunately, most bartenders weren't ready for it. Like the ones in the movie, they couldn't have cared less about old traditions and classic recipes. What they cared about was juggling.

As *Cocktail* ably showcased, the hot trend in bartending was "flair," a culmination of the 1970s conception of the bartender as camp counselor, where the goal was to keep the customers entertained with acrobatics, prestidigitation, choreography-- everything but mixology.

135

The drinks being juggled so dexterously were the same old Kamikazes, White Russians, and Long Island Iced Teas (a suburban New York club drink that first surfaced in 1976). Once novelties, these drinks had proliferated like kudzu, eventually choking out all but the thickest-skinned old classics: the Vodka Martini, the Margarita, the Highball.

Yet at the same time, one unlikely-looking Manhattanite was planning a counterattack. Restaurant visionary Joe Baum had a mandate to reopen the Rainbow Room, an old 1930s Art Deco nightclub high atop Rockefeller Center.

BASICALLY, YOU DO THE TRICKS AS ENTERTAINMENT FOR YOUR CLIENTELE AND TO GET EXTRA TIPS. IT DOESN'T MAKE BETTER DRINKS.

JUDIE SMART, INSTRUCTOR, INTERNATIONAL BARTENDING INSTITUTE, ALTAMONTE SPRINGS, FLORIDA, 1988

For it, Baum, whose Four Seasons and Fonda del Sol had transformed American fine dining, insisted on a real bar, with real drinks. Old people's drinks.

The kinds that got them through the world wars and the Depression.

By the time it reopened in 1987, the Rainbow Room had cost well over twenty million dollars, and it showed.

The center of the action was the bar, where the only flair involved was whatever came with doing things *right*.

Everyone who tasted the bar's resurrected classics agreed. The drinks were better. Better than anyone else's. Just maybe better than anything. It was the shock of the old.

Baum was exceptionally fortunate in his head bartender. Dale DeGroff, a former actor and a good one, was intelligent and hardworking and not only knew all the drinks but also had a deep curiosity about their origins and development.

Even better, he liked people and had a great deal of easy, unpretentious charm.

DeGroff was, in short, the perfect person to remind America what a cocktail could be in the hands of a real, old-school bartender. Not that he steered away from flair entirely: one of his signatures was the flamed orange twist with which he decked out his version of the Cosmopolitan, the hot new drink of the early 1990s.

He brought it to San Francisco in 1979, where it bubbled under in the gay community until the late 1980s.

It was in New York, however, that the Cosmo broke out, when Toby Cecchini at the popular, drop-dead-chic Odeon restaurant started making an upgraded version. It gave the folks who couldn't hack the rocket-fuel Martinis of the day a cocktail to pose with--and was delicious to boot.

Barnaby Conrad III (1988), William Grimes (1993), and Gary and Mardee Haidin Regan (1995) all offered well-researched, compelling writing on mixed drinks and their ingredients; something for the geek as well as the idly curious. All three books quickly earned cult followings.

Bartenders weren't the only ones driving the uptick of interest in classic mixology. The late 1980s and early 1990s saw the beginning of a new strain of cocktail-friendly drinks books that offered more than bare recipes and glossy pictures.

EARLY HEROES OF THE REVOLUTION (EHotR) 1999–2005*

EHotR

Portland, Maine
John Myers

Boston
Brother Cleve
Jackson Cannon
Lauren Clark
John Gertsen
Misty Kalkofen

New York
Jerri Banks
Martin Doudoroff
Eben Freeman
Charles Hardwick
Del Pedro
Sasha Petraske
Gary Regan
Audrey Saunders
Tony Yoshida

New Brunswick, New Jersey
Francis Schott
and Mark Pascal

Philadelphia
Katie Loeb

Cleveland
Paulius Nasvytis

Chicago
Charles Joly

New Orleans
Cheryl Charming

Kansas City
Harry Murphy

Seattle
Kathy Casey
Paul Harrington
Murray Stenson

Portland, Oregon
Peggy Boston
Marco Dionysos

EHotR

Sonoma, California
Scott Beattie
John Burton

San Francisco
Tony Abou-Ganim
Douglas Biederbeck
Jeff Hollinger
Julie Reiner
Alberta Straub

Los Angeles
Jeff "Beachbum" Berry
and Annene Kaye
Brian F. Rea

Melbourne, Australia
Matthew Bax

Tokyo
Kazuo Uyeda

Rome
Mauro Lotti

Munich
Charles Schumann

Trondheim, Norway
Pål Løberg

Lyon, France
Fernando Castellon

Amsterdam
Philip Duff

London
Douglas Ankrah
Dick Bradsell
Jared Brown
and Anistatia Miller
Salvatore Calabrese
Tony Conigliaro
Jonathan Downey
George Sinclair
Angus Winchester

> Yet all of this would have been a passing fad but for one thing...

DrCocktail
6/12/2000 1:47 AM

DB, you have the 1876 Jerry Thomas? I don't. I have the first and the 1880s one. Does the 1876 list the Martinez, or is the 1880s edition the first to do that?—Doc.

DrinkBoy
6/12/2000 2:00 AM
Message #4

Doc, finally a vintage book in my library that you don't have. I suppose I should go have a Martinez to celebrate! But I'll have to refer to a newer book than my 1876 edition for the recipe, since it doesn't have it.—DrinkBoy

The introduction of the World Wide Web in the early 1990s changed everything, of course. Now those who shared niche tastes could easily compare notes and build on their knowledge. Sometimes, that's not so good. As people went to sites such as AOL's cocktail board, moderated by Ted "Dr. Cocktail" Haigh, and Robert Hess's DrinkBoy forum and tried to hash out who invented the Margarita or the best vermouth for a Gibson, classic cocktails quietly grew from a fad into a revolution.

> NOW, I'M TOLD YOU CAN MAKE A JACK ROSE...
>
> WELL, SURE, I GUESS, IF YOU WANT THAT SORT OF THING.
>
> WE DO INDEED! WE'LL HAVE FOUR, PLEASE.

Inevitably, what started online was carried into the bars.

*THIS ROSTER IS FAR FROM COMPREHENSIVE.

Along with various old-film buffs, Raymond Chandler fans, and 1980s Martini cultists, the cultural wing had a strong contingent of...let's call them barflies. A mix of bartenders and bar drinkers, they were devoted to the traditions and culture of the bar and wanted to reforge the fragile connection between the modern bar and the bar as it was in its glory days (that is, before sour mix and electric guitars).

Rounding out the culinary wing were the antiquarians, who wanted to make drinks exactly as they were then (whenever "then" was). Cocktail-book collectors, junk-shop rummagers, dusty-bottle hunters, and (now) database searchers, they obsessed over resurrecting old recipes, ingredients, and techniques, no matter how weird or obscure.

The culinarians were more focused, although they, too, had their sects. The bar chefs, who believed that mixing drinks was one of the great culinary arts and should be acknowledged as such, tended to focus less on obscure old liquors and more on fruits and vegetables and such--farm to shaker.

The modernists, on the other hand, saw cocktails as ripe for the sort of high-tech tricksiness being practiced at the time by cutting-edge chefs. They also recognized it, not wrongly, as a field whose often-arbitrary methods and woolly conventions could use a bracing shot of STEM.

*ROTARY EVAPORATOR, A (HIDEOUSLY EXPENSIVE) LAB-TOP VACUUM STILL THAT WORKS AT ROOM TEMPERATURE.

The decisions all these new "cocktailians," as Gary Regan dubbed them, made when they began opening their own bars tended to show which of these pockets they fell into (to be sure, many managed to fall into more than one).

On the last day of 1999, Sasha Petraske, a twenty-six-year-old bartender, opened Milk & Honey on New York's Lower East Side. Built on a shoestring as a labor of love, M&H was dedicated to a nostalgic view of cocktail drinking at its most glamorous, but also to the idea that cocktail making was a craft like any other, demanding attention at every step.

A barfly and antiquarian with a well-concealed but wide modernist streak, Petraske kept his cocktails perfectly classic but rethought every step in their construction. He improved the shaker's efficiency by replacing the glass half with a second, smaller tin, brought back the jigger, and froze water into blocks that could be cut into custom shapes and sizes. Nobody had ever made cocktails exactly the way he and the crew he trained did, but they came out tasting as if Constante himself had mixed them.

When the Oar House caught on, Al Ehringer expanded the bar to fit all the new customers (see page 130). Petraske was made of different stuff: he changed M&H to reservations only, didn't publish a phone number, and instituted a strict set of rules for anyone who made it inside. If they didn't know how to act in a classic cocktail lounge--well, he'd teach 'em.

There were some hard months ("Never try to open a bar if you're not prepared to sleep in it"--Petraske). But then Milk & Honey--windowless, without signage, and in a rough part of town-- nonetheless caught on, drawing a large and boisterous crowd.

If Petraske was a secret modernist, Matthew Bax and his crew at Der Raum in suburban Melbourne, Australia, were anything but. You knew the place was different when you walked in: the back bar was full of lab equipment, and the bottles that belonged there were hanging over the bar from bungee cords. And they carbonated grapes and served you drinks in syringes.

Not surprisingly, the bar chefs tended to do their best work in restaurant bars. In 1999, when *The New York Times* featured the peripatetic cocktail consultant Jerri Banks's now-classic gin-lime-pomegranate Juniperotivo, she was heading the bar at Monzù, a chefy, luxe Sicilian restaurant in SoHo.

To find a pure antiquarian, one had to look at not a bar but an event: the Tribute to Jerry Thomas, a first-ever public celebration of the Professor's life and career. Organized by the New York chapter of the Slow Food organization (and me, in my capacity as *Esquire*'s drinks editor), it took place in March 2003 at the old Men's Bar of the Plaza hotel.

The tribute featured Thomas's drinks, made as accurately as possible by Dale DeGroff, Gary Regan, Sasha Petraske, Robert Hess, Ted Haigh, Audrey Saunders of the beloved Bemelmans Bar in New York, the Plaza's senior bartender George Papadakis, and yours truly.

Featuring such long-dormant drinks as the Blue Blazer, Tom & Jerry, Martinez (a wet, sweet-vermouth Martini), Gin Daisy, Brandy Crusta, Japanese Cocktail, and Arrack Punch, the tribute was covered extensively in the press, including a big article in *The New York Times*.

People were starting to pay attention.

By this point, many bars were pasting one or two of the drinks touted by the various cocktailians on their menus next to the omnipresent Cosmopolitan, which was getting heavy play in HBO's insanely popular *Sex and the City* (1998–2004). While these additions made them look hip, their execution of the drinks was rarely up to cocktailian standards.

A few other bars, such as Absinthe in San Francisco and Employees Only and the Flatiron Lounge in New York, became hugely successful by embracing the new fresh-juice aesthetic while soft-pedaling Petraske's type of retro evangelism.

Others, though, went full apostle. Alberta Straub, for example, donned retro flight-attendant garb to shake up Aviations--her specialty, naturally--and other classics at San Francisco's Orbit Room, bringing in her own gin, maraschino liqueur, and fresh lemon juice to do it.

...THAT'S RIGHT, THE STARLIGHT ROOM. SO, I HAD THIS THING, THE BARTENDER CALLED IT A CHARTREUSE SWIZZLE, AND I SWEAR IT REARRANGED MY DNA.

HUH. I MEAN, I KINDA LIKE MY DNA THE WAY IT IS-- A POOR THING BUT MINE OWN--BUT...I'M FREE THURSDAY.

It all added up. One balanced, delicious, and strong cocktail at a time, the smattering of cocktailian bartenders working in American bars were converting new people to the cause every day.

In 2005, Julie Reiner and her partners in the Flatiron Lounge recruited Audrey Saunders to head a new bar on the edge of Manhattan's chic SoHo neighborhood. Pegu Club (see page 82; no relation) was large, comfortable, and elegant, like a fancy big-city hotel bar of the 1930s, but without the hotel.

It was an instant hit. At Pegu Club, it was as if the Dark Ages had never happened.

Saunders, a barfly and culinarian at heart, was exacting and uncompromising about her drinks and every other aspect of the bar. And when the bartenders she trained moved on, they were like so many boozy dandelion seeds, opening excellent new bars wherever they landed.

PEAK COCKTAIL, 2005–2015

The opening of Pegu Club was like the starting gun for the cocktail revolution's victory lap. "Craft cocktails" (a term swiped from beer) weren't just a careful way of mixing drinks; they were a "movement."

In part, this new-old cocktail culture was popular for the simple reason that once you had a real drink, it was hard to go back to Jäger Bombs and Jack & Cokes.

But there was more to it. People huddle together in times of stress--and they drink. The attacks of September 11, 2001, and their aftermath were deeply unsettling, as, in a different way, was the internet's blitzkrieg conquest of seemingly every aspect of day-to-day life.

THE VIOLET HOUR, CHICAGO (2007)*

A good cocktail in a civilized bar was a little antidote. You couldn't download it or order it from Amazon. Somebody had to make it just for you, right in front of you, and you drank it surrounded by other, in-the-flesh humans, most of whom had put their BlackBerrys down and were actually talking to one another.

The next couple of years saw a wave of new speakeasy-style bars open in major cities, each with its particular twist on the hidden entrance and posted house rules.

Suddenly cocktail books were hip. Old ones were reprinted in painstaking facsimile editions; new ones achieved unprecedented depths of geekiness. Jeff Berry was able to devote a whole book to decoding the secrets of Donn Beach's Filipino bartenders, and my own 2007 *Imbibe!*, a very, very geeky dive into the life and drinks of Jerry Thomas, sold widely and even won a James Beard award, a cocktail book first.

In 2010, when Jim Meehan--the former Pegu Club bartender whose speakeasy-style PDT was one of the hottest bars in New York--mixed drinks for Jimmy Fallon, it was no anomaly. For a while there, it seemed like every week some bartender type was on one talk show or another, shaking up something classic and spouting snippets of cocktail lore.

*TOBY MALONEY, WHO OPENED THE BAR, HAD WORKED AT BOTH MILK & HONEY AND PEGU CLUB.

The drinks that had convinced everyone were mostly top-line classics, with the Manhattan, Old-Fashioned, and Daiquiri once again standing beside the gin Martini, which had never quite gone away. These were supplemented by a few old wild cards, but there was also a good smattering of new drinks, for the most part simple twists on the classics.

THREE NEW YORK CITY VARIATIONS ON THE MANHATTAN

THE BEDFORD
RYE, DUBONNET, COINTREAU, AND ORANGE BITTERS
(DEL PEDRO, GRANGE HALL, CIRCA 1999)

THE RED HOOK
RYE, MARASCHINO, AND PUNT E MES
(VINCENZO ERRICO, MILK & HONEY, 2003)

THE LITTLE ITALY
RYE, ITALIAN VERMOUTH, AND CYNAR
(AUDREY SAUNDERS, PEGU CLUB, 2005)

DRINKS AFIELD

REVOLVER
BOURBON, TIA MARIA, ORANGE BITTERS, AND FLAMED ORANGE TWIST
(JON SANTER, BRUNO'S, SAN FRANCISCO, 2004)

WHITE STAR IMPERIAL DAISY
ARMAGNAC, KÜMMEL, LEMON, SUGAR, AND CHAMPAGNE
(5 NINTH, NEW YORK, 2004)

PAPER PLANE
BOURBON, LEMON, AMARO NONINO, AND CAMPARI OR APEROL
(SAM ROSS, THE VIOLET HOUR, CHICAGO, 2008)

LONG AND ROCKY

HORSEFEATHER
RYE, GINGER BEER, LIME, AND BITTERS
(UNKNOWN, LAWRENCE, KANSAS, CIRCA 1990)

TOMMY'S MARGARITA
TEQUILA, LIME JUICE, AND AGAVE SYRUP
(JULIO BERMEJO, TOMMY'S MEXICAN RESTAURANT, SAN FRANCISCO, 1990)

GUNSHOP FIZZ
PEYCHAUD'S BITTERS, LEMON, SUGAR, STRAWBERRY, CUCUMBER, CITRUS PEEL, AND SANBITTÈR
(KIRK ESTOPINAL AND MAKSYM PAZUNIAK, CURE, NEW ORLEANS, 2009)

By the early 2010s, the success of the cocktail revolution had built enough momentum that it became hard to stop. You could see it in the way bars were set up; in the bottles kept in the "speed rack" or "well," where the ingredients for the most popular cocktails were stored; and in the bottles displayed on the shelves behind the bar.

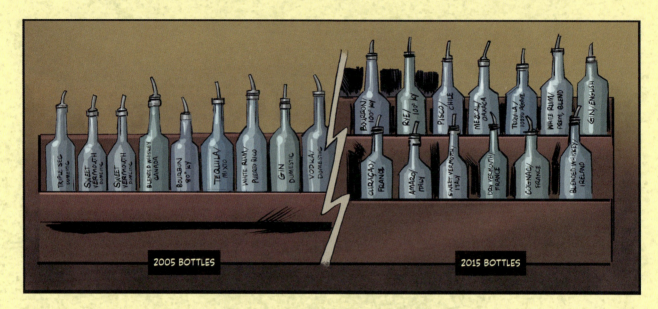

It took a wider, deeper, and better selection of spirits to make the retro-style cocktails now in vogue. Importers and distillers took note.

In 2005, vodka was still the fastest-growing spirit, and brands and bottlings were multiplying like mad. Ten years later, in high-end bars, most of the vodka slots would have gone to gin.

By 2015, the anemic top-shelf offerings of 2005--a couple of cognacs, single-malt Scotches, and maybe a grappa in a whimsical bottle--were joined by rare bourbons, special bottlings of extra-aged liqueurs, single-village mezcals, artisanal absinthes, and so on.

By 2010, the cocktailian trend had jumped the Atlantic.

SALVATORE CALABRESE

CHAS. SCHUMANN

Top-rank IBA-type professionals such as Salvatore Calabrese of the Playboy Club, London, and Charles Schumann of Schumann's Bar, Munich, gained appreciative new customers for their drinks and readers for their books.

The new, American retro-hipster style of mixology had already been introduced back in 2002, when the London bar entrepreneur Jonathan Downey had brought Petraske and DeGroff over to set up a (very swank) Milk & Honey London.

By the end of the decade, it was also on display in the inevitable new speakeasies in all the cool parts of town.

MILK & HONEY, LONDON

Meanwhile, American bars were moving on, as the ubiquitous (and easily parodied) Jerry-Thomas-meets-speakeasy aesthetic was supplanted by others--neo-tiki, Dr. Frankenstein's lab, drinking-as-fine-dining, like that.

At cocktail-themed gatherings such as New Orleans's Tales of the Cocktail and London Cocktail Week, mixologists, their most enthusiastic customers, and the booze-industry marketers seeking their favor met annually to get tipsy and pick up new ideas.

Karla & Jenn's Cocktails

Jenningway Daiquiri
no maraschino, Jenn's cherry bounce

SideKarla
applying the apple brandy

A Regular Old Negroni
gin, yadda yadda

The evolutions that the cocktail bar went through changed the home bar as well. Between books, drink-focused media such as *Imbibe* magazine, and, of course, the internet, the mildly interested home mixologist could easily develop into a raging hobbyist.

After a decade of full-on cocktail revolution, at least one thing had been accomplished: the (*clockwise from top*) Negroni, fresh-juice Daiquiri, rye Manhattan, Tommy's Margarita, and Old-Fashioned had all been normalized to the point that you could reasonably expect that any cocktail-bar bartender (and even many home mixologists) could quickly knock out at least two or three of these.

THE NEW NORMAL, 2015–PRESENT

Every revolution creates a new status quo. By the mid-2010s, there were craft cocktail bars in cities all around the world, and, in America, even in small towns.

The lost ingredients that early cocktailians had had to scratch-make, hand import, or kludge up could now be found at the local booze-geek liquor store or ordered online. The classic cocktail was back. Yet no sooner had it been resurrected than people began screwing with it.

In 2009, as an early preview of what was coming, New Orleans bartenders Kirk Estopinal and Maks Pazuniak self-published *Rogue Cocktails*, a manifesto with recipes explicitly aimed at bartenders who had already mastered the bottles behind the bar and knew their classics down to the DNA level.

"Where is the cocktail guide for the bartender who wants to introduce their customers to a drink that is challenging, complex, and most importantly, a new experience?" they asked. Yet complicated and strange as its recipes could be, *Rogue Cocktails* avoided house-made or otherwise unavailable ingredients; the drinks were makeable.*

I WOULD JUST *LOVE* A SIDECAR.

WE'VE GOT JUST THE THING ON OUR LIST--THE CLOWN CAR? ARTISANAL PEAR BRANDY, ACIDULATED BLOOD ORANGE JUICE, STREGA, AND A FLOAT OF LOCAL HEIRLOOM-PEAR CIDER. CAN I START ONE FOR YOU?

Alas, while the book's recipes proved highly influential, by the mid-2010s its preconditions--knowing your classics, mastering your ingredients, keeping your drinks reproducible--were widely flouted, as was its admonition that "a bar exists to serve customers, not cocktails."

Now, it wasn't enough to reproduce classic recipes precisely and well.

WELL, I'VE BEEN REALLY OBSESSING OVER A PLAIN OLD SIDECAR, IF YOU CAN DO THAT...

I GUESS. WE DO THOSE HERE WITH CAROLINA SCUPPERNONG BRANDY AND OUR HOUSE-MADE ORANGE CORDIAL...

To be cutting edge, a bartender or home mixologist had to generate new and unheard-of combinations-- pretty much as Cutty Cutsail had done at P. L. Cahoots, twenty years earlier (see page 131).

In the hands of a modern, educated mixologist who knows all the ingredients and what goes with what, or one who's just plain lucky, this approach to mixing drinks could indeed yield truly delicious, memorable cocktails.

But it also yielded a lot of misses, drinks that tasted muddy, awkward, or just plain weird. All too often, the answer to that was "serve it anyway."

Whether delicious or merely "interesting," these cocktails--unlike Cutsail's shooters--had to look good. In fact, with a camera in every customer's pocket and Instagram and Twitter calling, for the ambitious bartender looks were perhaps even more important than flavor.

*SEE ENDNOTES, PAGE 165.

"...BARTENDER SAID IT'S GINGER-RHUBARB SYRUP WITH FRESH LIME JUICE AND, UH, COCONUT WATER. AND SOME KIND OF CAYENNE TINCTURE. DAMN GOOD."

The ascendance of the baroque cocktail continued into the late 2010s, only now nonalcoholic creations were joining the high-octane ones on the bar.

Cocktails were more than a passing fad, and their makers had to consider those who were being left out of the fun.

Then, in 2020, came the COVID-19 pandemic and its associated lockdowns.

Some bars could limp along selling take-out cocktails, but many couldn't, including institutions such as Pegu Club, which closed in March 2020 and never reopened.

"KAT MADE US A COUPLE OF SAZERACS. SHE'S GOT 'EM DOWN."

"KILLING ME WITH THOSE! ALL I'VE GOT IS THIS STUPID G&T."

With bars closed, home mixology reached new heights as people gathered on Zoom and social media, or with their "pods," to share cocktails and companionship.

One thing to come out of the stocktaking that accompanied the pandemic was an intense discussion about inclusiveness in the cocktail world, accompanied by a stack of books showing how women and people of color had always been a part of it.

By the time cocktail bars finally resumed normal operations many of their old customers had gotten out of the bar habit, and many of their senior bartenders had found other work. That thinned the forest for a new generation to develop its own take on the cocktail and find its own heroes and inspirations.

JUKE JOINTS, JAZZ CLUBS, AND JUICE BY TONI TIPTON-MARTIN, *GIRLY DRINKS* BY MALLORY O'MEARA, AND *BLACK MIXCELLENCE* BY TAMIKA HALL

And thanks to the generation of tipsy revolutionaries that came before, they've got all the ingredients at hand from which to shake up something truly delightful. A thirsty world awaits.

A PARTING GLASS

All in all, it's hard to argue with those who call the 2010s and 2020s a new golden age for the cocktail, and, indeed, for spirits in general. (In 2022, spirits outsold beer in the American market for the first time in well over a century.) Cocktail bars are ubiquitous: you can drink well everywhere from Tres Monos in Buenos Aires to the Narrows in Juneau, Alaska; from Republic in Singapore to the Vintage Cocktail Club in Dublin, and too many places in between to count. That's a good thing.

But it's not all good news. As the veteran New York bartender Frank Caiafa posted in January 2024, "I'm still not confident in ordering something as simple as a Manhattan in every bar, even when on the island of Manhattan."

The emphasis in recent years on mixing drinks as a modern art, rather than as a traditional craft, and on creation over execution, sometimes makes for sketchy foundations.

The cocktail revolution brought back the ingredients and the attention to detail necessary for classic bartending, but it couldn't revive a mindset that was content to seek perfection through making the same drinks everyone else was making, over and over and over again (modern bars not only don't serve the same drinks as one another; they don't even serve the same drinks in June that they were serving in November).

Still, there are plenty of exceptions, and with our unprecedented access to spirits, mixers, tools, and recipes, if you can't find somebody to mix it exactly the way you want it, you can always do it yourself. And whether you mix it or some tattooed young philanthropist mixes it for you, a properly made cocktail is still one of the best things under the sun to help smooth, however briefly, the bumpy road we travel in life, just as it was in 1803.

MIXOLOGY: EL PANETÙN

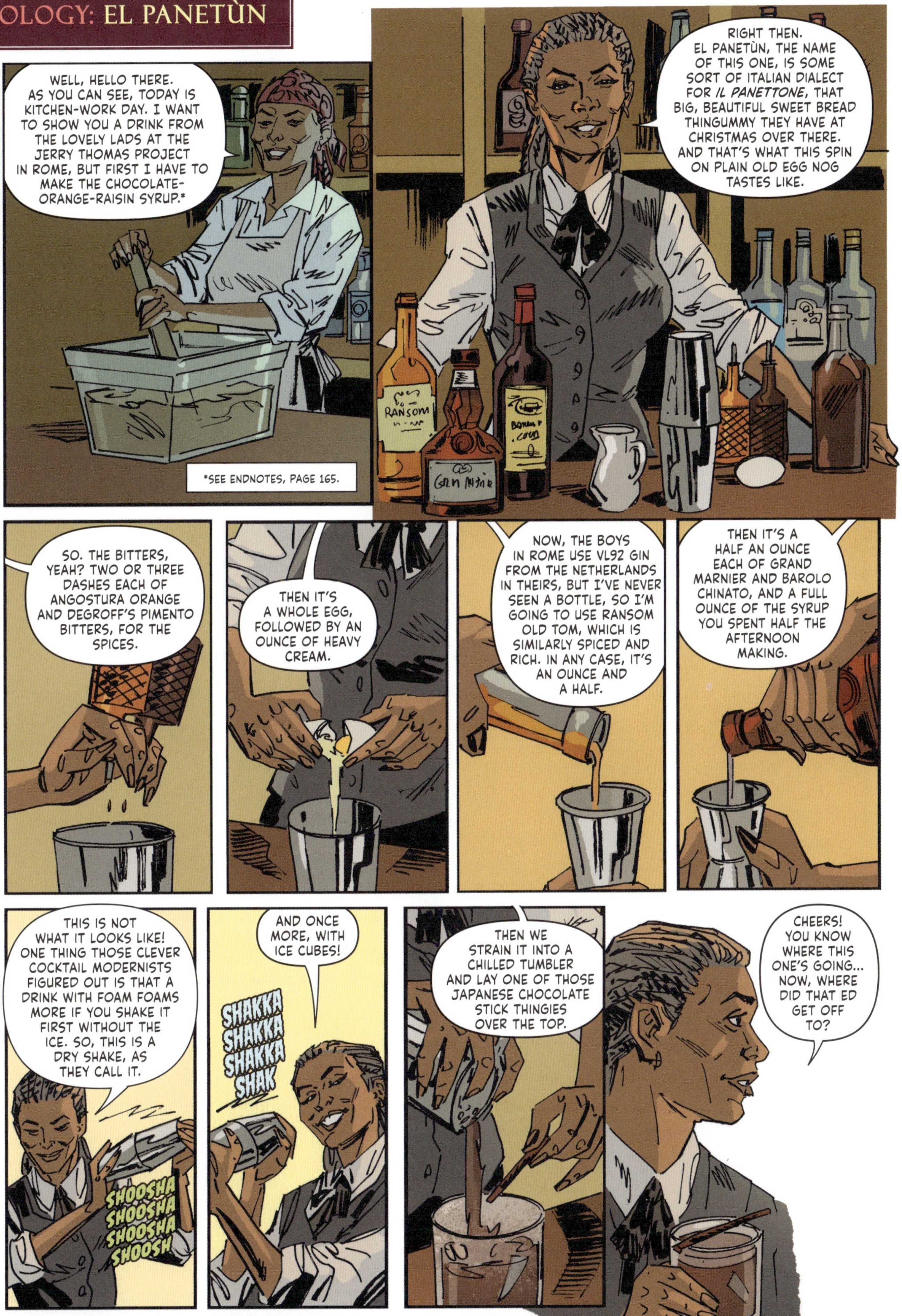

WELL, HELLO THERE. AS YOU CAN SEE, TODAY IS KITCHEN-WORK DAY. I WANT TO SHOW YOU A DRINK FROM THE LOVELY LADS AT THE JERRY THOMAS PROJECT IN ROME, BUT FIRST I HAVE TO MAKE THE CHOCOLATE-ORANGE-RAISIN SYRUP.*
*SEE ENDNOTES, PAGE 165.
RIGHT THEN. EL PANETÙN, THE NAME OF THIS ONE, IS SOME SORT OF ITALIAN DIALECT FOR *IL PANETTONE*, THAT BIG, BEAUTIFUL SWEET BREAD THINGUMMY THEY HAVE AT CHRISTMAS OVER THERE. AND THAT'S WHAT THIS SPIN ON PLAIN OLD EGG NOG TASTES LIKE.
RANSOM
SO. THE BITTERS, YEAH? TWO OR THREE DASHES EACH OF ANGOSTURA ORANGE AND DEGROFF'S PIMENTO BITTERS, FOR THE SPICES.
THEN IT'S A WHOLE EGG, FOLLOWED BY AN OUNCE OF HEAVY CREAM.
NOW, THE BOYS IN ROME USE VL92 GIN FROM THE NETHERLANDS IN THEIRS, BUT I'VE NEVER SEEN A BOTTLE, SO I'M GOING TO USE RANSOM OLD TOM, WHICH IS SIMILARLY SPICED AND RICH. IN ANY CASE, IT'S AN OUNCE AND A HALF.
THEN IT'S A HALF AN OUNCE EACH OF GRAND MARNIER AND BAROLO CHINATO, AND A FULL OUNCE OF THE SYRUP YOU SPENT HALF THE AFTERNOON MAKING.
THIS IS NOT WHAT IT LOOKS LIKE! ONE THING THOSE CLEVER COCKTAIL MODERNISTS FIGURED OUT IS THAT A DRINK WITH FOAM FOAMS MORE IF YOU SHAKE IT FIRST WITHOUT THE ICE. SO, THIS IS A DRY SHAKE, AS THEY CALL IT.
SHOOSHA SHOOSHA SHOOSHA SHOOSH
AND ONCE MORE, WITH ICE CUBES!
SHAKKA SHAKKA SHAKKA SHAK
THEN WE STRAIN IT INTO A CHILLED TUMBLER AND LAY ONE OF THOSE JAPANESE CHOCOLATE STICK THINGIES OVER THE TOP.
CHEERS! YOU KNOW WHERE THIS ONE'S GOING... NOW, WHERE DID THAT ED GET OFF TO?

MIXOLOGY: THE TRUSTY NAIL

HIYA. HERE'S SOMETHING I AIN'T USED TO: A DRINK INVENTED BY SOMEBODY WHAT AIN'T DEAD. LUCINDA STERLING'S GOT A COUPLE OF BARS IN NEW YORK: MIDDLE BRANCH, IN MIDTOWN, I THINK; AND WHATCHAMACALLIT, SEABORNE, OVER THERE IN BROOKLYN.

NOW, THIS ONE'S JUST TO SHOW THAT NOT EVERY MODERN DRINK'S A TRIP TO OUTER SPACE.

THE TRUSTY NAIL'S A QUICK TWIST ON THE RUSTY NAIL, BUILT RIGHT IN THE GLASS.

START WITH THE BITTERS. ANGOSTURA AND ORANGE-- A COUPLA DASHES OF EACH.

THEN THE BOOZE. AN OUNCE OF GENEVER TO START. YOU DIDN'T USE TO SEE NOTHIN' BUT CRAPPY GENEVER, IF THAT. NOW WE GOT SOME REAL GOOD STUFF, LIKE THIS OLD DUFF ONE. FOLKS SHOULD MAKE MORE GENEVER DRINKS.

AAAAND THE SCOTCH. NOW, THAT SOUNDS LIKE A KINDA ROUGH COMBINATION--GIN AND SCOTCH--BUT THE GENEVER'S PRETTY SCOTCHY AND THEY GET ALONG REAL WELL TOGETHER. AN OUNCE OF SCOTCH. IT SHOULD BE BLENDED, BUT USE SOMETHING NICE.

THREE-QUARTERS OF AN OUNCE DRAMBUIE TO FINISH IT OFF. SURE, IT'S JUST A RUSTY NAIL, BUT IT'S A REALLY GOOD RUSTY NAIL.

A QUICK STIR AND THEN IT'S TIME FOR THE BIG ICE. BIG. IF YOU AIN'T GOT THAT, REGULAR ICE WORKS, TOO. OH, AND STIR IT AGAIN, A BUNCH OF TIMES.

FINISH WITH A LEMON TWIST; GET SOME OF THAT BRIGHT LEMON OIL ON TOP.

MIXING ALL THESE DRINKS HAS BEEN THIRSTY WORK, SO IF IT'S OKAY WITH YOU, I'M GONNA TAKE CARE OF THIS ONE. CHEERS!

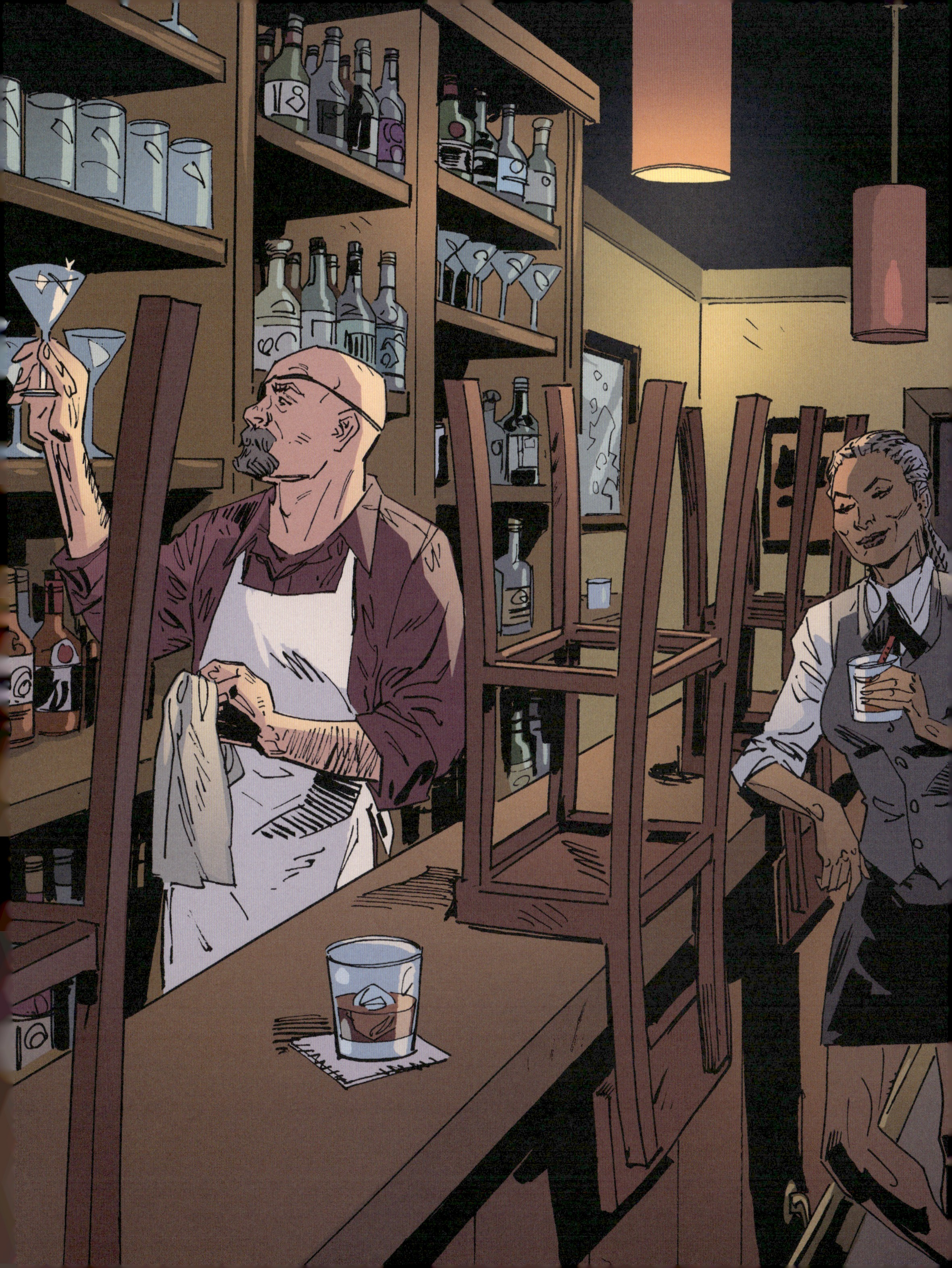

RECIPES: SOME DRINKS I HAVE ENJOYED (AND HOW TO MIX THEM)

For the most part, the drink recipes included so far in this book have been bedrock classics, the pillars of the mixologist's craft. Delicious, tried-and-true drinks that have withstood the test of time, and so on and so forth. But it's always nice to have a couple of other recipes in your repertoire, ones that are just as delicious, or nearly so, and far less known—just to keep things interesting.

Here are some of my back-pocket drinks, ones I've come across over the years (or, in the case of the final three, ones I've come up with) with which I like to surprise people sometimes. (And if three of these recipes contain Irish whiskey, what of it? They will help to make up for the dearth of it in the rest of the book.)

PIG & WHISTLE

This 1830s New Orleans creation is one of the oldest American "fancy drinks," and one of the simplest: French brandy and anisette stirred up with ice and strained into a little glass. The result is somehow both rich and cooling, particularly with a VSOP brandy and a good, imported anisette. Of course, if you just don't like anise, no ingredient upgrade will help. But if you do, share this with a friend.

1½ ounces VSOP-grade cognac or Armagnac

½ ounce imported anisette, such as Anis del Mono from Spain

Fill a mixing glass with cracked ice. Add cognac and anisette and stir well. Strain into a pair of small, stemmed liqueur glasses and drink to the Louisiana Purchase.

MR. GREEN'S MILK PUNCH

In August 1873, when the *New York Sun* interviewed a couple of expert New York bartenders about their work, the paper inaugurated a whole genre of writing. The man identified only as "Mr. Green," the patient zero for bartenders talking to reporters about their drinks, gave this recipe for Milk Punch, America's hangover cure par excellence, and it's a thoroughly sound one. (Though you don't need to be hungover to enjoy it.)

2 barspoons rich Demerara syrup (see Note)

1½ ounces rich, mellow rum, such as Plantation Fiji or Appleton Estate Reserve

½ ounce VSOP-grade cognac

2 to 3 ounces whole milk, depending on how milky or boozy you want it

Fresh nutmeg, for garnish

Add the syrup, rum, and cognac to a shaker and stir. Add the milk and shake well with ice. Strain into an ice-filled goblet and grate nutmeg over the top.

NOTE
To make rich Demerara syrup, stir 2 parts by volume Demerara sugar and 1 part water over a low flame until the sugar has dissolved. Let cool, bottle, and refrigerate. Store in the refrigerator for up to 4 weeks.

JAKE DIDIER'S IRISH ROSE

The subtle, honey-musk flavor of triple-distilled Irish whiskey—whether it's a pure pot-still such as Redbreast or a single-malt such as Bushmills—goes marvelously well with raspberries for some reason, as Binghamton, New York, bartender Jake Didier realized a little after the turn of the last century. He used raspberry syrup in his Irish Rose, but I prefer to just throw some fresh berries into the shaker and let the ice muddle them.

½ ounce fresh-squeezed lime juice

1 heaping barspoon sugar, preferably a fine-grained evaporated cane juice style

2 ounces triple-distilled Irish whiskey

6 ripe raspberries

½ ounce chilled sparkling water

Add lime juice to a cocktail shaker and stir in the sugar. Add the whiskey and raspberries and shake viciously with ice. Double strain into a chilled cocktail glass (i.e., use a Hawthorne strainer in the shaker and another fine-mesh strainer over the glass) and add sparkling water.

THE READING CLUB COCKTAIL

This suave minor masterpiece was a product of Buenos Aires's lively cocktail scene back around 1910. Recorded prosaically as the "Oporto Bianco" cocktail or enigmatically as the "Rending Club" cocktail (early Latin American cocktail books tended to suffer from the inexperience of local typesetters with English orthography), it turned a slightly unlikely roster of ingredients into a smooth and delightful whole.

1½ ounces rich blended Scotch whiskey

1½ ounces white port

½ barspoon orange curaçao

½ barspoon maraschino liqueur

1 dash (from a dasher or bitters bottle) green Chartreuse

1 maraschino cherry, for garnish

Fill a mixing glass with cracked ice and add the whiskey, port, curaçao, maraschino liqueur, and Chartreuse. Stir well. Strain into a chilled cocktail glass and garnish with a maraschino cherry.

THE OHIO COCKTAIL

Okay, yes, the Ohio Cocktail (see page 83) is about as American as Winnetou and Old Shatterhand (you know, the main characters of the first-person Western novels by Karl Friedrich May, who had been to the United States but once and never got west of Niagara Falls). But May's books nonetheless beguiled generations of German readers just as the Ohio Cocktail—which had no connection with Ohio, the Ohio River, or the continent in which those are found—delighted generations of German drinkers. With reason—it's perfectly delicious.

1½ ounces straight rye whiskey

¾ ounce red vermouth

1 barspoon imported orange curaçao

1 dash Angostura bitters

Chilled champagne, for topping

1 maraschino cherry, for garnish

¼ orange wheel, for garnish

Small piece of pineapple, fresh or canned, for garnish

Fill a mixing glass with cracked ice and add the whiskey, vermouth, curaçao, and bitters. Stir well. Strain into a chilled coupe, top off with champagne, and garnish with a cherry, a quarter orange wheel, and a small piece of pineapple.

THE PRESIDENTE VINCENT

Back in 1937, when the Caribbean cruise was a clever new idea, *Esquire* sent their drinks man, Murdock Pemberton, out to test the waters. He found them particularly fine at the Tourist Bar in Port-au-Prince, Haiti, where the nation's tourist director, Olympic long-jump champion Sylvio Paul Cator, introduced him to this lovely, refreshing drink. (Sténio Vincent was the president of Haiti from 1930 to 1941.)

1½ ounces Barbancourt Three-Star or Five-Star Haitian Rhum

¾ ounce Noilly Prat dry vermouth

½ ounce lime juice

¼ ounce rich Demerara syrup (see Note on page 153)

Lime, for garnish

Demerara sugar, for garnish

Fill a mixing glass with cracked ice and add the rhum, vermouth, lime juice, and Demerara syrup. Shake well, then strain into a chilled cocktail glass that has had its outside rim rubbed with lime and rolled in demerara sugar.

THE HUNTSMAN

In the 1950s and 1960s, if you maintained an interest in eating lead-poisoned game beasties, the Sports Afield Room at New York's Café Nino, on East 52nd Street just off 5th Avenue, was your place. Armadillo for four? How would you like that, sir? This was their house cocktail; I'm not sure if it's an over-and-under or a side-by-side, but it's definitely double-barreled.

1 barspoon superfine sugar

½ ounce lime juice

2 ounces vodka

½ ounce Smith & Cross or other high-proof, aged Jamaican rum

1 barspoon Bärenjäger or other honey liqueur

1 mint leaf, for garnish

Put the superfine sugar in a shaker, add the lime juice, and stir. Add the vodka, rum, honey liqueur, and ice. Shake and strain into a chilled cocktail glass. Float a mint leaf on top.

THE POONA CLUB

I've invented a great many cocktails over the last twenty-five years, the vast majority of them one-time improvisations that are pleasant enough but completely forgettable. But every once in a while, as the saying goes, even a blind pig finds an acorn, and the last three drinks here are some of those acorns: drinks that I have made and made again, and occasionally even other people have made. This one is an extra-citrusy riff on the Pegu Club (page 82) that I created in 2007 for the Fatty Crab, a New York restaurant dedicated to Asian-style street food.

1½ ounces lime-infused Plymouth gin (see Notes) or Tanqueray Rangpur gin

¾ ounce Martini & Rossi red vermouth

¾ ounce fresh-squeezed blood-orange juice (see Notes)

1 dash Angostura bitters

1 dash orange bitters

¼ blood-orange wheel

Fill a mixing glass with cracked ice and add the gin, vermouth, orange juice, Angostura bitters, and orange bitters. Shake well. Strain into a chilled cocktail glass and garnish with the blood-orange wheel.

NOTES

To make lime-infused Plymouth: slice 1 lime thinly, put it in a quart Mason jar, and add a 750-milliliter bottle of Plymouth gin. Let it steep for 4 hours, strain, and re-bottle. Keep this refrigerated for up to 2 months.

Unfortunately the season for blood oranges, December through April, is fairly brief. Regular orange juice also works, but the drink won't be nearly as striking.

THE GIACOMO JOYCE

James Joyce lived in the Austro-Hungarian port city of Trieste for a decade and a half, doing much of his most important writing there. Since the population was, and is, mostly Italian (indeed, the city has been part of Italy since World War I), and completely coffee-mad, it seems like a fitting liquid tribute to Joyce's time there to mix coffee liqueur, Italian semisweet vermouth, and the Irish whiskey with which he was intimately acquainted.

2 ounces John Powers or Black Bush Irish whiskey

½ ounce Carpano Bianco or other bianco/blanc vermouth (see Note)

½ ounce Varnelli Caffè Moka or other good coffee liqueur

2 dashes Peychaud's bitters

1 roasted coffee bean, for garnish

Fill a mixing glass with cracked ice and add the whiskey, vermouth, coffee liqueur, and bitters. Stir well. Strain into a chilled cocktail glass and drop in a roasted coffee bean.

NOTE

You want the semisweet white kind of vermouth from the Italian or French Alps ("bianco" or "blanc"), not the dry French kind ("seco" or "sec").

THE LEAVING OF LIVERPOOL

In January 2021, back when everybody was stir-crazy because of the pandemic, a bunch of people on Twitter became obsessed with sea chanteys (I know, I know). Anyway, a couple of them asked me to come up with an appropriate sea-chantey drink. I named this after one of the greatest of such songs (get the version by the Dubliners). It seemed to fit the bill.

1½ ounces Redbreast or other Irish pure pot-still whiskey

½ ounce Planteray Xaymaca or Smith & Cross Jamaican rum (i.e., pure pot-still)

½ ounce lemon juice

½ ounce cold black tea

½ ounce rich Demerara syrup (see Note on page 153)

Fresh nutmeg, for garnish

Fill a shaker with cracked ice and add the whiskey, rum, lemon juice, tea, and Demerara syrup. Shake well. Strain into a tall glass or tiki mug full of fresh ice and grate nutmeg over the top.

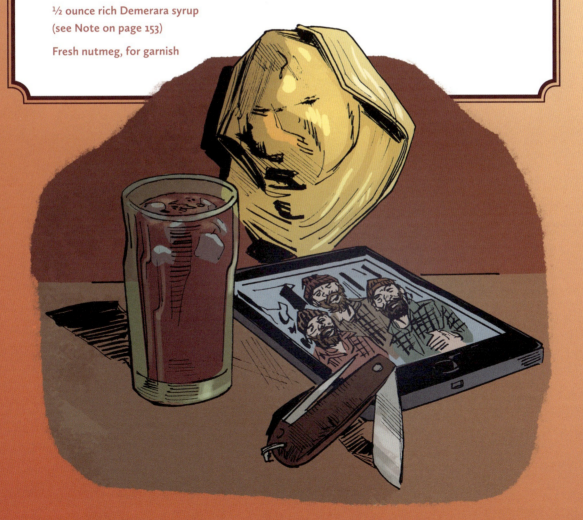

DATES, NOTES, AND FURTHER READING

Here you'll find birth and death years for most of the people mentioned in the text, where they're not already supplied and to the degree that such information is available (bartenders aren't always the easiest people to track down). You'll also find sources for any direct quotations, select facts (again, where not already supplied), and a few suggestions for further reading.

ABBREVIATIONS

It should come as no surprise that I've drawn on my previous writing for the information in this book, although much in here is new and everything else has been reconsidered, reframed, and re-researched. Nonetheless, I've leaned on these works the most.

> **Imbibe:** Wondrich, David. *Imbibe! Updated and Revised Edition: From Absinthe Cocktail to Whiskey Smash, a Salute in Stories and Drinks to "Professor" Jerry Thomas, Pioneer of the American Bar.* New York: Perigee, 2015.
>
> **OCSC:** Wondrich, David, ed. in chief, and Noah Rothbaum, associate ed. *The Oxford Companion to Spirits and Cocktails.* New York: Oxford University Press, 2021.
>
> **Punch:** Wondrich, David. *Punch: The Delights (and Dangers) of the Flowing Bowl.* New York: Perigee, 2010.

Note that second mentions of any source will be abbreviated.

PREHISTORY

Further Reading: See R. J. Forbes, *A Short History of the Art of Distillation* (Leiden: E. J. Brill, 1948); Nicole Austin, "Distillation, Process" in *OCSC;* Wondrich, "Distillation, History" and "Spirits Trade" in *OCSC;* Michele Savonarola, *I trattati in volgare della peste e dell' acqua ardente,* ed. Luigi Belloni (Rome: Società Italiana di Medicina Interna, 1953).

CHAPTER ONE

People: Robert Larkin (?–1616); James Ashley (1698–1776); Mary Gaywood (1714?–1770); Giuseppe Tortoni (1775?–1865?); Jasper Crouch (?–1860); Stephen Price (1782–1840); Stephen Limmer (1748–1818); John Collin (1769–1843).

Further Reading: *Punch;* "arrack, Batavia" and "Punch" in *OCSC;* Armin Zimmermann and Frank Arne Poremba, "From Gin Punch to Collins," parts 1–8, www.bar-vademecum.eu.

CHAPTER TWO

People: Murtagh Byrne (?–1822); Jim Cook (1808?–1870); John Dabney (1824?–1900); Albert Edward, Prince of Wales (1841–1910).

Quotes: Page 20, Julep poem: S. X. "A Short Poem on Hunting," *Virginia Gazette,* January 11, 1770, 2; Wig Wam Gardens: "Fire Works," *Norfolk Gazetteer and Publick Ledger,* May 4, 1807, 3. Page 22, Cook and Dabney's Juleps: Robert Cellem, *Visit of His Royal Highness the Prince of Wales to the British North American Provinces and United States* (London, 1861) 375.

Further Reading: *Imbibe;* Richard Barksdale Harwell, *The Mint Julep* (Charlottesville: University of Virginia Press, 1975); Robert F. Moss, *Southern Spirits* (San Francisco: Ten Speed Press, 2016); Elizabeth David, *Harvest of the Cold Months* (New York: Viking, 1994); David S. Shields, *The Culinarians* (Chicago: University of Chicago Press, 2017); Alba Huerta and Marah Stets, *Julep* (San Francisco: Ten Speed Press, 2018); Nicholas Faith, *Cognac* (Oxford: Infinite Ideas Limited, 2014); "Maturation," in *OCSC*.

CHAPTER THREE

People: Richard Stoughton (1665–1716); George Washington (1732–1799); Catherine "Kitty" Hustler (1762–1832); Harry Croswell (1778–1858); for Willard and Alexander, see page 21; Henry Cooke (of Peterborough, England), active 1844–1852; Joseph Santini (1818–1874).

Quotes: Page 27, "Pleasant (though bitterish) taste": *Proceedings of the Old Bailey,* October 14, 1695, 6; "Stoughton's Elixir Stomachicum": Stoughton's handbill, ca. 1705. Page 28, General Washington's wine and bitters: Smith, William, ed. William H. Sabine, *William Smith's historical memoirs 1777–1783* (New York: NY Times & Arno Press, 1971), 587. Page 29, "Cock-tail, then, is a stimulating liquor": Hudson, NY *Balance & Columbian Repository,* May 13, 1806, p. 2. Page 31, "Which are you for": Capt. J. E. Alexander, *Transatlantic Sketches* (London: 1833), 2:6; "Have you got any good gin?": Alexander, 2:120. Page 32, "Common cocktail": Henry Cooke, "Notes of a Loiterer in New York," *Bentley's Miscellany* 16, 1844, 597; "compounded of brandy": New York *Sunday Mercury,* rept. in New Orleans *Daily Picayune,* February 1, 1843, 2.

Further Reading: *Imbibe;* William Grimes, *Straight Up or On the Rocks,* 2nd ed. (New York: North Point Press, 2002); "Gin," in *OCSC;* William T. Harper, *Origins and Rise of the British Distillery* (New York: Edwin Mellen Press, 1999).

CHAPTER FOUR

People: Peter Bent Brigham (1807–1877); Martin Ackerman, active 1855–1859; John D. Hammack (1822–1867); Martha King Niblo, see page 21; Antonio Fernandez (1832–1917); Albert Haller Tracy (1834–1874); Randall Percy Otway Plunkett, Lord Louth (1832–1883).

Quotes: Page 40, "Hammack's": Washington *Evening Star,* April 16, 1863, 4. Page 41, "A Sherry Cobbler from her dainty hand": "Among the Actors," *New York Herald,* August 26, 1877, 7. Page 42, "When American meets American": Atlanta *Daily Constitution,* February 20, 1879, 2. Page 43, "The Famous Match at Cocktails": *New York Daily Tribune,* August 26, 1883, 4.

Further Reading: *Imbibe;* Grimes, *Straight Up or On the Rocks*; Wondrich, "The Greatest Drinking Match in History," TheDailyBeast.com, October 14, 2021.

CHAPTER FIVE

People: William Brisbane Dick (1827–1901); Laurence R. Fitzgerald (1826–1881); Jacob Martin Van Winkle (1812–1895).

Quotes: Page 46, "A Live Yankee": "King's Head," London *City Press,* August 1, 1857, 4. Page 47, "I was successfully launched": The Professor's monologue is stitched together out of what few bits of his speech have been preserved, various reminiscences of him, and details supplied by a myriad of contemporary periodicals, which I have shoehorned in according to my sense of how he might have phrased things. The most important sources: "Bibliology—the Notorieties of the Bar," San Francisco *Daily Alta California,* November 9, 1863, 3; "Jerry Thomas's Pictures," *New York Sun,* March 28, 1883, 2; Alan Dale, *Jonathan's Home,* chapter XV, Boston, 1885; "Jerry Thomas's Career," *New York World,* December 20, 1883, 23. Page 51, "Jerry Thomas was the best barkeeper" and "a genius at mixing drinks": in "Jerry Thomas's Career."

Further Reading: *Imbibe;* Lew Bryson, *Tasting Whiskey* (North Adams, MA: Storey Publishing, 2014); "whisky, bourbon" and "whisky, rye," in *OCSC.*

CHAPTER SIX

People: Frances Trollope (1779–1863); Katherine Jane Ellice (1813–1864); Willis G. Keeney (1821–1891); Leopoldo Bomboni, active 1850–1869; Paul Meade (1819–1868); Charlie Paul, active 1883–1912; Adam Worth (1844?–1902); Charles W. Bullard (1850?–1895?); Katherine Louise Flynn (1852?–1894); Giovanni Mitta, active 1898–1916; Otto Maier, active 1903–1934; Frank Meier (1884–1947); Albert Clavelot (1884–1976).

Quotes: Page 56, "It would, I truly believe": Frances Trollope, *The Old World and the New* (London, 1849), 1:318–19; "A large glass of Sherry Cobbler": Patricia Godsell, ed., *The Diary of Jane Ellice* (Canada: Oberon Press, 1975), 78, 83; "Mysteries of Gin-sling": Charles Dickens, *American Notes for General Circulation* (London: 1842), 1:141.

Further Reading: Ben Macintyre, *The Napoleon of Crime* (New York: Delta, 1997).

CHAPTER SEVEN

People: Edward S. Stokes (1841–1901); William F. Mulhall (1858–1941); Joseph F. McKone (1860–1914); Frederick E. Loud (1842–1907); Patrick H. McDonough (1850–1893); William T. Boothby (1862–1930); Harry Johnson (1845–1930); Vincent Miret (1847–1899); William Wilkinson (1854–1904); Leander Richardson (1856–1918); William Schmidt (1850?–1905); Duncan Nicol (1852–1926); Henry Carl Ramos (1856–1928); Louis Bustanoby (1873–1917); William A. Hayward (1838–1902?); Louis Deal (1867–?); C. Washington Wood, active 1898–1918; Chas. J. Edline, active 1896–1900; Edward Matthews, active 1898–1904; John Lewis, active 1900–1910; Robert R. Bowie, active 1898–1900; Thomas Bullock (1871–1964); Julian Anderson (1860?–1962); Prince Martin (1895–1965); James V. Forrestal (1892–1949).

Quotes: Page 67, "You cannot make a saloon too expensive" and "the more money a place": "Gorgeous Saloons," *Buffalo Commercial Advertiser,* October 2, 1883, 2. Page 68, "A beauty behind the board": "Before the Bar," *National Police Gazette,* November 14, 1885, 14; "Bald-headed snoozer": Frank Bellew, "Typical Gin-Mills," *Texas Siftings,* December 22, 1883, 8; "I wanted men": "Everybody Knows Them," New

York *Evening Telegram,* October 5, 1889, 6. Page 71, "Keep a line of cordials": Patsy McDonough, *McDonough's Bar-Keepers' Guide* (Rochester, NY: 1883), 7; "The handwritten formula": see *Imbibe,* 239. Page 72, "The Cocktail of Today": quoted in *Atlanta Constitution,* November 3, 1886, 4. Page 73, "The largest hennery": "People Talked About," *Leslie's Weekly,* January 19, 1899, 43. Page 74, "It is not good form": "Etiquette," *St. Louis Post-Dispatch Sunday Magazine,* April 13, 1902, 6. Page 75, "It grated on [his] nerves": "Last of the Barmaids," *New York Herald,* January 19, 1892, 7.

Further Reading: *Imbibe;* "Hoffman House," "Ramos, Henry Charles," and "Sazerac" in *OCSC;* Nicola Nice, *The Cocktail Parlor: How Women Brought the Cocktail Home* (Woodstock, VT: Countryman Press, 2024); Wondrich, "The Cunningest Compounders of Beverages: The Hidden History of African-Americans Behind the Bar," BitterSoutherner.com, January 12, 2016; Fulvio Piccinino, *The Vermouth of Turin* (Turin: Graphot, 2019).

CHAPTER EIGHT

People: Ciro Capozzi (1855–1938); Henry McElhone [sic, according to his books and his service record] (1890–1958); Ruth Burgess, active 1902–1925; Ada Coleman (1874–1966); Harry Crosby (1898–1929); Caresse Crosby (1892–1970); Cammillo [sic, according to his birth certificate] Negroni (1868–1934); Victor Vaughan Morris (1873–1929).

Quotes: Page 80, "I'm astounded to read": "How to Prepare Real Cocktails," *New York Herald,* Paris ed., April 27, 1898, 3; Charlie Paul's riposte, ibid., May 3, 1898, 2; "A book found in a drawer": George Wakefield, letter, ibid., April 30, 1898, 5.

Further Reading: "Ciro's," "Ada Coleman," "Victor Vaughan Morris," and "Singapore Sling" in *OCSC;* Isabelle MacElhone, *Harry's Bar: The Original* (New York: Stewart, Tabori and Chang, 2011); Luca Picchi, *Negroni Cocktail: An Italian Legend* (Florence: Giunti, 2015).

CHAPTER NINE

People: Henry Madden (1882–1948); Max Bilgray (1885–1958); Mary Lee Kelley (1890–1972); Oswald Haerdtl (1899–1959); Charles Wesley Price (1890–1962).

Quotes: Page 87, "I'm only gonna show you this once": The formula is the one Joe "the Markee" Madden had used in his New York speakeasy; see his self-published book, *Set 'Em Up!* (New York: 1939), 23. "1928 Tomato Juice Cocktail": "Newest Tomato Juice Cocktail," Bangor, ME *Daily News,* May 18, 1928, 17. Page 90, "Henry Madden's Mistake": "Grahams Sightseeing Southern California," Moville, IA *Mail,* July 23, 1936, 4; "Scientists": *Bottoms Up! Y Como!,* Agua Caliente, Mexico: 1933, 19.

Other: Page 89. The Prohibition drinks, clockwise from top of the bar: Corn Popper (corn whiskey, cream, and grenadine); White Cargo (gin and vanilla ice cream); Earthquake (gin, Scotch, and absinthe); Barbary Coast (gin, Scotch, cacao, and cream); Palm Beach (rum, gin, and pineapple juice); Maiden's Prayer (gin, lemon, egg white, and liqueur).

Further Reading: Daniel Okrent, *Last Call: The Rise and Fall of Prohibition* (New York: Scribner, 2011); J. C. Furnas, *The Life and Times of the Late Demon Rum* (New York: Putnam, 1965).

CHAPTER TEN

People: Jennings S. Cox Jr. (1866–1913); Robert Huntington Lyman Jr. (1867–1935); Emilio González (1868–1940); Edwin Woelke (1877–post 1938); Constante Ribalaigua y Vert (1888–1952); José "Sloppy Joe" Abeal y Otero (1886–1942); José "Joe" Mustaros y Salas (1898–1989); Ernest Raymond Beaumont Gantt (1907–1989); Monroe Proser (1904–1973); Victor Bergeron (1902–1984); Cora Irene Sund (1909–1974); Raymond Realista Buhen (1909–1999); Ching Kui On/Robert Ching (1911–1968); Robert Chester Ruark Jr. (1915–1965); Elvezio Grassi (1880?–post 1944); Giuseppe Scialom (1910–2004); John Durlesser (1911–1971).

Quotes: Page 100, "Cuba's greatest contribution": this account is inspired by the one R. H. Lyman gave in G. Selmer Fougner's "Along the Wine Trail" column, *New York Sun,* February 11, 1935, 29. Page 102, "1915 Cuban cocktail book": John B. Escalante, *Manual del Cantinero* (Habaña: Imprenta Moderna, 1915); "General en jefe": Enrique Coll, "Al Pie de la 'Barra,'" Havana *Diario de la Marina,* October 20, 1916, 1; "Bilingual recipe booklet": *Bar la Florida Cocktails,* issued annually 1934–1939 and then in 1946, 1952, and 1955, roughly (all editions are undated). Page 103, "The Mecca of Every American": "Havana," Galveston *Daily News,* November 23, 1924, 21. Page 104, "Perfect Burlesque of a South Seas Dive": Mollie Merrick, "Ziegfeld Film a Worry," *Kansas City Star,* September 17, 1935, 8; "Secret 1934 recipe," Jeff Berry, *Sippin' Safari* (San Jose, CA: Club Tiki Press, 2007), 115–24. Page 109, "A matter of uncut fact": Robert Ruark, "Is Vodka Being Forced Upon Us?," *Miami Herald,* July 31, 1950, 18-B. Page 109, "Opening list at Ciro's": Sir Affable, "Then—And Now," *The Sporting Times,* September 25, 1915, 2; "'75' Cocktail": Harry McElhone, *"Harry" of Ciro's ABC of Mixing Cocktails* (London: Odhams Press, 1922), 65. Page 110, "According to *Esquire*": "Painting the Town with *Esquire*," *Esquire,* December 1944, 56; "Inspiration for Milo Minderbender": see, e.g., "Air Rest Camp Is Run by Famed Restaurateur," Columbia, SC *Columbia Record,* December 14, 1944, 7, and Robert Ruark, "This Beach-Comber Is Rich and Has Had Nothing But Fun All His Life," *El Paso Herald,* April 11, 1945, 20; "Invented by Joe Scialom at Shepheard's": "Joe, the Suffering Bar Steward," *Esquire,* August 1947, 83. Page 111, "Documented field expedient": Mrs. Frank O'Brien [sic], "Friend and Foe Dine at Ankara Restaurant," Baltimore *Sun,* May 23, 1943, 3.

Further Reading: Basil Woon, *When It's Cocktail Time in Cuba* (New York: Horace Liveright, 1928); Berry, *Sippin' Safari;* N.E. Beveridge, *Cups of Valor* (Harrisburg, PA: Stackpole Books, 1966).

CHAPTER ELEVEN

People: Giuseppe Cipriani (1900–1980); Joseph A. Sheridan (1909–1962); Bernard DeVoto (1897–1955); Helen Cromell (1886–1969); Mariano Licudine (1907–1980); Takao Yamaguchi (1916–2014); Harry Yee/Yee Lin Kwai (1918–2022); Valentino Clementi (1914–1996); Edwin John Clarke (1908–1992); Maria Dolores Boadas (1935–2017); Gustave Tops-Schmit (1903–post 1968); Frank Kane (1912–1968); Gaspare Campari (1828–1882); Leonetto Capiello (1875–1942); Jeffrey Ong/Ong Swee Teik (1948–2019).

Quotes: Page 115, "Leaves you breathless": Smirnoff vodka, advertisement, Santa Barbara, CA *News-Press,* June 14, 1949, 6. Page 116, "A slug of whiskey": Bernard DeVoto, "The Easy Chair: For the Wayward and Beguiled," *Harper's,* December 1949, 68; "Get cursed out," Helen Cromell with Robert Dougherty, *Dirty Helen* (Los Angeles: Sherbourne Press, 1966), 268. Page 121, "The art of mixing drinks is a lost cause": Frank Kane, *Anatomy of the Whisky Business* (Manhasset, NY: Lake House Press, 1965), 14.

Further Reading: "Irish Coffee," "Margarita," and "Negroni" in *OCSC;* Giuseppe Cipriani, *L'angolo dell' Harry's Bar* (Milano: Rizzoli, 1978); Sean Muldoon et al., *When Whiskey Met Its Match: How Irish Coffee Captivated the World* (New York: Dead Rabbit, 2022).

CHAPTER TWELVE

People: (In the interest of privacy I have only supplied dates for those mentioned who are deceased.) Henry Hampton Riddle (1926–1989); Ramón López Irrizary (1897–1982); Albert Thomas Ehringer; Alan Stillman; Norman Hobday (1933–2011); David Smith (1942–2019); Paul Goiffon (1912–1990); Lawrence "Cutty" Cutsail Jr.; Mariano Martinez; John Tourtellotte, active 1982; Paul Prudhomme (1940–2015); Kay Hinrichs (1944–1993); Jeffrey Morgenthaler.

Quotes: Page 126, "Matarratas": George Arfeld, "Throats Seared in Havana These Days," *Miami News,* August 4, 1963, 10. Page 130, "Bartenders—due to promotion Henry's Africa": advertisement, San Francisco *Examiner,* December 7, 1972, 45; Page 131, "Years ago, Chartreuse": Carl Cannon, "Swampwater and What?" Corpus Christi, TX *Times,* June 16, 1976, 9C; "Training Bras, Neutron Bombs and Frednecks," Frederick, MD *News-Post,* October 9, 1981, C-5.

Other: Page 132. The Piscola, Kalimotxo, and Batanga are mixed with Coca-Cola; the Paloma, with grapefruit soda; and the Chuflay, with ginger ale. The last three usually add lime.

Further Reading: William Grimes, *Straight Up or On the Rocks: The Story of the American Cocktail,* 2nd ed. (New York: North Point, 2001).

CHAPTER THIRTEEN

People: (In the interest of privacy I have only supplied dates for those mentioned who are deceased.) Judith "Judie" Smart (1957–2021); Joseph H. Baum (1920–1988); Gary Lee Regan (1951–2019); Mardee Haidin Regan (1949–2013); Sasha Nathan Petraske (1973–2015); George Papadakis, active 1953–2003.

Quotes: Page 140, "Never try to open a bar": conversation with the author, circa 2010. Page 146, "A bar exists to serve customers": ibid., 4.

Further Reading: Dale DeGroff, *The New Craft of the Cocktail* (New York: Clarkson Potter, 2020); Paul Clarke, *The Cocktail Chronicles: Navigating the Cocktail Renaissance with Jigger, Shaker & Glass* (Nashville, TN: Spring House Press, 2015); Robert Simonson, *A Proper Drink* (Berkeley, CA: Ten Speed Press, 2016); Ted Haigh, *Vintage Spirits and Forgotten Cocktails,* 2nd ed. (Beverly, MA: Quarry Books, 2009); Gary Regan, *The Joy of Mixology,* 2nd ed. (New York: Clarkson Potter, 2018). Cheryl Charming, "Who Created the Cosmopolitan Cocktail?" MissCharming.com.

A PARTING GLASS

Quotes: Page 149, footnote: Muddle an ounce of dried golden raisins and the peels of three bitter oranges in a pint of very hot water. Strain through a "superbag" fine-mesh strainer, dissolve half a pound of powdered bitter chocolate in the liquid, strain it again, and stir in four cups of sugar over a low heat until it has dissolved. Bottle and refrigerate. Makes one quart syrup. Use within one month.

ACKNOWLEDGMENTS

I think the First Law of Acknowledgments is that half the people who actually helped a book get written, edited, and printed never make it into the acknowledgments. That said, the half who both should and will be thanked by name here include, first and foremost, Dean Kotz, whose intricate, animated drawings have brought this story to life. With Dean, I'd also like to thank Brad Simpson, who has supplied the vivid colors that make the drawings glow on the page. Of course, without Julie Bennett, who edited the book and guided it along, and Chloe Rawlins, who supervised the art, there would be no book at all. I have always relied upon the patience of editors. I do regret trying theirs as much as I did and am deeply grateful that they stuck with me as I did my best Poky Little Puppy impression.

I discussed much of the research in here with Noah Rothbaum, whose wise advice was, as always, invaluable. Jeff Berry helped with the Tikiverse, and Tim Glazner kindly shared some of his extensive research on Don the Beachcomber, and, as a lagniappe, Bob Ching.

My dear wife, Karen, has to put up with a lot when I'm finishing one of these things, and I'm eternally thankful that she doesn't just rent herself an apartment in Paris for the duration.

And for the half who should be but won't be thanked here, I am sorry. Drinks are on me when I see you.

ABOUT THE CONTRIBUTORS

As the drinks columnist for *Esquire* from 2000 to 2016 and *The Daily Beast* from 2016 to 2022, **David Wondrich** was perfectly placed not only to observe the modern cocktail revolution but to help push it along. A former English professor with a PhD in comparative literature, he put his studies to good use in writing books, such as the James Beard Award–winning *Imbibe!*, a biography-with-recipes of pioneering bartender Jerry Thomas, and editing *The Oxford Companion to Spirits and Cocktails*, which the American Library Association deemed the best reference book of 2021. On top of that, Wondrich has helped to train literally thousands of bartenders; has been a television guest of Conan O'Brien, Stephen Colbert, and Rachel Maddow; partnered in developing several award-winning spirits (plus his own line of barware); and was voted the #3 most influential person in the bar world by a thousand of his peers. He lives in Brooklyn, New York, and Trieste, Italy.

Originally from Northampton, Pennsylvania, **Dean Kotz** has been working in comics since 2009. He's drawn books for numerous publishers on titles, such as *Krampus!*, *Warlord of Mars Attacks*, and *The Butcher of Paris*. He currently lives in Brooklyn, New York, with his girlfriend and their pet spider.

INDEX

A
Ackerman, Mart, 40
Albert "Bertie" Edward, Prince of Wales, 22, 60, 65, 80
Alexander, Cato, 21, 30, 127
Amaretto Sour (No. 2), 134
Americano, 83
Anderson, Julian, 76
Armstrong, Louis, 92
arrack, 18
Ashley, James, 13, 127

B
Banks, Jerri, 140
Barbary Coast, 89
bartenders
 Asian and Pacific Islander, 106, 118–19, 142
 Black, 22, 75–76, 130, 147
 as entertainers, 135–36
 as "mixologists," 46
 women as, 41, 75, 81, 95, 111, 130, 147
 See also individual bartenders
bar tools, 64
Baum, Joe, 136
Bax, Matthew, 140
Beach, Donn, 104–6, 108, 110, 117, 142
Bedford, 143
Bees' Knees, 63, 92
Bellini, 114
Benjamin Menéndez Special, 107
Bergeron, Victor "Trader Vic," 105–6, 117, 118
Bermejo, Julio, 143
Berry, Jeff "Beachbum," 104, 142
Beiderbecke, Bix, 92
Bilgray, Max, 91
bitters, 27
Black Russian, 120, 127, 131
Bloody Mary, 89, 105, 115
Blue Blazer, 4, 46, 48, 53, 54, 141
Blue Hawaiian, 126
Boadas, Maria Dolores, 120
Bomboni, Leopoldo, 57
Boothby, "Cocktail Bill," 71
Boothby Cocktail, 71
Bouguereau, William-Adolphe, 68
bourbon, 54, 55

Bowie, R. R., 75
brandy, 25–26
Brandy Cocktail, 50
Brandy Julep, 24
Brigham, Peter Bent, 37, 41, 57
Bring Another Smurf!, 3
Brougham, John, 41
B2C2, 111
Buhen, Ray, 106, 118
Bullard, Charles, 62
Bullock, Tom, 76
Burgess, Ruth "Kitty," 81
Bush, George H. W., 76
Bustanoby, Louis, 74

C
Caiafa, Frank, 148
Cajun Martini, 133
Calabrese, Salvatore, 145
Campari, 114, 123
Campari, Gaspare and Davide, 123
Camparinete, 63
Cape Codder, 133
Capozzi, Ciro, 79–80, 82, 120
Cappiello, Leonetto, 123
Carnation, 97
Cator, Sylvio Paul, 157
Cecchini, Toby, 137
Champagne Cocktail, 33
Chaplin, Charlie, 97
Ching, Robert, 106, 108
Chocolate Snow Bear, 132
Churchill, Lord Randolph, 80
Ciro's, 79–80, 82, 109
Clark, Eddie, 120
Clavelot, Albert, 63
Clementi, Valentino, 120
cocktail
 definition of, 29–30
 etymology of, 28
 popularity of, 42
 renaissance of, 137–147
 variations on, 30–33, 72, 80
cocktail books, 50, 59, 85, 137, 142, 146, 147
Cognac, 25
Coleman, Ada "Coley," 81, 84, 120
Collin, John, 15

Conrad, Barnaby, III, 137
Cook, Jim, 22
Cooke, Henry, 32
Corn Popper, 89
Cosmopolitan, 3, 137, 141
Cox, Jennings, 100–101
Craddock, Harry, 120
Cromell, "Dirty Helen," 116
Crosby, Harry and Caresse, 81
Croswell, Harry, 29
Crouch, Jasper, 15, 21
Cuba Libre, 100
Cuban drinks, 83, 90, 99–104, 126
Cutsail, Cutty, 131, 146

D
Dabney, John, 22
Daiquiri, 100–101, 103, 104, 143, 145
Deal, Louis, 75
de Fleury, R., 85
DeGroff, Dale, 136–37, 141, 145
Delaplane, Stanton, 114
DeVoto, Bernard, 116
Dick, Bill, 49, 57
Dickens, Charles, 56
Didier, Jake, 154
Dirty Martini, 133
distillation, 5–7
Don the Beachcomber, 104, 106, 110, 117, 118. See also Beach, Donn
Downey, Jonathan, 145
Durlesser, Johnny, 114

E
Earthquake, 89
East India, 71
Edline, Charles J., 75
Ehringer, Al, 130, 140
Elizabeth I, Queen, 8
Ellice, Janie, 56
Ellington, Duke, 92
El Panetùn, 149
El Presidente, 101–102
Engel, Leo, 59, 60, 61, 79, 120
Errico, Vincenzo, 143
Estopinal, Kirk, 143, 146

167

F

Fernandez, Antonio "Panama Joe," 42–43
Fisk, Big Jim, 68
Fitzgerald, Larry, 49, 57
Floridita, 102–103, 120
Flynn, Kitty, 62
Forgione, Larry, 135
Forrestal, James, 76
Francis, Kay, 97
French 75, 89, 96, 109

G

Galsini, José Valencia "Popo," 119–120, 122, 126
Gellhorn, Martha, 102
Gelli, Elsie, 95
Giacomo Joyce, 160
Gibson cocktail, 70
gin, 35–36, 144
Gin and Tonic, 3, 133
Gin Buck, 4
Ginebra Compuesta, 83
Gin Fizz, 73
Ginsberg, Allen, 127, 129
Gin Sling, 82
glassware, 95, 97
Godchild, 131
Godfather, 126, 127
Godmother, 131
Goiffon, Paul, 131
González, Emilio "Maragato," 101
Grassi, Elvezio, 110
Greyhound, 111
Grimes, William, 137
Gunshop Fizz, 143
Guy, William, 21

H

Haerdtl, Oswald, 95
Haigh, Ted "Dr. Cocktail," 138, 141
"Hail-Storm" Julep, 21, 23
Haimo, Oscar, 85
Hall, Tamika, 147
Hammack, John D., 40
Hanky Panky, 84
Hannah, Chris, 96
Harry's New York Bar, 61, 63, 110
Harvey Wallbanger, 125
Hawthorne Café, 64
Hayward, W. A., 75
Heller, Joseph, 110
Hemingway, Ernest, 102
Hess, Robert, 138, 141
Hinrichs, Kay, 133

Hobday, Norman, 130
Holiday, Billie, 92
Hollywood, 97–98
Horsefeather, 143
Huerta, Alba, 23
Huntsman, 158
Hustler, Catherine "Kitty," 28

I

ice, 14, 20–21, 127
Improved Holland Gin Cocktail, 34
Improved Whiskey Cocktail, 51, 71
International Bartenders Association (IBA), 120–121, 130
Irish, John, 68
Irish Coffee, 114
Irish Rose, 154

J

Jahangir, Emperor, 5–7
Japanese Cocktail, 51
Jersey Cocktail, 33
John Collins, 15
Johnson, Harry, 71
Johnson, James W., 85
Jones, Stan, 85
Joyce, James, 160
Jungle Bird, 123
Juniperotivo, 140

K

Kamikaze, 136
Kane, Frank, 121, 125
Keaton, Buster, 97
Keeney, Willis, 57
Kelley, Mamie, 91
Kir Royale, 133
Koeppler, Jack, 114

L

Larkin, Captain, 10–11
Leaving of Liverpool, 161
Leland, Charles, 46
Leopold Bros., 55
Lewis, John, 75
Licudine, Mariano, 118
Little Italy, 143
Loeb, Robert, Jr., 85
Long Island Iced Tea, 136
López, Ramón, 126
Loud, Fred, 68
Lowe, Paul E., 85
Lowe, Thaddeus, 49
Loy, Myrna, 97

M

Madden, Henry, 90
Madonna, 137
Madras, 133
Maiden's Prayer, 89
Maier, Otto, 63
Mai Tai, 117, 118
Maloney, Toby, 142
Manhattan, 68–70, 143, 145
Margarita, 90, 114, 132
Marguerite, 63
Martin, Prince, 76
Martinez, 141
Martinez, Mariano, 132
Martini, 70, 77, 116, 121, 133, 143
Mary Pickford, 101
Matthews, Edward, 75
May, Karl Friedrich, 156
McDonough, Patsy, 71
McElhone, Harry, 63, 80, 105, 109
McGarry, Malachi, 26
McKone, Joe, 68
McMorris, Charles, 112
Mead, Paul, 59
Meehan, Jim, 142
Meier, Frank, 61, 63
Merrick, Mollie, 104
Milk & Honey, 140, 142, 145
Milk Punch, 153
Million Dollar Cocktail, 82
Mint Julep, 4, 19–21, 23, 56
Miret, Vincent, 71
Mitta, Johnny, 63
Mojito, 101, 105
Morgenthaler, Jeffrey, 134
Morris, Victor, 83
Morrissey, John, 52
Moscow Mule, 98, 112, 115
Muddled Martini, 133
Mulhall, Billy, 68
Murray, Neal, 137

N

Negroni, 83, 113, 114, 123, 145
Negroni, Count Camillo, 83, 113
Negroni Sbagliato, 2
New York Sour, 45
Niblo, Martha King, 21, 41
Nicol, Duncan, 73, 74
Noilly, Joseph, 78

O

Ohio Cocktail, 83, 156
Old-Fashioned, 72, 91, 116, 127, 143, 145
O'Meara, Mallory, 147

Ong, Jeffrey, 123
Overholt, Abraham, 54

P
Palm Beach, 89
Papadakis, George, 141
Paper Plane, 143
Patton, George S., 112
Paul, Charlie, 60, 80, 81
Pazuniak, Maksym, 143, 146
Pedro, Del, 143
Pegu Club, 82, 110, 142, 143, 147, 159
Pemberton, Murdock, 157
Petraske, Sasha, 140, 141, 145
Pharmacy Cocktail, 140
Pig & Whistle, 152
Piña Colada, 126, 127, 132
Pink Gin, 35
Pisco Punch, 73
Pisco Sour, 83, 105
Planter's Punch, 91
Plunkett, Randall Percy Otway (Lord Louth), 42–43
Pollard, Othello, 21
Poona Club, 159
Powell, William, 97
Presidente Vincent, 157
Price, Stephen, 15
Price, Wes, 98
Prohibition, 54, 55, 86–94
Proser, Monte, 106
Prudhomme, Paul, 133
punch, 4, 10–17

R
Rainbow Room, 136
Ramos, Henry Carl, 73, 74
Raymond, Henry J., 61, 62
Reading Club Cocktail, 155
Red Hook, 143
Regan, Gary and Mardee Haidin, 137, 140, 141
Reiner, Julie, 142
Revolver, 143
Ribalaigua y Vert, Constante, 102–103, 105, 107, 120
Rice, William, 21
Riddle, Hank, 126
Rose, 63
Ross, Sam, 143
Ruark, Robert, 109
rum, 18
Rum and Coke, 100
Rusty Nail, 126, 127
rye whiskey, 54, 55

S
San Martín, 83
Santer, Jon, 143
Santini, Joseph, 21, 32, 33
Sardi, Vincent, 85
Saturn, 119, 122
Saunders, Audrey, 141, 142, 143
Savonarola, Michele, 5–7
Savoy Hotel, 60, 81, 84, 85, 110, 120
Sazerac, 3, 51, 71, 89
Schmidt, "The Only William," 4, 73, 75, 131
Schumann, Charles, 145
Scialom, Joe, 110
Screwdriver, 111, 115
"75" Cocktail, 109
Shea, George, 85
Shepheard's, 81, 110
Sheridan, Joe, 114
Sherry Cobbler, 41, 44, 56
shooters, 131
Short Drink, 60, 65
Sidecar, 26, 63, 92
Smart, Judie, 136
Smirnov, Pyotr, 124
Smith, David, 131
Soda Cocktail, 33
speakeasies, 87–89, 91–92
Sterling, Lucinda, 150
Stillman, Alan, 130
Stokes, Edward S., 67–68
Stone Sour, 76
Stoughton, Richard, 27
Straub, Alberta, 141
Suffering Bastard, 110
Sund, Cora "Queen Sunakora," 105, 117
Swampwater, 131

T
Tequila Daisy, 90
Tequila Sunrise, 90, 127
Third Degree, 70
Thomas, Jerry, 4, 34, 46–52, 54, 57, 58, 59, 68, 71, 79, 80, 127, 141, 142
tiki bars, 117–119, 126
Tipton-Martin, Toni, 147
Ti' Punch, 3
Tom and Jerry, 51, 141
Tom Collins, 15, 110
Tommy's Margarita, 143, 145
Tops, Gustave "Gus," 120
Tourtellotte, John, 133
Tracy, Albert Haller, Jr., 42–43
Trader Vic's, 105–7, 117, 118
Trollope, Frances, 56
Trusty Nail, 150

U
Upside-Down Margarita, 132

V
Vennigerholtz, Johann George, 21
vermouth, 69, 78
Vermouth Cocktail, 41
Vincent, Sténio, 157
vodka, 115, 124, 127, 144

W
Walker, William, 21
Washington, George, 28
Waters, Alice, 135
Welles, Orson, 113
Wells, Charles H., 61, 62
Wells, Kitty, 61, 62
whiskey, 54–55, 116
Whiskey Sour, 42
White Cargo, 89
White Lady, 92
White Russian, 131, 136
White Star Imperial Daisy, 143
Wilkinson, Billy, 71
Willard, Orsamus, 21, 29
Woelke, Eddie, 85, 95, 101, 102
women
  as bar customers, 41, 66, 74–75, 130
  as bartenders, 41, 75, 81, 95, 111, 130, 147
Wood, "Wash," 75
World War I, 109–10, 112
World War II, 55, 105, 106, 109–12, 115
Worth, Adam, 62

Y
Yamaguchi, Takao "Taka," 118
Yee, Harry, 118, 126

Z
Zombie, 3, 104, 106, 108

Ten Speed Graphic
An imprint of the Crown Publishing Group
A division of Penguin Random House LLC
1745 Broadway, New York, NY 10019
tenspeed.com
penguinrandomhouse.com

Text copyright © 2025 by David Wondrich
Illustrations copyright © 2025 by Dean Kotz
Penguin Random House values and supports copyright. Copyright fuels creativity, encourages diverse voices, promotes free speech, and creates a vibrant culture. Thank you for buying an authorized edition of this book and for complying with copyright laws by not reproducing, scanning, or distributing any part of it in any form without permission. You are supporting writers and allowing Penguin Random House to continue to publish books for every reader. Please note that no part of this book may be used or reproduced in any manner for the purpose of training artificial intelligence technologies or systems.

Ten Speed Graphic colophon is a registered trademark of Penguin Random House LLC.

Typefaces: Comiccraft's Victory Speech; Palmer Type Company's New American Gothic; Monoype's Felix Titling; Exlibris's Calluna Sans

Library of Congress Cataloging-in-Publication Data
Names: Wondrich, David author | Kotz, Dean illustrator. Title: The comic book history of the cocktail : five centuries of mixing drinks and carrying on / David Wondrich ; illustrated by Dean Kotz. Other titles: Five centuries of mixing drinks and carrying on Identifiers: LCCN 2024052757 (print) | LCCN 2024052758 (ebook) | ISBN 9781984860330 hardcover | ISBN 9781984860323 ebook Subjects: LCSH: Cocktails—History—Comic books, strips, etc. | LCGFT: Graphic novels | Nonfiction comics | Recipes
Classification: LCC TX951.2 .W66 2025 (print) | LCC TX951.2 (ebook) | DDC 641.87/4—dc23/eng/20250214
LC record available at https://lccn.loc.gov/2024052757
LC ebook record available at https://lccn.loc.gov/2024052758

Hardcover ISBN: 978-1-9848-6033-0
Ebook ISBN: 978-1-9848-6032-3

Editor: Julie Bennett | Production editor: Natalie Blachere
Designers: Francesca Truman and Chloe Rawlins
Art director: Chloe Rawlins
Colorist: Brad Simpson
Letterer: Micah Myers
Production: Dan Myers | Compositor: Hannah Hunt
Proofreaders: Kate Bolen, Ann Roberts, Carol Burrell, Miriam Taveras | Indexer: Ken DellaPenta
Publicist: Maya Bradford | Marketer: Paola Crespo

Manufactured in China

10 9 8 7 6 5 4 3 2 1

First Edition

The authorized representative in the EU for product safety and compliance is Penguin Random House Ireland, Morrison Chambers, 32 Nassau Street, Dublin D02 YH68, Ireland, https://eu-contact.penguin.ie.